Tolley's Personal Pensions for The Financial Adviser

by

David Wicks BA, FCII, FInstSMM
Finance Industry Training Limited

Members of the LexisNexis Group worldwide

United Kingdom	LexisNexis UK, a Division of Reed Elsevier (UK) Ltd, 2 Addiscombe Road, Croydon CR9 5AF
Argentina	LexisNexis Argentina, BUENOS AIRES
Australia	LexisNexis Butterworths, CHATSWOOD, New South Wales
Austria	LexisNexis Verlag ARD Orac GmbH & Co KG, VIENNA
Canada	LexisNexis Butterworths, MARKHAM, Ontario
Chile	LexisNexis Chile Ltda, SANTIAGO DE CHILE
Czech Republic	Nakladatelství Orac sro, PRAGUE
France	Editions du Juris-Classeur SA, PARIS
Germany	LexisNexis Deutschland GmbH, FRANKFURT and MUNSTER
Hong Kong	LexisNexis Butterworths, HONG KONG
Hungary	HVG-Orac, BUDAPEST
India	LexisNexis Butterworths, NEW DELHI
Ireland	Butterworths (Ireland) Ltd, DUBLIN
Italy	Giuffrè Editore, MILAN
Malaysia	Malayan Law Journal Sdn Bhd, KUALA LUMPUR
New Zealand	LexisNexis Butterworths, WELLINGTON
Poland	Wydawnictwo Prawnicze LexisNexis, WARSAW
Singapore	LexisNexis Butterworths, SINGAPORE
South Africa	LexisNexis Butterworths, Durban
Switzerland	Stämpfli Verlag AG, BERNE
USA	LexisNexis, DAYTON, Ohio

First published in 2003
© Reed Elsevier (UK) Ltd 2003

A CIP Catalogue record for this book is available from the British Library.

ISBN 0 7545 2161 3

Typeset by Phoenix Photosetting, Chatham, Kent
Printed and bound in Great Britain by Hobbs the Printers Ltd, Totton, Hampshire

Visit LexisNexis UK at www.lexisnexis.co.uk

Preface

There are already a number of reference books which relate to personal pensions, and adding a further new book may seem superfluous. However, the opportunity to do something genuinely different greatly appealed to me, and I hope that readers find the book of value.

This handbook is aimed very firmly at advisers, and although it covers the technicalities of personal pensions, the intention has been to concentrate on practical aspects which may figure in, and may influence, the advice given to clients and prospective clients. There are therefore a large number of examples dealing with the application of the theory to practical situations. It has been both interesting and enjoyable to put the content together with this practical basis at the forefront at all times.

There is constant publicity relating to the need for greater retirement saving, and much of the problem is probably due to potential investors feeling dissociated with pensions generally. Relating the still very substantial advantages of these arrangements to the particular circumstances of the individual is a necessary step in solving this problem.

The proposals for simplification of the tax treatment of pension arrangements are under consultation at the time of writing, though it looks like being some time before they come to fruition. Assuming they are put into effect in broadly their original form, these will also have a major impact on pension planning and advice. In the meantime, it remains important that best use is made of the existing rules, and this handbook should also help advisers to ensure that this is done.

The simplification proposals themselves are discussed in the final chapter, though inevitably they will be amended during consultation.

Finally, I would like to record my thanks to Rob Gaines for his help during the writing of this handbook. As well as being a source of encouragement and a useful sounding board for ideas, Rob's detailed and constructive comments helped improve the final outcome considerably.

David Wicks
BA, FCII, FInstSMM

Finance Industry Training Limited

Contents

Table of Statutes

Table of Statutory Instruments

1 — Background to Personal Pensions

Introduction 1.1

Retirement planning as a whole has undergone massive change in recent years, and is now recognised as one of the most important financial considerations for most people. Personal pensions, and stakeholder pensions (which are a sub-group of personal pensions more generally), are fundamental to this consideration in many cases.

Influences on change 1.2

A major factor in increasing the importance of retirement planning has been the dramatic change in life expectancy over the last century. At the start of the twentieth century, an average newborn male child had a life expectancy of only about 45 years, whereas now the figure is close to 75 years (Source: *Government Actuary's Quinquennial Review of National Insurance Fund Expenditure: February 2000*).

Advances in medical science have contributed to this increase, as have improvements in living standards, and a greater awareness of health issues. It is now common for people to live long into retirement and to be active, which in turn increases the need for substantial financial resources. Those planning ahead for retirement often see these years as an opportunity to fulfil long held ambitions; perhaps to travel, or to take up new interests, rather than to passively spend their time at home.

In addition, retirement as a concept is now much more flexible than it has been previously. Some people retire much earlier than generally would have been feasible in the past, sometimes on a voluntary basis and sometimes through circumstances such as enforced redundancy. Other individuals choose to carry on working well beyond the usual retiring age range of 60 to 65, but often with a reduced time commitment, and therefore a reduced earned income. As a result, retirement planning has had to become more flexible to cater for these varied scenarios.

Non-earners 1.3

There are also groups of individuals who are not currently working, but for whom retirement planning remains important. These might be individuals who have suffered incapacity, and so are receiving income from the State and perhaps also from a permanent health insurance or income protection arrangement. This could be through their employment, or on a personal basis. Because benefits from these arrangements commonly run out at what would have been the individual's expected retirement age, there is a need to plan to replace at least some of that income eventually.

Others have broken careers because of commitments to others, for example those bringing up young children, or caring for elderly and infirm relatives. Retirement planning during these periods also remains relevant (though the level of disposable income may make such provision difficult).

The length of time during which people will rely on the proceeds of their retirement planning will vary considerably from individual to individual. Some will not survive long after retirement, but many will do so, and it is by no means uncommon for the period of retirement to extend for 30 years or more.

State benefits   1.4

Most people will qualify for State pension benefits, although even these are subject to minimum National Insurance contribution requirements. The State basic pension, which is £77.45 per week for a single person from April 2003, and £123.80 per week for a married couple, is pitched at a low level. These equate to an annual income of approximately £4,025 or £6,440 respectively, and the basic pension certainly would not, on its own, support the kind of retirement which most people would want.

The State Second Pension (S2P) provides additional benefits, but only for employees. Even those who qualify for maximum S2P benefits as well as the State basic pension will still only receive a modest income in retirement. The maximum for a single person would be around £9,300 per year in today's terms, and for the self-employed – who qualify for basic pension only – the position is much worse. Although total State provision, including S2P, is probably more than most people appreciate, it remains important for individuals to build more significant resources for themselves.

The basis of S2P is described in detail in section **12.8**, which includes various examples of expected benefit levels based on different earnings figures.

There are additional State benefits, such as the Minimum Income Guarantee, which are means tested, but the intention of these benefits remains to support very basic living standards.

At the time of publication there has recently been a great deal of publicity about the savings gap (the fact that individuals are not saving to a sufficient extent to provide for the future, and in particular are not providing sufficiently for retirement).The size of the problem is clear when one considers that most people will have a working lifetime of perhaps 45 years or so, and during this period they need to create sufficient wealth not only to support themselves during that working lifetime, but for, possibly, a further 30 years thereafter. Even for someone who starts to save for retirement at a very early age, the effect is still in a sense that each year's income will have to support them for between one and a half and two years.

Given the other financial pressures, particularly on those just starting work, who will often wish to buy a house, and perhaps raise a family, it is not surprising that few people are in a position to save as much as they would in an ideal world.

Tax advantages   1.5

Successive governments have for many years sought to encourage the use of pension arrangements which are specifically geared to provide retirement benefits. Restrictions are imposed to ensure that the arrangements are used for the intended purpose, and in return a range of tax advantages is available.

Essentially the same tax advantages apply to both occupational pension schemes (which are established, and contributed to, by the employer) and personal pensions (which are established by the individual, though an employer can also contribute), and these are summarised in the checklist below.

Checklist – Main tax advantages of pension schemes

- Contributions paid by an individual qualify for tax relief at his highest rate(s) of income tax.
- Contributions paid by an individual's employer will be treated as a deductible business expense, so that the employer will benefit from tax relief on them.
- Employer contributions are not treated as remuneration of the employee, either for tax or National Insurance purposes.
- The investment return achieved by the pension fund is tax advantaged in that there is no UK tax to pay on income or capital gains, though the ability to reclaim dividend tax credits was abolished with effect from 2 July 1997.
- At retirement, part of the benefit is generally available as a tax free lump sum.
- On death before taking retirement benefits, lump sum death benefits can be provided, and can usually be paid free of all tax, including inheritance tax.

The way in which these tax advantages are applied, and in some cases the operation of the restrictions on them, vary between the different types of pension arrangement, and in this book we explore in particular the position under personal pension schemes.

Although the tax advantages are very powerful, it must be recognised that one of the most important of them, the availability of tax relief on contributions, is in the main only a deferment of tax liability. This reflects the fact that, although part of the total benefit at retirement can be taken in the form of tax free cash, the remainder must be taken as income, which is taxed as earned income under PAYE. This reduces the tax advantage of pension schemes, and so means that retirement planning must be considered as a much wider concept than just pension planning. Other tax advantaged investments can also be used to great effect, and sometimes may be more flexible.

Alternatives to pensions   1.6

When an individual reaches retirement, he will certainly have other assets as well as any pension arrangements, and these will contribute to his overall financial resources in retirement. The balance between pension arrangements and other assets will vary from individual to individual, and some of the main alternatives likely to be used in financial planning for retirement are considered below.

Individual Savings Accounts   1.7

The most obvious alternative to pension arrangements is the Individual Savings Account (ISA).

The tax advantages of ISAs are different from those which apply to pensions, but they can be almost as powerful. There is no tax relief on contributions made to the ISA, but neither is there any tax to pay when the individual takes benefits. In the meantime, the investment return is tax advantaged in the same way as the return within a pension fund, but with the slight added advantage that dividend tax credits can be reclaimed until 5 April 2004.

Example – Reclaim of dividend tax credit

Suppose a holding of shares within an ISA produces a dividend payment, net of tax credit, of £720 in 2003/04.

The tax credit is 10% of the gross dividend (ie the net dividend plus the tax credit), so here, the gross dividend would be £800, and the tax credit is £80, giving the net dividend of £800 − £80 = £720.

The ISA can reclaim the tax credit, and so will receive, in total, income of £800.

A similar holding within a pension fund would only produce £720, because the dividend tax credit cannot be reclaimed.

In purely tax terms, assuming the individual is subject to the same rates of tax whilst working and in retirement, the total tax reliefs on pensions will be more favourable, because of the influence of the tax free cash sum.

Example – Personal pensions or ISAs I

A higher rate taxpayer expects to remain so, even during retirement. They intend to invest £1,800 from their income net of higher rate tax, ie the equivalent of £3,000 gross.

If they choose an ISA, they will invest £1,800 (because there is no tax relief on the contribution). Suppose that, as a result of investment returns, this doubles over the period to retirement. They will then be able to take the fund of £3,600 with no tax liability.

If they choose a personal pension instead, the amount invested would be £3,000. If we again assume this doubles in the period to retirement, their pension fund will then be £6,000. If this all had to provide taxable income benefits, its net worth would be only £3,600 (ie after a 40% reduction to allow for the tax liability). This is the same as the value of the ISA.

However, 25% of the fund (£1,500) is available as tax free cash. The balance of £4,500 will provide taxable income, so its net worth is £2,700. This gives a total of £4,200.

(This and our remaining examples in this section ignore the slight advantage to ISAs of the ability to reclaim tax credits on dividends received in 2003/04.)

Where there is a differential between the tax rate applicable whilst working and that in retirement, this will affect the balance of advantage. The fairly common situation where an individual is a higher rate taxpayer whilst working, but in retirement becomes a basic rate taxpayer, boosts the argument in favour of pensions.

Example – Personal pensions or ISAs II

Suppose that our example above, although being a higher rate taxpayer whilst working, now expects only to be liable to basic rate tax in retirement.

The contributions and eventual fund sizes at retirement are unchanged. However, the reduction in tax liability on their pension income means that the net worth of the pension fund is increased:

Tax free cash	£1,500
Net worth of residual fund	£3,510 (ie £4,500 x 78%)
Total net worth	£5,010

This compares with the value of the ISA fund, which would be £3,600, as before.

This example shows an ideal situation for the use of pensions as opposed to ISAs.

On the other hand, if tax rates are higher in retirement the reverse is true. It would be relatively unusual for an individual to be in receipt of a higher level of income in retirement than whilst working, though this is not impossible (for example if the individual receives an inheritance which provides significant levels of investment income).

This situation is more likely to arise if tax rates in general are increased, as a result of government policy. For example, before 6 April 1988, the highest rate of income tax was 60% rather than the current level of 40%. If a higher rate taxpayer believed that the 60% rate was likely to be re-introduced in the future, the 40% relief available on personal pension contributions today would be unattractive relative to the tax liability he expects to have on the eventual pension payments.

Example – Personal pensions or ISAs III

Suppose now that our example remains a higher rate taxpayer in retirement, but that higher rate tax increases to 60% by then. The position is therefore:

Tax free cash	£1,500
Net worth of residual fund	£1,800 (ie £4,500 x 40%)
Total net worth	£3,300

This now compares unfavourably with the position under the ISA, where the fund is still worth £3,600 at retirement.

If an individual wishes to consider whether pension arrangements or ISAs are more tax efficient, he would have to take a view not only on what his own personal tax situation in retirement is likely to be, but also on the level of tax rates in the economy as a whole.

Position on death 1.8

There is a further important point to take into account from a tax perspective. As mentioned in section **1.5** above, death benefits under pension arrangements will usually be payable free of tax, including inheritance tax. This subject is considered in more detail in **Chapter 8: Death Before Retirement**.

ISAs on the other hand do not enjoy this advantage. With effect from the death of the individual, the tax advantages applicable to the ISA investment fund are lost, and the value of the ISA forms part of the individual's estate. If the estate is liable for inheritance tax, and if the nil rate band has already been used, this will mean that 40% (at current rates) of the ISA fund will be lost to the Inland Revenue in inheritance tax.

Example – Position on death

A higher rate taxpayer has made retirement planning provision by means of a personal pension arrangement. They are approaching retirement, and they have built up a fund of £200,000.

If they were to die shortly before retirement, the £200,000 could be paid as a lump sum immediately, and would be free of inheritance tax.

Had ISAs been used instead of personal pensions, the fund would have been smaller, because their contributions would not have qualified for tax relief. Allowing for 40% relief throughout on pension contributions, it would be reasonable to assume an alternative ISA fund size of £120,000.

If they died, this would form part of their estate, and the potential inheritance tax liability at 40% would be £48,000. This would leave a net £72,000 for their heirs.

Even if there is no inheritance tax liability, perhaps because the value of the estate is below the inheritance tax threshold, or because it is passing to an exempt recipient, such as a legally married spouse, there will still be a delay before the money becomes available, because of the necessity to await the grant of probate before distribution.

Particularly where a substantial fund builds up over a number of years, this inheritance tax aspect will be an important one, and needs to be taken into account in the individual's estate planning arrangements.

Note that the examples above assume that the whole of the fund under the personal pension could be paid as a lump sum, though, as discussed in **Chapter 8: Death Before Retirement**, it will sometimes be required that some benefits are paid in income form.

Death after retirement 1.9

If death occurs after retirement, the position under a pension arrangement is different. If an individual is receiving income from an annuity, the death benefits will reflect the basis of that annuity. Under personal pension arrangements, however, although the annuity income may continue either for a defined period or for the lifetime of a spouse or dependant, there will be no lump sum payment. The income benefit would remain subject to income tax.

If income is being taken by way of income withdrawals from the fund itself, as an alternative to annuity purchase, then a lump sum will usually be payable, but will be subject to 35% tax at source (see section **6.11**). Even though there would still be no inheritance tax on the payment, this considerably reduces the advantage of the pension arrangement in this situation.

With an ISA, the treatment of the residual fund on death remains the same, whether or not any benefits have been taken.

Flexibility 1.10

Although the tax position generally favours pensions over ISAs, there can be considerably more flexibility with ISAs and this will redress the balance for some investors.

One of the areas where this is most apparent is in the form in which benefits can be taken. With an ISA, there are no restrictions. Thus, if the individual so chooses, they can take the whole of the ISA fund in the form of a lump sum, at a single point in time.

Alternatively, the individual can arrange to take regular withdrawals, and these will be completely free of tax, even though, for practical purposes, they take on the form of income payments.

It is also possible for the individual to choose to draw benefits from time to time as required, with no necessity for either regularity in timing or consistency in amount. These aspects give the individual much more control than is possible with a pension arrangement, where income once started cannot be stopped, and where there is limited scope to vary the level of income payments from time to time.

Access is another important area where ISAs offer more flexibility. Pension benefits cannot generally be accessed before the age of 50, whereas ISA benefits are available whenever the individual wishes. This can also mean that there is a temptation to draw on an ISA fund before retirement, to fund short term expenditure. The lack of accessibility of pension fund monies, particularly for younger potential investors, can therefore have advantages.

However, it is much more likely that a 20 year old will be prepared to put money into an ISA where, if necessary, it can be withdrawn, rather than making the commitment to place money into a pension arrangement, where it will be irretrievable for a period of 30 years.

Form of benefits 1.11

There is no requirement to take benefits from an ISA in any particular form, and in particular, there is no requirement for annuity purchase. Many people feel that annuities are insufficiently flexible, and perhaps also that currently they do not represent good value for money. The need to purchase an annuity can therefore be seen as a considerable disadvantage of pension arrangements.

Although the extent of the disadvantage has been lessened by the ability to take income withdrawals from the fund (see **Chapter 6: Income Withdrawals**), it remains the case that an annuity must be purchased by age 75 at the latest. (The proposals currently under consultation for the simplification of the tax treatment of pensions include a proposal that under some types of pension arrangement, the requirement to buy an annuity at age 75 will be removed. However the application of this will not be certain until the simplification proposals are finalised. These proposals are discussed in **Chapter 15: Simplification of Tax Treatment**.

The income withdrawal option is also generally only available to those with relatively large pension funds, whereas the flexibility of drawing benefits from an ISA is available at much lower levels.

Investment 1.12

Investment for retirement planning purposes will usually be long term, and will usually have a strong equity bias, as discussed in more detail in **Chapter 7: Investment Considerations**. ISAs also allow equity investment and can therefore, in principle, match a pension arrangement in this way.

There are however some disadvantages, depending on the detailed requirements of the investor. In particular, some investment areas cannot be accessed by means of an ISA, for example, commercial property.

Also, because the maximum amount which can be invested in insurance ISAs is only a small part of the total contribution limit, the ability of an ISA investor to make use of with profits funds (see section **7.33**) is very limited. For those investors to whom this concept appeals, ISAs will therefore not be an ideal solution to retirement planning, unless contribution levels are quite modest.

A further difficulty with ISAs is that money, once committed, must be allocated to one of the three investment components, and cannot subsequently be moved to another component. The components are:

(*a*)   stocks and shares;
(*b*)   cash; and
(*c*)   life insurance.

Although it is possible to hold cash within, for example, the stocks and shares component, on a temporary basis, any interest earned outside the cash component is subject to tax deducted at source at the rate of 20%, which removes a significant part of the tax advantage of the ISA. (There is however no further liability to tax, even for a higher rate taxpayer.)

Where an investor wishes to have the flexibility to move money from one sector to another, so as to control the timing of his exposure to the equity market, pension arrangements will usually prove more adaptable.

ISA limits   1.13

The limits on contribution levels to ISAs and to pension arrangements are entirely different. The ISA limits are expressed in monetary terms as a maximum annual figure, with subordinate limits applicable to the cash and life insurance components, and also to the stocks and shares component if the individual invests through mini–ISAs rather than maxi–ISAs.

Maxi-ISA and mini-ISA annual limits

Maxi-ISA annual limits:	Maximum total contribution: £7,000 (reducing to £5,000 from 6 April 2006) of which
Maximum to cash component:	£3,000 (reducing to £1,000 from 6 April 2006)
Maximum to insurance component:	£1,000

(If there is no investment in the cash and insurance components, the full £7,000 can be invested in the stocks and shares component of a maxi–ISA.)

Mini-ISA annual limits:

Stocks and shares mini–ISA:	£3,000
Cash mini–ISA:	£3,000 (reducing to £1,000 from 6 April 2006)
Insurance mini–ISA:	£1,000

Pension contributions on the other hand are generally limited in relation to an individual's earnings and age. In some cases the ISA limits will be greater, whilst in others the pension limits will be greater, depending on the individual's circumstances. This difference will also influence the choice in some cases.

Eligibility 1.14

The eligibility requirements for personal pensions are more restrictive than those which apply to ISAs, though in terms of retirement planning, this is no longer as big an issue as it was. This is partly because changes to the personal pension eligibility conditions were made from 6 April 2001, and from that date, those with no earnings can nevertheless contribute (see section **2.15**).

The upper age limitation, which requires contributors to be under the age of 75, is also unlikely to be a problem in this context.

Otherwise, the main group of individuals who are ineligible for personal pensions are those who are members of an occupational pension scheme provided by their employer, and who do not meet the requirements of the concurrency rules (see section **2.20**). Given that in these circumstances, provision is being made through the occupational scheme itself, this again is unlikely to be a practical drawback.

Overall comparison 1.15

As can be seen from the above, there are advantages and disadvantages on both sides of the comparison between pension arrangements and ISAs. Broadly, the tax position favours pensions, but the more flexible features of ISAs tend to redress the balance.

Over the years, there has been a sometimes heated debate regarding the relative merits of these two prime candidates for retirement planning. In reality, the needs of most individuals are probably best met by a combination of the two.

This would enable an individual to use pension arrangements to maximise the tax advantages on amounts which they are prepared to commit to retirement planning on an irrevocable basis, whilst other funding, to which access might possibly be required in an emergency, could be housed within ISAs.

Property 1.16

For many people, property is a major asset, even if only in the form of the house in which they live. Although retirement does not mean that the individual no longer requires a roof over his head, many people anticipate that they will move house in retirement and trade down to a smaller, or at least less expensive property.

This can release a substantial amount of capital, particularly if any mortgage commitment has been already paid off. This capital, which is then free to be invested, can provide a substantial financial resource in retirement.

The attraction of this approach to retirement planning is increased by the fact that any capital gain made in respect of an individual's principal UK residence is entirely free of tax. This exemption from CGT does not apply to other property, and this will detract from the net return available in such cases, but property has proved to be a very attractive investment for many people.

It would be unwise to rely entirely on a single property as a means of retirement planning. This is because the timing of the disposal of the property may be difficult to control, in the sense that the individual may not be able to delay his retirement simply because the property market is depressed. Similarly, it will not be possible to spread the disposal over a period in the way that it would be possible to spread, for example, the disposal of an equity portfolio.

Sale of a business 1.17

Those who work in their own business, whether as a sole proprietor or partner, or as a shareholding director of a limited company, will often expect to provide for a substantial proportion of their retirement needs by the sale of their business, or their share in it. This can work extremely well, and where the business has a substantial value, the individual may feel that they have no need of any other form of retirement planning.

There are considerable tax advantages which apply on the sale of a business, even though retirement relief has now been phased out. Generally business taper relief will be available, and this will mean that, subject to a requirement that the business must have been owned for two years, the amount of the gain which is subject to capital gains tax (CGT) is reduced by 75%. As a result, the effective rate of CGT is, at most, 10%.

However, there are considerable uncertainties. For example, it is very difficult to establish what the value of the business will be in advance, and this makes it very difficult for the individual to plan ahead. In reality, the range of potential purchasers for a small business is often very limited, and as a result it may not be possible to establish a value for the business on an objective basis. Instead, the value will simply be whatever the ultimate buyer is prepared to pay.

As long as the seller of the business has a degree of flexibility as regards timing, and the business is a desirable and profitable one, he may be in a position to negotiate from a point of strength and so achieve a good price. However, if the situation is more of a forced sale, perhaps because the individual, or their partner, has experienced a deterioration in health, it is likely to be far more difficult to obtain a good price.

The amount realised may also suffer if the business has gone into a period of unfavourable trading conditions. This is likely to damage profitability, therefore making the business less valuable, and possibly even making it impossible to sell at all. If the poor trading conditions are likely to be temporary, it may be possible for the individual to bide their time until profits increase. However for someone who would ideally like to retire, keeping a business going in such circumstances is difficult. In addition, the business might lag behind its competitors if the owner becomes less inclined to innovate and to take on new market developments, because of any imminent retirement plans.

A further factor which may create difficulty is that often the success of the business is very much tied to the influence and work of the individual who is now seeking to retire. Often such an individual will have an extremely optimistic view of the sale price which could be achieved for the business, perhaps ignoring the loss of their own ongoing involvement in it.

Overall, then, when this approach to retirement planning works, and the business is sold for a large sum, the individual may do extremely well. However the extent of uncertainty and the difficulty in planning mean that it could be extremely ill-advised to rely on the sale of the business as the sole or main form of retirement planning.

It is also possible that the current favourable tax environment for the disposal of businesses and business assets could be replaced with less attractive provisions at some future date, perhaps without warning.

Other investments   1.18

Although the investments discussed above are the main alternatives to pension arrangements for retirement planning, in reality any investments could be used. These can include deposit accounts, equities (and related collective investments such as unit trusts, Open Ended Investment Companies (OEICs), and investment trusts), gilts and other fixed interest investments, and investment orientated life insurance policies. National Savings & Investments products could also fulfil a useful role.

In general, the tax attractions of pension arrangements and ISAs will make them a better first choice than other investments which do not enjoy the same tax advantages. However other products should not be ruled out entirely. Where, for example, an individual is firmly against the idea of being forced to purchase an annuity at any stage, it may be that once he has exhausted his ISA allowance, he will prefer to invest in (say) OEICs, without any tax advantaged wrapper, rather than putting money into a pension arrangement. If the OEIC chosen produces a relatively low level of income, and if the individual does not already use his CGT annual exemption, there is scope for tax free capital gains up to the level of the exemption. The tax disadvantage may therefore be slight.

Employer involvement   1.19

A factor which will almost always make pension arrangements more attractive than any alternative is the availability of employer contributions. Whether the scheme is an occupational pension scheme or a personal pension, it is possible for the employer to contribute and, as mentioned in section **1.5** above, any employer contribution will not create a tax or National Insurance liability for the employee.

An employee is not required to participate in any pension arrangements made by the employer, but few employers will make the amount of any employer contribution available to the employee in any other form. If the employee chooses not to participate therefore, they will forego benefits that would otherwise have been provided by the employer.

Sometimes the employee is required to contribute personally as a condition of membership of the scheme, and this may act as a disincentive for some employees to join the scheme. However the employer will often either match the employee contribution or pay in a greater amount. Given that the employee contribution qualifies for tax relief, the real cost of the scheme will be small relative to the amount invested in total.

Example – Cost to employee

An employee has the opportunity to join a personal pension to which their employer will contribute. Employees are required to make a contribution equivalent to 4% of their basic salary, before allowing for tax relief, and the employer will then match this amount.

The employee's basic salary is £20,000, so their contribution would be 4% of £20,000 = £800. This would qualify for tax relief and for the employee, who is a basic rate taxpayer, this would be worth 22% of £800 = £176.

The net cost to the employee would therefore be £624.

The total invested for the employee's eventual benefit would be £800 (from their contribution) plus a further £800 (from the employer) ie £1,600 in total. This is more than two and a half times the net cost to the employee.

The involvement of the employer is required under the provisions introducing stakeholder pensions, though they are not required to contribute. These provisions are covered in detail in section **1.25** below.

Structure of personal pensions 1.20

Personal pensions can only be arranged on a money purchase (ie defined contribution) basis. This is logical, since benefits can only be provided by contributions invested, and there is no shared fund to allow cross-subsidy as would be the case with a defined benefit occupational scheme.

Prior to 6 April 2001, personal pension schemes could be offered only by one of a relatively small number of authorised pension providers, including insurance companies, friendly societies, banks and building societies. This basis is still the most common today and a list of the institutions which can act as authorised pension providers is given in the table below.

These schemes are referred to as contract-based schemes, because they involve a contractual relationship between the member and the provider.

Definition of 'authorised pension provider'

Institutions which can act as an authorised pension provider are:

(*a*) a person who is authorised under *Chapter III* of *Part I* of the *Financial Services Act 1986* (*FSA 1986*) to carry on investment business and who carries on business of the following kind:
  (i) issuing insurance policies or annuity contracts, or
  (ii) managing unit trust schemes authorised under *s 78(1)*, *FSA 1986*;
(*b*) an EC company which:
  (i) lawfully carries on long term business in the United Kingdom (i.e. through a branch in respect of which such of the requirements of *Part I* of *Schedule 2F* to the *Insurance Companies Act 1982* (*ICA 1982*) as are applicable have been complied with), or
  (ii) lawfully provides long term insurance in the United Kingdom (i.e. such of the requirements of *Part I* of *Schedule 2F, ICA 1982* as are applicable have been complied with in respect of the insurance);

(c) a building society within the meaning of the *Building Societies Act 1986 (BSA 1986)*;

(d) a pension company within the meaning of the *Building Societies (Designation of Pension Companies) Order 1987 (SI 1987/1871)* which is an associate of a building society within the meaning of *s 18(17), BSA 1986*;

(e) an institution authorised under the *Banking Act 1987 (BA 1987)*;

(f) a body corporate which is a subsidiary or holding company of an institution authorised under the *BA 1987*, or is a subsidiary of a holding company of such an institution;

(g) a recognised bank or licensed institution within the meaning of the *Banking Act 1979*; or

(h) an institution which:

   (i) is a European institution within the meaning of *regulation 3(1)* of the *Banking Co-ordination (Second Council Directive) Regulations 1992 (SI 1992/3218)* and

   (ii) conforms with the conditions and requirements of those Regulations.

Source: *Inland Revenue Guidance Notes IR76*

An authorised corporate director (ACD) of an OEIC is not included within this list, but is nevertheless regarded as being acceptable. This is because the tax regulations governing OEICs allow a reference to an authorised unit trust scheme to be regarded as including a reference to an OEIC (*paragraph 5(1)(b), Open-Ended Investment Companies (Tax) Regulations 1997 (SI 1997/1154)*).

It is also possible for other organisations to establish a personal pension scheme, under trust, subject to a number of conditions. The schemes must generally have applied for registration as a stakeholder pension scheme, and their ability to act as an authorised pension provider will be dependent on that registration taking place.

Trust-based schemes of this sort have been established by a few large employers, seeking to provide a tailor-made scheme for employees, or might be established by an industry body where the intention is to appeal specifically to employees working in a particular industry, or by an affinity group.

Whether the scheme is contract-based or trust-based, the pension provider establishes the scheme, and individuals are invited to become members of it.

Scheme administrator   1.21

In relation to any scheme, it is a requirement under *section 638(1)* of the *Income and Corporation Taxes Act 1988 (ICTA 1988)* that 'there is a person resident in the United Kingdom who will be responsible for the management of the scheme'. This person is the 'scheme administrator' and must be named in the scheme documents.

The *Inland Revenue Guidance Notes (IR76)* specify that the scheme administrator may be one of:

(*a*) the provider;
(*b*) an employee of the provider;
(*c*) a committee of management;
(*d*) a corporate body; or
(*e*) in the case of a scheme established under irrevocable trust, the trustee.

It is the scheme administrator that the Inland Revenue would look to if any of the requirements of the legislation are not met, for example the requirement for contributions to be within limits, and for this to be checked by the administrator.

The member may have rights under a number of contractual arrangements under the same personal pension scheme. In the past, an individual applying for membership of a personal pension scheme will often have entered into a large number of such arrangements automatically, in order to facilitate the taking of benefits from different arrangements at different times (see section **5.5** for a discussion of phased retirement).

This practice may become less popular in future because it is now possible for benefits under a single arrangement to be taken in tranches, thus making the use of multiple arrangements redundant.

Group personal pensions   1.22

Personal pensions are by their nature individual arrangements where the member is in control. It is for the member to decide when to take benefits, and in what form, subject only to the constraints imposed by the governing legislation. Similarly it is for the member to decide (within the options available under the particular arrangement concerned) where the fund is invested.

Many employers however offer group personal pension facilities to their employees. Sometimes the employer contributes, and sometimes contributions are paid solely by the employees.

In many ways a group personal pension facility can seem very like an occupational pension scheme and may be promoted to employees in a similar way by the employer. However, whether or not the employer contributes, the scheme remains individual to the member and remains in the member's control.

Stakeholder pensions 1.23

Stakeholder pensions were introduced from 6 April 2001 and are a sub-category of personal pensions, to which particular requirements apply, for example, in relation to charges.

Despite these requirements, it is important to understand that there are no differences in the tax treatment of stakeholder pensions, nor in the calculation of contribution limits as compared to personal pensions generally.

The motivation behind the introduction of stakeholder pensions from a governmental point of view was to ensure that individuals had access to personal pensions which met specific standards in relation to charges, access and terms. These standards are known as CAT standards.

CAT standards 1.24

The Government felt that, prior to April 2001, personal pensions generally were complex and expensive, and were sometimes not sufficiently flexible to meet the needs of potential investors, particularly those on modest incomes. The imposition of CAT standards under the *Stakeholder Pension Schemes Regulations 2000 (SI 2000/1403)* is intended to address these problems, and the main standards are summarised in the checklist below.

Checklist: Main stakeholder pension CAT standards

Charges

- The maximum annual charge is 1% per year of the fund (which can be taken at the daily rate of 1/365%).
- No other charges can be made for the running of the scheme, except in respect of additional services provided to the member.
- Any such additional services cannot be compulsory.
- There can be no entry or exit charges, nor any bid/offer spread, nor any special charges for transfers into or out of the scheme.

Access

- If the provider chooses to impose a minimum contribution level, this cannot exceed £20.
- There can be no requirement for regularity of contributions.
- There can be no prohibition on contributions stopping or re-starting, increasing (subject to normal limits) or reducing (subject, if the provider wishes, to the £20 minimum).

Terms

- If money is held on deposit (other than short term, pending dealing), the interest rate must be no less than bank base rate less 2%, with increases in the rate reflected within one month.
- If there is a with profits fund available, its assets must be ring-fenced from any other with profits fund(s) of the provider.
- The scheme must allow members to contract out of S2P (see **Chapter 12: Contracting Out**).
- It must be willing, if a member wishes, to accept or receive transfer payments to or from other approved pension schemes.
- Members must not be forced to make investment decisions, so there must be a default fund choice for those who prefer not to do so.

CAT standards are compulsory for stakeholder pensions, but many providers choose to offer personal pensions which do not fully meet the standards and which cannot therefore be described as stakeholder pensions. One reason for this is that the cap on charges at 1% *per annum* is regarded by many providers as being too low to support an arrangement which offers anything like the full range of facilities permitted by the personal pension legislation.

The Government is content for more complex products with higher charge levels to be available for more sophisticated investors, alongside generally simpler stakeholder products from other providers, which will be sufficient to meet the needs of other investors, particularly those on lower pay, who are likely to be making lower contributions.

This is also reflected in the low minimum contribution which must apply under stakeholder pensions. Providers must be prepared to accept a contribution of £20, without any requirement for a commitment to regularity.

Employer involvement   1.25

The cap on charges means that there is less scope for adviser remuneration and therefore less incentive for advisers to seek out situations where stakeholder pensions might be appropriate. In order to assist in the distribution of stakeholder pensions therefore, the Government recognised that it was important for employers to be involved. It is therefore required under the *Stakeholder Pension Schemes Regulations 2000 (SI 2000/1403)* that employers, with a number of exceptions, designate a stakeholder pension scheme for its employees.

The requirement for designation is that the employer must choose a scheme and provide employees with access to it. This requirement is not particularly well defined, though in practice the employer is likely to make descriptive literature available, and probably provide access for a representative of the provider to speak to interested employees regarding the operation of the scheme.

The employer is relieved of any obligation to investigate or monitor investment performance by *section 3(8)* of the *Welfare Reform and Pensions Act 1999 (WRPA 1999)*. Designation of a scheme is not investment advice and does not require the employer to be authorised under the *Financial Services and Markets Act 2000 (FSMA 2000)*.

The employer must also provide the facility for employees to have contributions deducted from their salaries through payroll, with the employer remitting the amounts deducted to the product provider. This must be done by the 19th of the month following that in which the deduction was made.

The employee must be able to vary the amount of the contributions deducted through payroll, but it is possible for the employer to limit the administrative complications of this by restricting the ability to do so to no more than once in each six month period.

Exempt employers   1.26

Employers will be exempt under *para 22* of the *Stakeholder Pension Schemes Regulations 2000 (SI 2000/1403)* from the requirement to designate a stakeholder pension scheme if one of the following conditions applies, namely:

(a)   the employer has fewer than five employees; or
(b)   all employees are eligible for membership of a group personal pension scheme which meets particular requirements.

In order to allow the employer to be exempt on the grounds that all employees are eligible for a group personal pension arrangement, it is necessary for the arrangement to have an employer contribution of at least 3% of the basic salary of members. Employee contributions can be required as a condition of entry of the scheme, but the level of contributions required from them must not exceed the employer contribution. In addition, it cannot exceed 3% of basic pay in the case of employees who joined the scheme on or after 6 April 2001.

This does not prevent the employer encouraging employees to contribute more on a voluntary basis, for example by matching higher contributions.

In addition, the group personal pension arrangement must not apply any exit charges, and the employer must be prepared to deduct contributions through payroll, remitting them to the product provider in the same way as is required under the stakeholder pension provisions.

In some ways the requirement for a 3% contribution from the employer is a peculiar provision, in that there is no requirement for employers to contribute to stakeholder pension arrangements.

In addition, as can be seen in section **1.27** below, employees who are eligible for membership of an occupational scheme are excluded from the requirements to designate a stakeholder scheme. Although an employer must contribute to an occupational pension scheme, there is no requirement for those contributions to be at a particular level, nor for the benefits to reach any set standards, in order for this exclusion to apply.

However under personal pensions, charges may well be higher than those which apply under a stakeholder pension scheme and this provision is in place to ensure that members are not disadvantaged as a result.

Note that in order for the employer to be exempt, one of the conditions above must be satisfied fully. The conditions cannot be used in conjunction with each other. In other words, if an employer has, for example, 20 employees, 18 of whom are eligible for a personal pension scheme but the other two are not, then the employer is not exempt. The fact that he has less than five employees who are not eligible for the personal pension scheme does not provide exemption.

Excluded employees   1.27

If an employer does not satisfy the requirements for exemption as discussed in section **1.26** above, then a stakeholder scheme must be designated for 'relevant employees'. *Section 3(9)* of the *WWRPA 1999* excludes from this definition any employees who are:

(*a*)   eligible for membership of an occupational scheme of the employer; or

(*b*)   whose earnings are below the Lower Earnings Limit ($£77$ per week in 2003/04).

These exclusions are extended slightly by *para 23* of the *Stakeholder Pension Schemes Regulations 2000 (SI 2000/1403)*. Also excluded under these regulations are:

- employees who would be eligible for an occupational scheme if they had completed 12 months service, but have not yet done so;
- employees who would be eligible for an occupational scheme were it not for the fact that they are under the age of 18, or within five years of their expected retirement date;
- those who have been eligible for an occupational pension scheme of the employer, but who have declined to join and are excluded as a result;
- those who have been employed for less than three months;

- those whose earnings have fallen below the Lower Earnings Limit for one week (or more) in the last three months;
- those who are ineligible to contribute to a stakeholder pension scheme under the law or Inland Revenue practice.

Decision trees 1.28

The Financial Services Authority has developed decision trees which are intended to help individuals to decide whether stakeholder pensions are suitable for their needs. These decision trees are a recognition that in many cases individuals will not receive personalised financial advice in relation to these arrangements. These decision trees can be viewed online at http://www.fsa.gov.uk/consumer/decision_trees/index.html.

CAT standards (see section 1.24 above) should limit the individual's risk in investing in a stakeholder pension scheme, though the decision trees do suggest that further advice be sought where required. Where advice is given, this must be by a person who is authorised to do so under the *FSMA 2000*, but it is not necessary to be authorised in order merely to help an individual use the decision trees.

Note that where a recommendation is made for a personal pension which is not a stakeholder pension scheme, the suitability letter issued to the client must state why the personal pension is at least as suitable for the client's needs as a stakeholder pension would have been. This means that, for example, if the charges under the personal pension scheme are higher than those which would have been made under a stakeholder pension scheme, there would need to be compensating advantages which are relevant to the particular client's circumstances.

Personal pension scheme design 1.29

The introduction of stakeholder pensions has had a major impact on the design of personal pensions generally. In particular, the level of charges under personal pension schemes has tended to reduce significantly and is now generally at, or close to, the levels permitted under stakeholder pension schemes. If this were not so, it would be difficult for non-stakeholder schemes to compete. Nevertheless, higher charges may be supportable to an extent, if the product allows more complex features than are generally available under stakeholder schemes. This could, for example, be the availability of a particularly wide range of fund links – including specialist funds – where the levels of investment research necessarily undertaken are higher than normal.

Personal pension schemes usually also allow contributions to start or stop, increase or decrease, without penalty, and allow one off contributions. In the past, penalties have tended to apply if contributions were not maintained for at least a minimum period.

In addition, personal pensions are also becoming more flexible regarding the drawing of retirement benefits. Although most have allowed access to benefits within the age range permitted by the legislation, in the past it has been common to apply sometimes substantial penalties if benefits are drawn early. This is not permitted under stakeholder pension schemes and is becoming less common under all personal pension schemes.

Application of rules to occupational schemes 1.30

Although this handbook is concerned with personal pension schemes rather than occupational pension schemes, it is relevant at this point to note that it is possible for the trustees of an occupational pension scheme to opt for the scheme to be covered by the contribution limits and rules applicable under personal pension scheme legislation. This is generally referred to as the 'defined contribution regime' or simply the 'DC regime'.

If this is done, the benefit based limitations which generally apply under occupational pension schemes cease to apply, so there is no limit on the totality of benefits which can be provided. In addition, the limit on tax free cash at retirement conforms with personal pension rules, and is therefore 25% of the fund, rather than the final remuneration related basis which applies under occupational schemes.

Note however that the scheme remains an occupational pension scheme. As a result, for example, its investment is the responsibility of the scheme trustees. It is also necessary for such a scheme to have an employer contribution.

Similarly, if the scheme contracts out, the scheme will be treated not as an Appropriate Personal Pension Scheme (see **Chapter 12: Contracting Out**) but as a Contracted Out Money Purchase Scheme (COMPS). This means, amongst other things, that part of the reduction in National Insurance Contributions which results from contracting out will be handled through payroll rather than all of it being dealt with through a rebate from the National Insurance Contributions Office.

Where such a scheme is contracted out, protected rights benefits will be accrued in respect of contracted out service and, as with most personal pension arrangements, protected rights will be excluded from the calculation of tax free cash benefits at retirement.

2 — Eligibility

Introduction 2.1

The eligibility conditions for personal pensions changed significantly from 6 April 2001, and now cover a much wider group than was previously the case. However, at the same time, the conditions, which are covered in *section 632A* of the *Income and Corporation Taxes Act 1988* (*ICTA 1988*) (as amended) have become more complex as a result.

The main groups which are now eligible are:

(*a*) those with relevant earnings, which includes the self-employed and employees who are not in pensionable employment;

(*b*) those with no earnings; and

(*c*) those who are in pensionable employment, but who meet the conditions under the concurrency rules.

There is one over-arching requirement which must always be satisfied. This is that the individual must be under the age of 75 (simply because retirement benefits must be taken no later than the individual's 75th birthday). There is no minimum age requirement, though some special conditions apply to arrangements taken out for minors. These are covered in section **2.16** below.

Note that in this chapter, and throughout most parts of this book, reference is made to personal pensions. This term includes stakeholder pensions, which are essentially personal pensions, but with additional requirements, including the CAT standards described in section **1.24**. Eligibility for stakeholder pensions is identical to that for personal pensions.

Relevant earnings 2.2

Perhaps the most important eligibility category consists of those with relevant earnings within the tax year in respect of which contributions are made. The term 'relevant earnings' is defined in *s 644, ICTA 1988*.

Individuals who are in receipt of relevant earnings are:

(*a*) the self-employed who are carrying on a trade, profession or vocation which produces income which is chargeable under Schedule D. Both sole proprietors and working partners within a partnership fall into this category; or

(*b*) employees with earnings chargeable under Schedule E from an office or employment which is not regarded as pensionable employment, as defined in *s 645, ICTA 1988*. In general, this means employees who are not members of an approved occupational pension scheme. However, the question of membership of such a scheme is not always a straightforward one, and is dealt with in some detail below.

The intention behind pension arrangements, and the reason for the availability of tax advantages in relation to them, is to encourage individuals to make their own provision for retirement. This is necessary because they will need to replace earnings which they are likely one day to become too old to continue to generate themselves.

Linking eligibility to the existence of a source of relevant earnings is therefore a logical provision. Until 6 April 2001, this was the only way in which eligibility for a personal pension could be established.

The Inland Revenue has provided a summary of what does and what does not constitute relevant earnings, and this is reproduced at the end of this chapter.

Overseas aspects 2.3

To be regarded as relevant earnings for personal pension purposes, the income concerned must be chargeable to UK income tax.

100% deduction 2.4

In some cases (now applicable only to seafarers working overseas, though of wider application in the past), income may be chargeable to income tax, but be subject to a 100% deduction, so no tax is actually paid. These earnings can still qualify as relevant earnings, because they are chargeable to income tax.

Because contributions by individuals are payable net of basic rate tax (see section **4.1**), those subject to the 100% deduction still benefit from tax relief on their contributions, even though they may pay no tax.

Foreign emoluments 2.5

Where an individual receives foreign emoluments, as defined in *s 192, ICTA 1988* (broadly income of a non-UK domiciled individual, employed in the UK by an employer who is not resident in the UK), this income will in some cases be chargeable to UK tax and could rank as relevant earnings. However, if the individual is a member of an overseas pension scheme which the Inland Revenue regards as corresponding to a

UK approved scheme or statutory scheme, the foreign emoluments are excluded from the definition of relevant earnings. (This needs to be checked in relation to the circumstances of any particular case, since there is some scope for the Inland Revenue to take a view in this area.)

Non-residents   2.6

If an individual is resident outside the UK for tax purposes, and has no net relevant earnings, they are not eligible to join a personal pension scheme. However, if they are already a member (having joined whilst resident and ordinarily resident in the UK), they can continue to contribute for a period. The requirement is that the individual must have been resident and ordinarily resident in the UK at some time during the tax year in which the contribution is made, or during the five preceding tax years.

Pensionable employment   2.7

Whether an individual is a member of an approved occupational pension scheme is a matter of fact. If the individual is currently accruing retirement benefits under such a scheme, they are in pensionable employment.

It is important to note that membership of a scheme means that all earnings arising from the employment are excluded from the definition of relevant earnings. This is so even though in many cases the occupational pension scheme provides benefits linked only to part of an individual's total Schedule E remuneration.

Example – Earnings from pensionable employment

An individual is a member of their employer's occupational pension scheme, which provides benefits of 1/60th of final pensionable salary for each year of scheme membership. Pensionable salary is defined as basic salary only.

In addition to their basic salary of £20,000, the employee also receives overtime and bonus payments totalling £5,000, and benefits in kind which are valued for tax purposes at £3,000.

Although the occupational pension scheme only provides benefits linked to £20,000 of the employee's total Schedule E income of £28,000, none of their earnings from the employment count as relevant earnings.

There are a number of situations where it is less obvious whether an employment is pensionable.

Unapproved schemes   2.8

If an individual belongs to a scheme provided by their employer, but the scheme is an unapproved retirement benefits scheme, this alone will not result in the employment being regarded as pensionable. The earnings from the employment will therefore be relevant earnings.

In reality, unapproved schemes are usually provided for high earners as an additional to an approved scheme, where the benefits which can be provided under the approved scheme are limited by the earnings cap. In such a case, the membership of the approved scheme would render the employment pensionable in the normal way.

Contributions by an employer to a Funded Unapproved Retirement Benefits Scheme (FURBS) are taxed as income of the employee concerned. If the employee is not also a member of an approved scheme, the employer contributions to the FURBS will themselves count as relevant earnings for personal pension purposes, in addition to the other remuneration arising from the employment.

Death benefits only   2.9

Some employees are covered under the terms of an occupational scheme only for benefits arising on death in service, and not for retirement benefits.

This sometimes arises on a permanent basis, where only limited categories of employees (for example, monthly paid staff) are covered for retirement benefits as well as death benefits, but other employees are included for death benefits only. It may also arise on a temporary basis, where employees are covered for death benefits whilst they complete a waiting period prior to entry to the scheme for full benefits.

Membership for death benefits only does not result in the employment being regarded as pensionable, and does not exclude the resulting earnings from the definition of relevant earnings for personal pension purposes.

Whether the occupational scheme death benefits are provided in the form of a lump sum or in the form of income for a spouse and/or dependant(s) makes no difference.

Waiting periods   2.10

The eligibility conditions for occupational schemes commonly include a waiting period, in other words a minimum period of service which must be completed before an employee is invited to join the scheme. Similarly there are often minimum age requirements which must be met.

In these circumstances the periods of service completed by an employee before joining the occupational scheme are not regarded as pensionable employment and the earnings arising prior to joining the scheme constitute relevant earnings.

Under some occupational schemes (though only a minority) once the employee becomes a member, benefits may be backdated to cover all or part of the service the employee completed whilst waiting to become eligible. This has no effect on the interpretation of pensionable employment, and earnings arising before the individual actually becomes a member of the scheme still rank as relevant earnings. In practical terms however, there may be rather less incentive for the employee to make personal pension provision during this period, because they know that benefits under the occupational scheme will be provided on a backdated basis.

Joining an occupational scheme 2.11

Once an individual joins an approved occupational pension scheme and is accruing retirement benefits, the employment becomes pensionable and the earnings arising from it cease to be relevant earnings. However, where the individual joins the scheme part way through a tax year, the earnings derived before joining remain within the definition of relevant earnings. As a result, subject to normal contribution limits (see **Chapter 3: Contribution Limits**) the individual can continue to make personal pension contributions through the remainder of the tax year.

Indeed, again subject to contribution limits, they can continue to make contributions until 31 January in the following tax year provided that these contributions are carried back to the year in which there was a source of relevant earnings.

Example – Entering pensionable employment

An employee joins their employer's occupational pension scheme on 1 August 2003, having completed the required waiting period of twelve months. The employee has been contributing £50 per month to a personal pension throughout this period.

Earnings from 1 August 2003 are not relevant earnings but those received before that date remain so. As the employee has a source of relevant earnings during the tax year 2003/04, they remain eligible and can continue contributions until April 2004.

During the tax year 2004/05, even though the employee remains a member of the occupational pension scheme, they can continue to make contributions to their personal pension until 31 January 2005, provided they carry them back to tax year 2003/04 during which they were eligible.

Full details of the operation of carry back are given in section **4.13**.

Leaving an occupational scheme 2.12

Usually, if a member of an occupational pension scheme leaves the scheme before benefits become payable, there will be preserved rights held for them under the scheme, or a transfer value will be paid to an arrangement chosen by the member instead.

Once the member leaves the scheme, pensionable employment ceases. If they stay in the same employment, their subsequent earnings will therefore be relevant earnings. Whether they leave the scheme of their own volition, or whether they are forced to leave for example because the scheme closes, makes no difference.

If they leave the employment, and start to generate earnings from another source, this source will be considered separately and the earnings will be relevant earnings if the normal conditions discussed above are met. Personal pension contributions can commence once they have a source of relevant earnings, subject to normal contribution limits.

Example – Leaving pensionable service I

An employee joined their employer's pension scheme on 1 April 1999, and left the scheme and the employment on 30 June 2003. They take a month off, and then enter a new employment, where there is no occupational pension scheme, on 1 August 2003. Their earnings from the first employment in the 2003/04 tax year are £10,000 and from the second employment are £20,000.

Their relevant earnings for 2003/04 are £20,000.

However, note that if a member leaves the occupational scheme before completing two years' qualifying service (which is generally service qualifying for benefits under the scheme), there is no legal requirement to provide any preserved benefits. Instead, if the member has paid contributions, these can be refunded (after deduction of income tax at 20%). If there were no member contributions (ie the scheme was non-contributory), there would be no refund, nor any preserved benefits.

If no preserved benefits are provided (nor an alternative transfer payment made) the employment ceases to be regarded as pensionable, with retrospective effect, and the earnings from it become relevant earnings. Personal pension contributions can therefore be paid, based on all earnings from the employment in the tax year of leaving. It may be possible to pay contributions in respect of the previous tax year as well, using the carry back option (see section **4.13**).

It is open to the scheme to preserve benefits even for those with very short service, though few do so because of the potential administration problems of dealing with large numbers of small pensions. If a preserved pension is provided, then the period of employment whilst a member of the scheme continues to be regarded as pensionable.

Example – Leaving pensionable service II

An employee joined their employer's pension scheme on 1 December 2001, and left the scheme and the employment on 31 August 2003. The scheme was non-contributory.

On leaving, they are told that the scheme does not provide a preserved pension benefit because they have completed less than two years' qualifying service.

Their earnings from the employment were £12,000 in 2003/04. These now constitute relevant earnings, and provide the basis of eligibility for personal pensions in 2003/04.

Their earnings from the employment were £25,000 in 2002/03. These are also now regarded as relevant earnings, and a contribution based on them could be paid any time up to 31 January 2004, provided it is carried back to 2002/03.

See section **4.13** for details of carry back.

Controlling directors   2.13

Generally, the rules relating to controlling directors are the same as those applicable to other employees, but there is an exception to this under *s 644(6B)(a), ICTA 1988*.

This section excludes from the definition of relevant earnings any amounts which arise from a company of which the individual is a controlling director, where in the same tax year the individual is in receipt of benefits (in cash or pension form) from an approved occupational scheme, in respect of previous service with that company.

If benefits originally accrued under an occupational scheme in these circumstances are transferred to a personal pension or section 32 buy-out arrangement, or to an occupational scheme of a subsequent employer, these would also be caught when in payment under *ss 644(6C)-644(6E), ICTA 1988.*

Definition of controlling director

For the purposes of *s 644, ICTA 1988*, the term 'controlling director' means a director who is, either on their own, or with one or more associates, the beneficial owner of, or able, directly or through the medium of other companies or by any other indirect means, to control 20% or over of the ordinary share capital of the company.

An individual will continue to be regarded as a controlling director if they are within this definition at any time in the tax year concerned, or at any time in the preceding ten tax years.

See also section **2.18** below regarding controlling directors of investment companies.

More than one source of earnings 2.14

Many situations arise where individuals have earnings from more than one source. If one (or more) of those sources of earnings is either a self-employment, or an employment to which no occupational pension scheme relates, then the earnings from that source or sources constitute net relevant earnings, and will support eligibility for membership of a personal pension.

The effect on contribution limits in these circumstances is dealt with in section **3.11**.

No relevant earnings 2.15

Before 6 April 2001, only those individuals with relevant earnings were eligible to contribute to a personal pension arrangement. However one of the most important departures from previous practice which came into effect at that time was the widening of eligibility to include non-earners, under *s 632A, ICTA 1988.*

Much of the intention behind this change was to allow those with a broken earnings pattern to continue to contribute. This would cover, for example, those who have temporarily stopped working in order to look after and raise young children, or to care for a sick relative.

Contribution limits had always until this point been linked to earnings, and this change of eligibility was facilitated by the introduction of a minimum contribution allowance (rather oddly known as the 'earnings threshold') which can be paid irrespective of the level of earnings (or lack of earnings) by those who are eligible. This is discussed in more detail in section **3.7**.

Although the ability to pay contributions to personal pensions in these circumstances is welcome, the difficulty in many such cases is the availability of sufficient funds to pay the contribution, rather than the eligibility conditions themselves. It is early yet to say whether the extension of eligibility has impacted to any great degree on this target group.

Note that to be eligible, an individual with no net relevant earnings must be under the age of 75 and must, for at least part of the tax year in question, not be in pensionable employment.

Example – No relevant earnings

An employee has worked for JKL Ltd for five years and has always been a member of the company's occupational pension scheme. They leave service at 31 July 2003, because they have been offered a position with RFG Ltd. This does not start until 1 September 2003, and they will join the RFG occupational pension scheme immediately on starting in the new position. They have no employment for August 2003, and so the individual takes this as their annual holiday.

If the individual wishes, they can contribute to a personal pension in 2003/04, with a contribution up to the earnings threshold of £3,600. (Both employments are pensionable, so they have no relevant earnings in 2003/04, but in August they were not in pensionable employment.)

In addition the individual must be:

(a)   resident and ordinarily resident in the UK in the tax year in respect of which the contribution is paid; or

(b)   resident and ordinarily resident in the UK at some time in the five preceding tax years; or

(c)   a Crown servant working overseas, but treated as working in the UK under *s 132(4), ICTA 1988*; or

(d)   the spouse of such a Crown servant.

As discussed in section **2.6** above, a non-resident can contribute under (*b*) above only if already a member of a personal pension scheme, but cannot join a scheme for the first time unless in receipt of relevant earnings at some point in the current tax year.

Children 2.16

Children, whatever their age, can be in receipt of income and may be tax-payers in their own right. They may therefore have a source of relevant earnings, and although it is relatively unusual for young children to have significant earnings, it is not impossible, particularly where the child is active in, for example, acting or modelling. In some circumstances, a child may have income from playing sports on a professional basis and this may also constitute relevant earnings.

Where a minor is in receipt of relevant earnings, they will be eligible to make personal pension contributions based on those earnings in the normal way (though as discussed below, the legal guardian will generally need to take responsibility for the arrangement). Where there are no net relevant earnings, the introduction of the earnings threshold and the widening of eligibility to non-earners will mean that personal pension contributions can be paid for the benefit of children.

Where contributions are to be paid in respect of an individual who is under 16, or 18 if not employed, it is only possible for the contract to be established by the child's legal guardian. The Inland Revenue requires that it must be the legal guardian who:

(*a*) completes the application form and any accompanying declarations;
(*b*) is responsible for ensuring that contribution limits are not exceeded; and
(*c*) is responsible for the contract until the child reaches 18 (irrespective of whether they are working).

The legal guardian must also sign a separate declaration confirming their understanding that it is not possible for the contributions made to be returned except in accordance with normal personal pension provisions, governing both the form and timing of benefits.

Since April 2001, there has been a considerable amount of business trans-acted where contributions are paid for the benefit of minors. Sometimes the contributions are paid by a parent, sometimes by a grandparent or other relative, and sometimes by unrelated individuals such as godparents.

There are certainly attractions from a tax point of view for making finan-cial provision in this way. In particular, the tax advantaged growth which is enjoyed by pension funds will be particularly powerful over the potentially very long period involved before benefits are taken. Many people take the view that making financial provision in this way for a minor provides a uniquely attractive way of making a gift with a long term financial impact.

Some commentators have expressed the view that the popularity of this approach runs counter to any governmental intention of focusing tax relief towards lower earners, since inevitably such provision has generally been made by the relatively well off. Whilst this must be true to a certain extent, the building up of potentially substantial retirement rights for future generations will inevitably reduce the potential burden which could fall on the state in future, and may as a result take some pressure off the National Insurance fund in the long term. It seems unlikely therefore that there will be any attempt to legislate against any such provision.

It is worth making clear at this stage that where contributions are paid by one individual on behalf of another (whether a minor or otherwise) the availability of tax relief reflects the position of the member of the personal pension (ie the eventual recipient of benefits) rather than the tax position of the individual funding the contribution.

Also, the payments could be regarded as potentially exempt transfers from an inheritance tax point of view, though they will usually be capable of being covered by an exemption, for example the normal expenditure exemption if payments are regular in nature.

Spouses, partners etc   2.17

Contributions may also be paid in a similar way by one individual for the benefit of a spouse, partner (or indeed any other individual). This could occur where the spouse, partner etc has no source of earnings in their own right, but where it is nevertheless attractive to build up pension rights, at least partly because of the tax reliefs available.

It can also be very effective to provide a pension arrangement so that use can be made of tax allowances and bands once benefits are drawn, particularly if the individual might otherwise have no income in retirement.

Controlling directors of investment companies   2.18

Prior to 6 April 2001, controlling directors of investment companies – in the absence of relevant earnings arising from any other source – have not been eligible to contribute to a personal pension. This is because earnings received in this capacity are excluded from the definition of relevant earnings under *s 644(5), ICTA 1988*.

For this purpose, the term 'director' is defined as including any person occupying the position of director by whatever name they are called.

Here, 'controlling' means that the individual, either alone or together with any other persons who are or have been at any time directors of the company, controls the company (ie essentially controls a majority of the voting rights). Note that this definition is not the same as that which applies in other circumstances, for example, in dealing with the restrictions under *s 644(6B)(a), ICTA 1988* (see section **2.13** above).

An investment company is defined as one whose income consists wholly or mainly of investment income (ie income which, if received by an individual, would not be regarded as earned income).

Although it remains the case that such income is excluded from relevant earnings, this does not prevent a controlling director of an investment company making contributions up to the earnings threshold of £3,600 per year, provided he or she is otherwise eligible.

Controlling directors in receipt of occupational scheme benefits 2.19

Where the earnings of a controlling director do not count as relevant earnings because he is in receipt of occupational scheme benefits (see section **2.13** above), contributions up to the earnings threshold are still permitted, subject to the normal eligibility conditions.

Concurrency 2.20

A further major development which took place with effect from 6 April 2001 was the introduction of the concurrency rules (sometimes known as the partial concurrency rules). This for the first time allowed an individual to also contribute to a personal pension in some circumstances, provided they:

(*a*) have no relevant earnings; and
(*b*) are accruing benefits under an occupational pension scheme.

There are a number of conditions which must be met, including the normal requirement that the individual must be under the age of 75. In addition, he must be resident and ordinarily resident in the UK, or be overseas as a Crown servant or the spouse of a Crown servant, at some time in the tax year.

Controlling directors 2.21

There are then two conditions which are specific to the concurrency rules, and both conditions must be met. The first is that the individual is not a controlling director at any time in the tax year when the contribution is paid or in any of the five preceding tax years, but excluding years before 2000/01. This is a condition that excludes certain individuals, in the sense that someone who has been a controlling director at any time in the relevant period, irrespective of the length of time involved, is entirely excluded.

Note that the terms of the exclusion relate to being a controlling director of any company, not simply the company which provides the occupational pension scheme.

Example – Concurrency I

A controlling director of a company (CXZ Ltd) for a short period from February to March 2001 left following a disagreement with the other directors of the company, and sold all their shares.

They are now employed by GFD Ltd and are a member of their occupational scheme. They are neither a director or a shareholder of GFD, nor of any other company.

Under the concurrency rules, they cannot however contribute to a personal pension in 2003/04, because they have been a controlling director during the relevant period (the previous five years excluding years before 2000/01).

The short period as a controlling director will continue to exclude the individual from using the concurrency rules in tax years up to and including 2005/06.

Earnings condition 2.22

The second condition relates to earnings, and requires that, in at least one of the five tax years preceding the tax year in which the contribution is paid, but excluding tax years before 2000/01, the individual must have earnings of £30,000 or less.

The £30,000 maximum earnings figure is known as the remuneration limit, and is given in *s 632B(4)(c), ICTA 1988*. Provision is made for this to be varied by Treasury order. However, there is no defined basis upon which this is required to occur – there is for example no automatic indexation of the remuneration limit.

For this purpose, earnings are 'aggregate grossed up remuneration' which is defined in *s 632B, ICTA 1988*, and the *Personal Pension Schemes (Concurrent Membership) Order 2000 (SI 2000/2318)*. The earnings taken into account are those which are used for P60 purposes, in other words essentially payments received in monetary form. Benefits in kind, even if taxable, are not included.

Example – Concurrency II

An individual (who has never been a controlling director) earns £32,000 in 2002/03. They are a member of their employer's occupational pension scheme, and contribute 5% of pay as member contributions, which are required as a condition of membership.

P60 earnings are calculated after deduction of member contributions and any in-house additional voluntary contributions (AVCs). Their member contributions are £32,000 x 5% = £1,600, giving P60 earnings of £30,400.

However, if they made in-house AVCs of £400 in 2002/03, this would reduce P60 earnings to £30,000. This level of earnings would provide the basis of eligibility under the concurrency rules and would mean that the individual could make personal pension contributions in the years 2003/04 to 2007/08 inclusive.

Note that only the employment or employments held on 5 April in each tax year are taken into account for the purposes of this test.

The definition allows for the earnings figure to be grossed up where an individual holds the relevant office or employment for less than a year. In these cases, the process is:

(a) the number of months for which the office or employment is calculated, rounded up to the next higher month; and

(b) the result is then divided into 12 to determine the grossing up factor, which is then applied to the earnings received.

Example – Concurrency III

An individual worked for XYZ Ltd for a number of years, and throughout their period of employment was a member of their occupational pension scheme.

They left the employment of XYZ Ltd on 31 January 2003, and their earnings to that date were £45,000. They joined a new employer, GHL Ltd, on 1 February 2003 and immediately entered their pension scheme. The position was not as senior as the previous one, involving less responsibility, and the individual only earned £7,000 from this employment during the remainder of the tax year 2002/03.

They are not, and never have been, a controlling director of any company, and earnings in each of the tax years 2000/01 and 2001/02 exceeded £30,000.

For the purposes of dealing with the limit on aggregate grossed up remuneration under the concurrency rules, it is only the employment(s) held on 5 April which are relevant. In this case therefore, we are concerned only with earnings from GHL Ltd.

The period of employment with GHL Ltd is two months and five days, which, for calculation purposes, is rounded up to three months.

The grossing up factor is therefore 12/3 for the GHL Ltd earnings, and applying this factor gives grossed up remuneration of £7,000 x 12/3 = £28,000

This is within the remuneration limit (£30,000), and the individual is eligible to contribute to a Personal Pension under the concurrency rules.

The fact that their earnings in total during the year exceeded £30,000 does not exclude them, as it is only earnings from GHL Ltd which are relevant. In this case, the fact that it is only the employment(s) held on 5 April which is/are taken into account favours the individual. The next example shows a situation where the reverse is the case.

Example – Concurrency IV

Take the same details as before, except that this time, assume that the individual's new position with GHL Ltd is a more senior role. Suppose earnings with XYZ Ltd were £15,000, and with GHL Ltd were £8,000 in 2002/03.

Applying the grossing up factor of 12/3 to the GHL Ltd earnings gives a figure of £8,000 x 12/3 = £32,000.

This exceeds the remuneration limit (£30,000), so in this situation, the individual is not eligible to contribute under the concurrency rules, even though their total actual earnings in 2002/03 were only £23,000.

Where the individual holds more than one employment on 5 April, the earnings from each (grossed up appropriately if the employment has not been held throughout the tax year) are aggregated to arrive at aggregate grossed up remuneration.

Example – Concurrency V

An individual is employed by two companies, ABC Ltd and FGH Ltd, each on a part-time basis. Both companies have occupational pension schemes, and they are a member in each case.

Their salary from ABC Ltd is £20,000 and from FGH Ltd is £15,000.

The aggregate grossed up remuneration is the total of the P60 earnings from both employments (ie £35,000).

This exceeds the remuneration limit (£30,000), and does not allow the individual to make concurrent personal pension contributions.

If an individual is eligible to contribute to a personal pension solely as a result of the concurrency rules, it is important to appreciate that their earnings still constitute earnings from pensionable employment and are not relevant earnings. It is therefore reasonable and logical that the legislation limits contributions to the earnings threshold of £3,600.

Where an individual has earnings from any source during a tax year which constitute relevant earnings, the concurrency rules will not be applicable, because the existence of relevant earnings during the tax year provides the necessary eligibility anyway.

The remuneration rules act to include rather than exclude since it is required only that the individual has one year within the relevant period (the previous five tax years excluding years before 2000/01) in which earnings do not exceed £30,000 in order to be eligible. The levels of earnings in other years are of no consequence.

Note also that the level of earnings in the year when the contribution is made is of no consequence either. These earnings cannot be used as the basis of eligibility under the concurrency rules (and neither will the earnings from the current year exclude anyone from eligibility under the concurrency rules).

Example – Concurrency VI

An individual (who has never been a controlling director) is in pensionable employment. They have aggregate grossed up remuneration as follows:

2000/01	£26,000
2001/02	£35,000
2002/03	£120,000
2003/04	£130,000

The individual is eligible to pay contributions to a personal pension under the concurrency rules in 2003/04 because their aggregate grossed up remuneration was no more than £30,000 in 2000/01.

They will continue to be eligible on the basis of their 2000/01 earnings up to and including 2005/06.

Declaration 2.23

An individual who intends to contribute under the concurrency rules must make a concurrency declaration to the product provider. This confirms that the criteria set out under the concurrency rules are satisfied and the necessary details are set out in the *Personal Pension Schemes (Concurrent Membership) Order 2000 (SI 2000/2318)*. The aspects which must be covered in the certificate are:

(a)   the qualifying year (ie the year in which earnings did not exceed £30,000) must be identified and must be one of the immediately preceding five tax years, excluding years before 2000/01;

(b)   it must be confirmed that aggregate grossed up remuneration did not exceed the remuneration limit in the year identified;

(c)   it must be confirmed that total contributions will not exceed the earnings threshold in the current tax year or any subsequent year to which the certificate relates;

(d)   the full name and address of the employer in relation to each office or employment held must be given; and

(e)   The certificate must confirm that the individual is not, and has not been, a controlling director in the current tax year or any of the five immediately preceding tax years (but ignoring years before 2000/01).

The *Personal Pension Schemes (Concurrent Membership) Order 2000 (SI 2000/2318)* defines 'certificated years' as the five tax years immediately following the qualifying year in which earnings did not exceed £30,000. This suggests that further certificates of eligibility would be required from concurrent members at five year intervals.

However, in the Inland Revenue guidance notes (IR76), paragraph 3.19, it is stated that:

'The scheme administrator should ensure that the declaration by the individual contains a form of words along the lines of "I understand that to continue to be eligible to make contributions under concurrency, I must have earned £30,000 or less in one of the five previous tax years, but ignoring tax years earlier than 2000/01. I will let you know immediately if I cease to be eligible on this basis."'

The Inland Revenue then does not require the position to be rechecked for any subsequent tax year, unless the individual notifies them of any change in their circumstances which may affect their eligibility.

Attractions of concurrency   2.24

There are many attractions of contributing to a personal pension under the concurrency rules, rather than the alternative of additional voluntary contribution (AVC) schemes under occupational pension rules. These are considered in detail in section **11.13**, as part of the discussion of the interaction between personal pensions and occupational schemes.

Transfers   2.25

Personal pension arrangements can receive transfers from other pension arrangements, including occupational pension schemes, retirement annuity contracts and other personal pensions.

Such transfers do not require the individual concerned to be eligible in the normal way, because no contributions are being paid by the individual.

Contracting out   2.26

Personal pensions can be used to contract out, as described in **Chapter 12: Contracting Out**.

In order to contract out only, it is not necessary to meet the eligibility rules as described in this chapter. So, an individual who is a member of an occupational scheme which is not itself contracted out can choose to contract out on an individual basis using a personal pension arrangement. The National Insurance rebate would be paid to the personal pension by the National Insurance Contributions Office of the Inland Revenue.

The individual could only pay additional contributions himself if he was eligible, either under the concurrency rules, or because of a separate source of relevant earnings.

Proof of eligibility   2.27

The requirements for proof of eligibility are designed so as not to create a major administrative burden on product providers, though it remains the provider's responsibility to determine eligibility.

Residence   2.28

For UK residents, a declaration to this effect is all that is required. Non-residents other than Crown servants and their spouses will need to provide proof that they have a source of relevant earnings. This can be in the form of a payslip for the current year, or a declaration from their employer.

For a self-employed individual who is not UK resident, copies of the accounts, a self-assessment tax return, or a written statement from the accountant, solicitor or auditor dealing with the individual's tax affairs is required.

Earnings   2.29

Evidence of earnings is not required if contributions do not exceed the earnings threshold.

For higher contributions, evidence will be required and the form of that evidence is covered in section **3.32**.

Concurrency   2.30

For individuals who are eligible under the concurrency rules, a concurrency declaration is also required (see section **2.23** above).

Summary of eligibility requirements

An individual is eligible to contribute to a personal pension if:

(*a*)   they have a source of relevant earnings;

    or if not,

(*b*)   they are UK resident and ordinarily resident, or a Crown servant, or the spouse of a Crown servant; and

(*c*)   they have no relevant earnings; and

(*d*)   they are not a member of an approved occupational scheme throughout the tax year;

    or if not,

(*e*)   they are a member of an approved occupational pension scheme; and

(*f*)   they are not a controlling director in the tax year concerned or in any of the previous five tax years, excluding years before 2000/01; and

(*g*)   they have earnings (as taken into account for P60 purposes) not exceeding £30,000 in at least one of the previous five tax years, excluding years before 2000/01.

Checklist – Income regarded as relevant earnings

The following income counts as relevant earnings.

- Profits chargeable under Schedule D immediately derived from a trade, profession or vocation.
- Salary, wages, bonus, overtime, commission.
- Benefits in kind which are chargeable to tax under Schedule E (applies to employees earning over £8,500, and to directors).
- Profit related pay (including the part which is not taxable).
- Statutory Sick Pay (SSP) and Statutory Maternity Pay (SMP) provided it is paid by the employer and chargeable under Schedule E.
- Permanent Health Insurance (PHI) payments paid by the employer whilst the individual is still in employment.
- Furnished holiday lettings chargeable under Schedule D Case VI for the years 1982/83 to 1994/95.
- Furnished holiday lettings chargeable under Schedule A for the years 1995/96 onwards.
- Salary paid by way of Government Securities.
- Enterprise Allowance payments chargeable under *s 127, ICTA 1988*.
- Post-cessation receipts which qualify as earned income under *s 107, ICTA 1988*.
- Remuneration paid in the form of units in an authorised unit trust provided it is treated, on receipt, as a taxable emolument of the individual.
- Income from woodlands provided it is treated for tax purposes as immediately derived from the carrying on of a trade.
- Patent rights treated as earned income under *section 529*.
- Sub-postmaster's retirement gratuities.
- Payments made to local councillors which are chargeable under Schedule E.
- Amounts deducted from salary to purchase partnership shares in a share incentive plan provided they qualify as such under *paragraph 83* of *Schedule 8* of the *Finance Act 2000*.
- Employer contributions to a funded unapproved retirement benefit scheme (FURBS) which are assessable on the employee, provided the FURBS is the only scheme of the employer of which the employee is a member.

Source: *Inland Revenue Guidance Notes IR76*.

Checklist – Income not regarded as relevant earnings

The following income does not count as relevant earnings.

- Income from an employment which is pensioned under an occupational pension scheme (*s 645, ICTA 1988*).
- Redundancy and termination payments chargeable to tax under *s 148, ICTA 1988* (golden handshakes).
- Income arising from the acquisition or disposal of shares or an interest in shares or from a right to acquire shares.
- Emoluments received by an individual as a controlling director of an investment company.
- Earnings falling within *s 644(6A), ICTA 1988*.
- Pensions (a pension is not remuneration from an office or employment).
- All benefits paid by the State, including Invalid Care Allowance, Working Family Tax Credit and Disabled Person's Tax Credit.
- Grants paid by local authorities to foster parents.
- Statutory Sick Pay and Statutory Maternity Pay paid by the DWP.
- Except for directors, benefits in kind where earnings from the employment are less than £8,500 (such benefits are not taxable).
- Permanent Health Insurance (PHI) paid directly to the individual by the insurance company after the employment has ceased.
- Partnership retirement annuities.
- Client's account interest assessed under Schedule D Case III.
- Earnings from international organisations which are exempt from UK tax by reason of a statutory instrument, including the:
  - United Nations;
  - World Health Organisation;
  - International Sugar Organisation;
  - International Coffee Organisation;
  - International Cocoa Organisation; and
  - International Maritime Satellite Organisation.
- 'Foreign emoluments' chargeable under *s 192, ICTA 1988* where the individual is a member of a 'corresponding' overseas pension scheme.
- Employer contributions to a funded unapproved retirement benefit scheme (FURBS) where the employee is also a member of an approved occupational pension scheme.

Source: *Inland Revenue Guidance Notes IR76*

3 — Contribution Limits

Introduction

3.1

Although personal pension arrangements are generally thought of as arrangements to which an eligible individual contributes, it is also possible for contributions to be paid by others.

Who can pay contributions?

3.2

Increasingly, personal pension arrangements are being used as part of an employee's remuneration package. It is important therefore that an employer can contribute, in order to provide benefits for an employee.

Contributions can also be paid by the National Insurance Contributions Office (NICO) of the Inland Revenue, where the personal pension is used to contract out of the State Second Pension Scheme (S2P). Contracting out is dealt with in detail in **Chapter 12: Contracting Out**.

Employer contributions are dealt with later in this chapter, though it is important to note that these contributions, when aggregated with any contributions paid by the individual, must lie within normal limits.

It is possible for a personal pension to be funded entirely by employer contributions (there is no requirement for the employee to contribute). Similarly, it is possible for an employer to fund a personal pension arrangement with one provider whilst the employee is contributing to a personal pension arrangement with an entirely separate provider (always subject to normal limits on the overall contributions being paid).

The Inland Revenue also allows contributions to be paid by one person on behalf of another (though strictly speaking this is not allowed for in the legislation). This may arise in a number of ways, for example:

(a) where an employer deducts contributions from an individual's pay and passes them to the product provider on the member's behalf (this is distinct from an employer contribution in that the cost of the contribution is borne by the individual rather than the employer);

(b) it is also possible for contributions to be paid for an individual by the employer of that individual's spouse;

(c) contributions may be paid by a parent on behalf of a minor, or by one spouse on behalf of the other;

(d) a building society draft made payable to the personal pension scheme can be accepted as being a payment by the individual;

(e) contributions can be paid by cheque drawn on a business account (or a direct debit or standing order from such an account) provided the scheme administrator receives confirmation in writing from the business that the individual has reimbursed the amount involved; and

(f) similarly, a contribution can be paid by means of a cheque drawn on a partnership account (or a direct debit or standing order) subject to the partnership confirming in writing that the payments come from the individual's share of partnership profits.

The Inland Revenue has confirmed that it is happy to allow scheme administrators to accept contributions in all these, or in similar circumstances.

Payment date   3.3

There will be occasions when the precise date on which a contribution can be regarded as paid is of great importance, for example in determining the way in which tax relief can be claimed. The Inland Revenue provides details in relation to this in the *Personal Pension Schemes Guidance Notes (IR76)*.

As an overriding consideration, the personal pension arrangement must be in force before a contribution can be considered paid, although it is possible for the scheme administrator to hold a contribution temporarily if it is received before the arrangement comes into force. It will then be treated as paid on the first day that the arrangement is in force.

In order for the arrangement to come into force, there must be a fully completed application with any necessary documentation such as proof of earnings, and these items must have been accepted as valid by the scheme administrator. A contribution which is paid by cheque is regarded as being paid on the date that the cheque is given to, or is received through the post by the scheme administrator. However, if the cheque is not honoured when presented, then the contribution cannot be regarded as having been made.

Payments can also be made by debit or credit card, and the payment date is the date on which the relevant card details are received by the scheme administrator.

Direct debits   3.4

Where payments are made by direct debit, it is the scheme administrator who takes the action necessary to draw the amount involved from the account. In general terms, it is the date on which this action is taken that will count as the payment date.

However the first payment can be regarded as made on the date when the administrator receives the direct debit instruction (subject as always to the requirement that the personal pension arrangement is in force).

The situation can arise where a payment due just before the end of a tax year is not in fact collected until just after the start of the following tax year, because direct debits will not be paid on Saturdays, Sundays or Bank Holidays. Where this is so, the payment can be regarded as being made in the earlier tax year.

Example – Direct debit payment date

An individual pays monthly personal pension contributions by means of a direct debit, which has been in force for some time, and is due for payment on the 5th of each month.

The payment due on 5 April 2003 (which was a Saturday) was not collected until the following Monday (7 April 2003).

Although the payment was not therefore collected until after the start of the 2004/05 tax year, it will be treated for tax purposes as paid on its due date of 5 April 2003, which fell in the 2003/04 tax year.

However the Inland Revenue does specifically point out that this treatment is not available if:

(*a*)   the payment is due on or after 6 April;

(*b*)   the direct debit was originally presented in the earlier tax year but was not paid, and was re-presented after the start of the next tax year; and/or

(*c*)   where the failure to collect the direct debit on or before 5 April resulted from the personal pension scheme's administrative arrangements, for example where contributions are only collected weekly, etc.

It is also possible for a contribution to be made by directly transferring shares into the personal pension scheme where they have been acquired under an SAYE share option scheme, an approved profit sharing scheme, or a share incentive plan. A 90 day window is available within which such a transfer can be made, and the payment date will be the date of actual transfer.

The amount contributed in such cases is taken as the market value of the shares, as defined in *section 272* of the *Taxation of Chargeable Gains Act 1992 (TCGA 1992)*. For quoted shares, this will be the lower of:

(*a*)   the lower of the two prices shown in the daily official list, plus one quarter of the difference between the two prices; and (*b*)   halfway between the highest and lowest prices at which bargains took place on the relevant day.

Note that there are no other circumstances in which shares can be transferred directly into personal pension arrangements as a contribution (though shares may form part of a transfer *in specie* between schemes in some cases).

Benefits in payment   3.5

In principle, contributions cannot be paid to a personal pension arrangement if retirement benefits are already being taken from it.

When an individual establishes membership of a personal pension, it is very often the case that a number of separate arrangements (perhaps 10, 100 or 1,000) come into force at the same time. This is usually done to facilitate the taking of benefits from different arrangements at different times, where the individual decides that they wish to phase in their retirement benefits (see section **5.5**).

In such a case, if benefits are being taken from some arrangements, but not from all arrangements, it is perfectly possible for contributions to continue to those arrangements from which benefits are not being taken.

With effect from 6 April 2001, it became possible for the first time for benefits from a single arrangement to be phased in a similar way. The effect is essentially the same, and once benefits start to be taken from a part of the personal pension arrangement, that part effectively becomes a separate arrangement. In these circumstances also, provided there is a part of the personal pension arrangement from which benefits are not being taken, contributions can continue to that part.

Contribution limits   3.6

Note that the structure of limits on personal pension contributions changed significantly from 6 April 2001, but that the new basis, as described in this chapter, applies to all contributions paid on or after 6 April 2001. The date the personal pension arrangement was established, even if before that date, makes no difference.

This contrasts with the changes made to term assurance (see section **8.20**) and waiver of contribution (see section **9.10**) where the old rules have been retained for arrangements entered into before 6 April 2001.

The new structure does not however apply to retirement annuities, where wholly different rules apply. These are covered in **Chapter 14: Retirement Annuity Contracts**.

Maximum contributions 3.7

Provided an individual is eligible to contribute to a personal pension, as discussed in **Chapter 2: Eligibility**, contributions can be made up to the level of the earnings threshold (currently £3,600) in each tax year. This figure is given in *section 630(1)* of the *Income & Corporation Taxes Act 1988 (ICTA 1988)*, and was initially set at this level for the tax year 2001/02. Although it can be amended by Treasury Order, no change has so far been made.

If greater, contributions can be paid in accordance with the age and earnings related scale below:

Age at 6 April	Maximum contribution as % of Net Relevant Earnings
up to 35	17.5%
36 to 45	20%
46 to 50	25%
51 to 55	30%
56 to 60	35%
61 to 74	40%

For this purpose, age means the age attained by the individual on 6 April in the relevant tax year. This means that the level of maximum contribution does not change during the tax year when an individual reaches, for example, their 51st birthday, but will only do so from the following 6 April.

Example – Age for contribution limits

An individual reaches their 51st birthday on 27 June 2003.

Their maximum contribution on the age and earnings related scale is 25% of net relevant earnings in the tax year 2003/04, but will be 30% of net relevant earnings in the tax year 2004/05.

Basis of limits 3.8

The limits described in section **3.7** above apply to the level of gross contributions to personal pensions, before allowing for tax relief.

Within these limits, it is possible for contributions to be paid to an unlimited number of personal pension arrangements.

The limits cover contributions paid by the individual and any paid for their benefit by others, including an employer. However, minimum contributions paid by the National Insurance Contributions Office if the individual has contracted out (see **Chapter 12: Contracting Out**) do not count towards the limit.

Net relevant earnings 3.9

Net relevant earnings (NRE) means relevant earnings (see section **2.2**) less deductible business expenses, losses and capital allowances arising from business activities.

The full definition is given in *s 646, ICTA 1988*. A detailed consideration of the issues involved in quantifying NRE appears later in this chapter.

Earnings cap 3.10

The net relevant earnings figure is subject to an overall maximum known as the 'allowable maximum' or, more commonly, the 'earnings cap', defined in *s 640A, ICTA 1988*.

This was introduced with effect from the 1989/90 tax year, when the figure was set at £60,000. Generally the earnings cap is increased each year to reflect the increase in the Retail Prices Index (measured over the twelve month period to the September preceding the start of the tax year), and is rounded up to the next higher multiple of £600.

It is open to the Chancellor each year to override the indexation requirement, though this has so far only occurred once, when the earnings cap for 1993/94 was fixed at the same level as had applied for 1992/93.

For 2003/04, the earnings cap is £99,000.

Although indexation in line with the Retail Prices Index ensures that the earnings cap maintains its real value in terms of its relationship to prices, earnings tend to increase faster than prices. As a result, it is likely that over the years, an increasing number of people will be affected by the earnings cap.

The table below shows the earnings cap for each year since its introduction up to 2002/03, together with the index of average earnings (all employees) as published by the Office for National Statistics (ONS). The final column shows the level the earnings cap would have reached had it been maintained in line with the increase in average earnings rather than prices (but with no rounding up). This clearly shows that the growth in the cap has lagged behind the growth in earnings.

Tax year	Earnings Cap Earnings (all employees) at start of tax year	Index of Average adjusted in line with average earnings index	Original Cap
1989/90	£60,000	71.2	£60,000
1990/91	£64,800	77.9	£65,646
1991/92	£71,400	84.4	£71,124
1992/93	£75,000	89.6	£75,506
1993/94	£75,000	92.9	£78,287
1994/95	£76,800	95.7	£80,646
1995/96	£78,600	99.5	£83,848
1996/97	£82,200	102.8	£86,629
1997/98	£84,000	106.7	£89,916
1998/99	£87,600	112.9	£95,140
1999/2000	£90,600	117.5	£99,017
2000/01	£91,800	122.8	£103,483
2001/02	£95,400	128.8	£108,539
2002/03	£97,200	133.8	£112,753

It is also true that many individuals experience increases in their personal earnings in excess of the average rate. This simply reflects the fact that, as they get older and more experienced, they are more likely to take on positions of increased responsibility. This may also widen the impact of the earnings cap over time.

Multiple sources of earnings 3.11

There are often cases where an individual has more than one source of earnings, and this can affect the way in which the earnings cap is applied. There are various situations which we consider in turn.

Associated employments 3.12

The treatment of employments in some cases depends on whether or not the employers are associated. For this purpose, employers are associated if (directly or indirectly) one is controlled by the other or if both are controlled by the same third person.

All sources non-pensionable 3.13

The most straightforward situation is where all sources of earnings are non-pensionable. Here the earnings cap applies to the total of net relevant earnings from all sources.

It makes no difference whether the earnings from the various sources are taxed on a Schedule D (self-employed) or Schedule E (employed) basis, nor whether any of the employments are associated.

Pensionable employment and non-pensionable employment 3.14

If an individual has more than one employment, and provided the employments are not associated, then the earnings cap applies separately to each source of pensionable earnings, and again separately to the total of net relevant earnings arising from the non-pensionable employments.

Where the employments are associated, then the earnings cap applicable to net relevant earnings is reduced by earnings from the pensionable employment.

Example – Multiple employments

An individual has been employed by HKL Ltd for the last five years, and earns £60,000 from that employment. They are a member of the company's approved occupational pension scheme.

They are also employed by STR Ltd, where they earn £150,000. There is no occupational pension provision in respect of this employment.

The employment at HKL Ltd is pensionable and so these earnings are not relevant earnings. The individual's earnings will be subject to the earnings cap under the occupational scheme.

The earnings from STR Ltd count as relevant earnings. Assuming HKL Ltd and STR Ltd are not associated, there is no interaction between the two sets of earnings, and the net relevant earnings would be £99,000 (the earnings cap).

If the employments were associated, the net relevant earnings from STR Ltd would be reduced by the earnings from the pensionable employment at HKL Ltd. If this was the case, the net relevant earnings would be:

£99,000-£60,000 = £39,000

More than one pensionable employments, plus self-employed earnings 3.15

If an individual has several pensionable employments which are not associated, the earnings cap applies separately to each, and a separate earnings cap applies to any net relevant earnings arising from a separate self-employment.

If the pensionable employments are associated, only one earnings cap will apply to them in total, but a separate earnings cap remains available for the self-employment.

Using the earnings threshold 3.16

The ability to pay contributions up to £3,600 where an individual is eligible, irrespective of the level of their earnings is an important one, and one which has added a number of possibilities to the use of personal pensions.

Shareholding directors 3.17

As an example, it will often be the case that shareholding directors of private companies draw the majority of their income by means of dividends rather than salary, in order to reduce or avoid liability for National Insurance Contributions, both for the director and company. In many cases, the earnings drawn will be at a level of around £4,000 *per annum*, which is just above the Lower Earnings Limit, but below the threshold for National Insurance Contributions.

The effect of this is to allow the individual to accrue benefits under the State pension arrangements, but with no liability to National Insurance. If personal pension contribution limits were related solely to earnings, the scope for contributions would be very small. The ability to pay contributions up to the earnings threshold can therefore significantly increase the scope for using personal pensions.

Those with no relevant earnings 3.18

The earnings threshold is also applicable where the individual has no net relevant earnings. Contributions up to this level can therefore be paid each year on behalf on non–earners, which might include carers, but also minor children.

The earnings threshold is also the limit on the contributions which can be paid by those who are eligible under the concurrency rules (see section

2.20). Under these rules, some individuals who are in pensionable employment can contribute to a personal pension at the same time. The earnings from the employment still constitute pensionable earnings and are not net relevant earnings. It is therefore not possible for them to pay a contribution under the age and earnings related scale.

Until the introduction of the earnings threshold, controlling directors of investment companies were entirely excluded from making personal pension provision in respect of any income drawn from the investment company. It remains the case that such income is not within the definition of net relevant earnings, but it is now possible for these individuals to pay contributions up to the earnings threshold.

Life cover and waiver of contribution   3.19

It is possible to provide life cover, and in some cases waiver of contribution benefits, under personal pension legislation. Full details of these benefits are covered in **Chapter 8: Death Before Retirement** and **Chapter 9: Incapacity** respectively.

Contributions for life assurance benefits are subject to their own limits, but are also regarded as being part of the overall limits described in this chapter. Thus any contributions paid for life assurance will reduce the scope for contributions to build up retirement benefits.

Waiver of contribution (which provides continuation of contributions in the event of incapacity) can only be included within a personal pension where the cover was introduced not later than 5 April 2001, or where the facility to do so existed at that time, even if it is not taken up until later. In these circumstances, the cost of the waiver is again regarded as being part of the total personal pension contribution, which must lie within the limits discussed in this chapter.

Contracting out   3.20

Where an individual contracts out using a personal pension, payments are made to the personal pension by the National Insurance Contributions Office (NICO) in return for the individual giving up rights to accrue benefits under the State Second Pension (S2P).

As mentioned earlier in this chapter, these contributions (known as 'minimum contributions') are not taken into account as part of the contribution limits discussed above.

Contracting out is discussed in more detail in **Chapter 12: Contracting Out**.

COMPS 3.21

Note that where an occupational pension scheme has elected to be subject to the Defined Contribution (DC) regime in the same way as a personal pension for limit purposes, the situation is different. If such a scheme contracts out, it is treated as a COMPS (Contracted Out Money Purchase Scheme). In this situation, both employer and employee pay a lower level of National Insurance Contribution through payroll, and the employer must ensure that at least the total of the reductions in National Insurance is input to the COMPS (and may or may not recover from the employee an amount equivalent to the reduction in employee National Insurance).

These payments do count towards overall contribution limits.

An additional earnings related payment will be made to the COMPS from NICO, but this additional amount does not count towards limits.

Quantifying net relevant earnings for the self-employed 3.22

Net relevant earnings for the self-employed are based on the earnings which are brought into account for tax purposes in respect of any particular tax year. This can cause a certain amount of difficulty in some circumstances.

For example, generally, the earnings taken into account for tax purposes will be based on profits in the accounting period which ends in the tax year concerned. Where the end of the accounting period is shortly before the end of the tax year, this may mean that the level of net relevant earnings is uncertain for most, or sometimes all of the tax year. If it is intended to pay a contribution above the earnings threshold, linked to the age and earnings related scale, the result will be uncertainty as to the level of contribution permitted.

Example – Uncertainty of net relevant earnings figure

An individual has been self-employed for a number of years, and their accounting period runs from 1 February to 31 January. Their profits in the accounting period ending on 31 January 2004 will be the basis of their taxable income and net relevant earnings for 2003/04.

The accounts for this period will not be finalised until some time after 31 January 2004, and it is quite likely that they will not be finalised until after the end of the 2003/04 tax year.

Net relevant earnings may therefore not be precisely known until after the end of the tax year concerned.

Care is also necessary where the level of profit changes, in particular if the change is such that the individual is moving from basic rate to higher rate tax, or vice versa. There will often be a significant time lag between the point where profits increase and the point at which net relevant earnings are affected. If the intention is to maximise tax relief on contributions, it may sometimes be appropriate to delay payment until the start of the tax year when higher rate liability will apply.

Example – Changing tax position

An individual has been self-employed for some years and has an accounting period which runs from 1 May to 30 April. They have no other income of any sort.

Under the current year basis of assessment, their profits in the accounting period ending 30 April 2003 will be the basis of their taxable income for the tax year 2003/04, and will therefore also be the basis of their net relevant earnings for 2003/04.

Suppose the individual's profits for the accounting period ended 30 April 2003 were £20,000, but soon after the start of their next accounting period, they win a substantial and lucrative new contract. As a result, they anticipate that their profits in the accounting period to 30 April 2004 will be £100,000.

With higher profits, they may find the idea of making personal pension contributions very attractive, but they need to be careful about the timing of these contributions.

The individual will be a basic rate taxpayer in 2003/04, reflecting the £20,000 profit figure. Although they may feel the effects of their higher profits, and might increase their drawings from the business soon after the start of the new contract, they will only obtain basic rate tax relief on any contributions paid up to and including 5 April 2004.

They will become a higher rate taxpayer in the tax year 2004/05 and will obtain higher rate tax relief on contributions paid on or after 6 April 2004.

It may be best for the individual to delay any contributions until then.

Note also that contribution limits for 2003/04 remain based on their net relevant earnings of £20,000, and the limit will not increase until 2004/05.

Opening years 3.23

Net relevant earnings may also be difficult to quantify during the opening and closing years of the business.

In the tax year in which a self-employed business starts, the profit to be taxed is calculated on a proportionate basis from the profit in the first set of accounts, based on the length of time from the start of business until the end of the tax year.

For the second tax year, the profits taken into account will be those from the first set of accounts, assuming that the first accounting period was twelve months in length. This can create a considerable delay in establishing precisely the level of profits involved, and therefore precisely the level of net relevant earnings upon which contributions can be based.

Example – Opening years I

An individual starts up as a self-employed travel consultant on 1 July 2003, and prepares their first set of accounts to reflect the first twelve months of their business, to 30 June 2004.

Suppose these accounts show a profit of £24,000.

The taxable profit for 2003/04 is 9/12 x £24,000 = £18,000.

The taxable profit for 2004/05 is £24,000.

These figures will be the basis of net relevant earnings for these years. The accounts will probably not be finalised until some time after 30 June 2004, and NRE for 2003/04 and 2004/05 cannot be precisely quantified until they are finalised.

Where the first accounting period is not twelve months in length, further delays can arise.

If the first accounting period is less than twelve months, and ends in the second tax year during which the business has operated, the taxable profit for the second tax year will be based on profits in the first twelve months of the business. This will mean that the profits from the first set of accounts will be taken, together with a proportionate amount of the profit emerging in the second accounting period.

If the first accounting period is more than twelve months, and ends during the second tax year, taxable profits are based on the profits from the last twelve months of the accounting period, calculated on a proportionate basis from the profits shown in the accounts.

Situations can also arise where, because the first accounting period is longer than twelve months, there is no accounting period ending in the second tax year. In this case, taxable profit for the second tax year will be based on profit in the tax year, calculated on a proportionate basis from the first set of accounts.

For the third tax year, the figure will be calculated on a proportionate basis, from the profits in the accounts for the accounting period ending in the third tax year.

Example – Opening years II

An individual starts a self-employed business on 1 March 2004, and prepares their first set of accounts for the 15 month period to 31 May 2005. These show profits of £45,000.

There is therefore no accounting period ending in the tax year 2004/05.

The taxable profit for 2003/04 is 1/15 x £45,000 = £3,000

The taxable profit for 2004/05 = 12/15 x £45,000 = £36,000

The taxable profit for 2005/06 = 12/15 x £45,000 = £36,000

These figures cannot be precisely quantified until the finalisation of the accounts, some time after 31 May 2005, and net relevant earnings for 2003/04 and 2004/05, as well as 2005/06, will be uncertain until then.

Overlap profits and closing years 3.24

One result of the method used to tax a self-employed individual during the opening years of their business is that part of the profit generated is taxed more than once.

This is illustrated in the examples of opening years above. In the first example, the profit from the first accounting period formed the basis of taxable profit for both 2003/04 and 2004/05. The profit was £24,000, but the total amount taxed over those two years was £42,000.

In the second example, the profit in the first accounting period was £45,000, and this was used as the basis for calculating taxable profit for three tax years, with the total amount taxed being £75,000.

The excess of the amount taxed compared to the actual profit is known as 'overlap profit'.

When a business ceases – and sometimes if there is a change of accounting period – an adjustment is made to allow for the overlap profit. The effect over the entire lifetime of the business is to tax precisely the amount of profit that has been made. There is however no adjustment to allow for the effect of inflation on the profit initially taxed twice.

The method used is that for the final tax year in which the business operates, the profit made from the end of the accounting period falling in the previous tax year to the date of cessation is calculated, then the overlap profits are deducted.

Example – Closing years

Suppose that the individual used in the example above ('*Opening years II*') runs their business successfully for a number of years, and then ceases to trade at 30 April 2010.

The profits for the accounting period to 31 May 2009 would have been the basis of taxable profit for the tax year 2009/10. Suppose that the profits shown in the accounts for the period 1 June 2009 to 30 April 2010 are £50,000.

The overlap profits from their opening years detailed above were £75,000-£45,000 = £30,000.

The taxable profit for 2010/11 is therefore £50,000-£30,000 = £20,000.

This is also the basis of net relevant earnings for 2010/11.

(This example necessarily assumes that there will be no change in the basis of self-employed taxation before the assumed cessation of the individual's business.)

There should not generally be any significant delay in preparing the accounts for this period though if the date of cessation is towards the end of a tax year, it is again likely that net relevant earnings will not be known until after the end of the tax year. It is always important to take account of overlap profits in determining net relevant earnings and therefore maximum contribution limits during closing years.

Losses   3.25

Where a self-employed person makes a loss in an accounting period, this loss will be related to a tax year in the same way as a profit, so generally, a loss in an accounting period would be regarded for tax purposes as a loss for the tax year in which the accounting period ends.

Thus, assuming that the individual has been in business for some years, a loss made in an accounting period ended on 31 December 2002 would be regarded as a loss related to the tax year 2002/03.

The loss can be treated in various ways, but in particular may be carried forward and set against future profits from the same trade, or may be set against other income in the tax year in which it arose.

If the loss is set against future profits, the loss will reduce future net relevant earnings.

Example – Losses I

An individual is self-employed, having set up in business ten years ago. Their accounting period runs from 1 January to 31 December, and in the period ended 31 December 2002, they made a loss of £10,000. This is regarded for tax purposes as a loss for the tax year 2002/03.

They have no other income, and the loss is carried forward to set against future profits.

Suppose that in the accounting period ending 31 December 2003, they make a profit of £25,000. This is treated for tax purposes as income for the tax year 2003/04. The carried forward loss will be set against this income for tax purposes, and in determining net relevant earnings.

Their net relevant earnings are therefore:

2002/03	Zero
2003/04	£25,000-£10,000 = £15,000

If the individual has other income, for example from savings interest, the loss can be set against that income for tax purposes. This can be attractive, because relief is available more quickly, and with certainty, whereas if the loss is carried forward, it may turn out that there are no future profits against which to set it.

However, *s 646(5), ICTA 1988* requires that where the loss is set against income other than net relevant earnings, the loss must still be treated as reducing future net relevant earnings for personal pension purposes. The reduction must be made from net relevant earnings for the following years, strictly in order. This can therefore reduce the scope for future contributions.

Example – Losses II

Suppose that, in the example immediately above, the individual had interest income of £20,000 in 2002/03. They decide to claim relief on their trading loss by setting it against this interest income.

However, the loss will still reduce net relevant earnings in 2003/04, exactly as in the previous example.

Note that it is also possible to set a loss against the total income of the previous tax year, or in the case of a new business, against total income of the previous three tax years. Also, where a loss arises on the cessation of a business, the loss can be set against trading profit of the final tax year, with any excess being carried back against the trading profit of up to the three previous tax years (using the latest year first).

Quantifying net relevant earnings for employees 3.26

For employees in non-pensionable employment, net relevant earnings in general include all items of remuneration which are taxable under Schedule E. This includes regular items such as basic salary, but also non-regular earnings, such as overtime, bonuses and commission payments.

Benefits in kind are included to the extent that they are taxable. So for example, a P11D employee who is provided with a company car can include the scale charge made in respect of the car for tax purposes in the calculation of his net relevant earnings (assuming the employment is non-pensionable).

Items excluded from relevant earnings 3.27

There are two exceptions to this rule, which are specified in s *644(4), ICTA 1988.*

The first is that any amount that is taxable under Schedule E, but arises from the acquisition or disposal of shares, or an interest in shares, or from a right to acquire shares, is excluded from relevant earnings and therefore from net relevant earnings. This could cover rights under share option schemes where subject to tax under Schedule E.

The second exclusion is golden handshakes, ie payments made to an individual in connection with the termination of their employment. Generally such amounts up to £30,000 are not chargeable to tax (and are therefore excluded in any event) but any further amounts are also ruled out even though they would be taxable.

As already mentioned above, any amounts derived as a controlling director of an investment company are also excluded under s *644(5), ICTA 1988.*

Interestingly, profit related pay, which at one time could be paid to employees free of tax, nevertheless remained within the definitions of relevant and net relevant earnings. However the favourable tax treatment of profit related pay has now ended, and this is of historical interest only.

Overseas earnings   3.28

In very limited cases, it is possible for seafarers working overseas to have income which is chargeable to UK tax, but which is subject to a 100% foreign earnings deduction. An individual in this situation is eligible to pay personal pension contributions because the income is chargeable to UK tax, even though no tax is actually paid.

These earnings count as relevant earnings for limit purposes, before the application of the 100% deduction.

Doctors and dentists   3.29

Doctors and dentists working in general practice (as opposed to those employed by the NHS) are in a unique situation in that they are taxable under Schedule D, but are nevertheless included in the membership of the National Health Service Pension Scheme, which is an occupational scheme.

Special rules apply to the calculation of net relevant earnings for these individuals, and these are covered specifically in **Chapter 13: Special Occupations**.

Basis years   3.30

The basis year rules were introduced with effect from 6 April 2001. They are applicable for individuals who are paying contributions above the earnings threshold, and who therefore need to determine net relevant earnings in order to calculate the maximum permitted level of personal pension contributions.

The basis year rules allow an individual to nominate either the current tax year or any one of the previous five tax years as the basis year, and net relevant earnings for the current year will be based on earnings in that basis year.

The calculation of maximum contributions is made taking into account:

(a)   net relevant earnings from the basis year;
(b)   the earnings cap for the current tax year; and
(c)   age on 6 April in the current tax year.

At one time the Revenue held that it should be the earnings cap from the basis year which was used in the calculation of maximum contributions, but towards the end of the 2001/02 tax year it amended this ruling. It is therefore necessary to calculate net relevant earnings without regard to the earnings cap in the past year, but then to apply the earnings cap for the current tax year.

Note that the basis year may be any one of the previous five tax years without restriction. This may mean that the basis year is a year prior to the introduction of the new structure of contribution limits, which took effect from 6 April 2001.

It is not necessary for the individual to have been a member of a personal pension scheme during the basis year, but if he was, and made contributions at the time, these in no way affect the calculation of the limit for contributions in 2003/04.

Example – Basis years

An individual aged 47 at 6 April 2003 has net relevant earnings over recent years as follows:

1998/99	£30,000
1999/2000	£100,000
2000/01	£65,000
2001/02	£69,000
2002/03	£73,000
2003/04	£78,000

By choosing 1999/2000 as their basis year, they can contribute up to 25% of £99,000 as their contribution for 2003/04.

Note that the percentage limit is 25%, because their age at 6 April 2003 was 47. The age at 6 April 1999 (ie in the year when the net relevant earnings of £100,000 arose) is not relevant.

Also the earnings cap which applies is that for 2003/04, not the lower figure of £90,600 which would have applied in 1999/2000.

Effect on administration   3.31

From a practical point of view, the basis year rules have a major impact in easing the administration of personal pension schemes. Where an individual is required to provide proof of earnings in order to support contributions in excess of the earnings threshold (see section **3.7**) that evidence will be valid for the tax year to which the evidence relates and the following five tax years.

This avoids the need to seek further evidence of earnings each year, unless contributions are increased to a level which is not supportable, based upon the evidence of earnings already supplied.

However, note that if the individual becomes ineligible for a personal pension, as a result of entering an occupational pension scheme, they cannot use the basis year rules to support further personal pension contributions.

Evidence required 3.32

The *Inland Revenue Guidance Notes (IR76)* specify the form in which the scheme administrator must obtain evidence of earnings where required, and the evidence must always be retained by the scheme administrator.

The evidence must be supplied within 30 days of the payment of a contribution which takes total contributions for the tax year over the earnings threshold, or over the maximum that can be justified based on evidence previously supplied.

The acceptable forms of evidence are shown in the table below.

Checklist – Evidence of earnings

Where evidence of earnings is required, it must be supplied in one of the following forms:

Employees

- A copy of an end of tax year payslip (week 52) or form P60 showing relevant earnings for the basis year; or
- A declaration from the employer stipulating the amount of remuneration paid for the basis year; or
- A copy of the relevant parts of the self-assessment tax return, showing net relevant earnings for the basis year.

Self-employed

- A copy of the relevant parts of the accounts relating to the basis year; or
- A copy of the relevant parts of the self-assessment tax return, showing net relevant earnings for the basis year; or
- A written statement from the accountant, solicitor or auditor dealing with the individual's tax affairs, and showing net relevant earnings.

The Inland Revenue accepts that an individual who has recently become self-employed, and has no previous source of relevant earnings cannot supply evidence in the required form. In these circumstances, an estimate must be obtained, and must be supported by evidence provided by 31 January in the following tax year.

Application of basis years 3.33

The basis year rules are also of great value for individuals who have fluctuating earnings. They allow individuals to plan ahead in terms of their commitment to contributions without necessarily knowing the level of net relevant earnings for the current tax year. To some extent, therefore, the basis year rules provide at least a partial solution to some of the problems experienced particularly by self employed individuals in quantifying net relevant earnings.

In tax planning terms, this facility can also be used to great advantage by shareholding directors. It has already been mentioned that it is common for such individuals to take the majority of their income from a company in the form of dividends, rather than salary, in order to minimise or entirely avoid National Insurance liability.

In this situation, contributions up to the earnings threshold would be permitted in any event (assuming the employment is non-pensionable). However, by increasing salary for one year in every six, the basis year rules can be used to link contributions to that high salary figure, so significantly increasing the scope for personal pension contributions. In the intervening years, salary can again be reduced to low levels to avoid National Insurance liability.

Example – Fluctuating earnings

A shareholding director generally draws around £4,000 per year in salary, and £50,000 in dividends. However, in 2001/02, they drew a salary of £30,000 and £24,000 in dividends (so their gross income remained £54,000).

They nominate 2001/02 as their basis year, so their net relevant earnings (NRE) are as follows:

Tax year	Salary	Dividend	NRE
2001/02	£30,000	£24,000	£30,000
2002/03	£4,000	£50,000	£30,000
2003/04	£4,000	£50,000	£30,000
2004/05	£4,000	£50,000	£30,000
2005/06	£4,000	£50,000	£30,000
2006/07	£4,000	£50,000	£30,000

In 2007/08, they would no longer be able to use 2001/02 as their basis year, as it is no longer within the previous five tax years. The director must then either take a higher salary, or accept that their net relevant earnings would fall to £4,000.

A similar approach may be adopted where a spouse or partner works within a business, and draws a modest salary. If it is intended to pay personal pension contributions in excess of the earnings threshold, then the level of earnings would need to be sufficient to support them.

Cessation rules   3.34

There is an extension of the basis year rules which applies where an individual ceases to have a source of earnings. In some circumstances these rules mean that a single year's net relevant earnings can form the basis of the calculation of net relevant earnings and therefore maximum contributions for a period of up to eleven tax years.

Note that the cessation rules apply only where there is a true cessation of earnings, not merely a cessation of relevant earnings, for example where an individual moves from self employment to pensionable employment.

The last year in which there are relevant earnings is known as the cessation year, and the following year (in which there are no relevant earnings) in known as the break year. The break year must be 2001/02 or later in order for these rules to apply.

The cessation rules apply for the cessation year and the following five tax years. However, they will cease to apply if during that period there is a tax year in which the member once again starts to have relevant earnings or is a member of an occupational scheme throughout the tax year.

The five years following the cessation year to which the cessation rules apply are known as 'qualifying post cessation years'.

The effect of the cessation rules is that during the five qualifying post cessation years, net relevant earnings can be taken from the cessation year or any of the previous five tax years. In other words, any tax year which could have been used as the basis year for contributions in the cessation year can also be used throughout the five qualifying post cessation years. These years are known as the 'reference years'.

Maximum contributions will however be based on the appropriate percentage reflecting the age of the individual on 6 April in the tax year in which any contribution is made.

Example – Cessation rules

An individual has been self-employed for a number of years, but retires in December 2006, on their 60th birthday, after which time they will have no earned income. Their net relevant earnings and contribution limits are as follows:

	Tax year	Actual NRE	Basis year chosen	Basis year NRE	Age at 6 April	% limit	Cont limit
	2001/02	£60,000			54	30%	£18,000
	2002/03	£55,000			55	30%	£18,000
Reference years	2003/04	£56,000			56	35%	£21,000
	2004/05	£53,000			57	35%	£21,000
	2005/06	£32,000			58	35%	£21,000
	2006/07 Cessation year	£21,000	2001/02 in all cases	£60,000 in all cases	59	35%	£21,000
Qualifying post-cessation years	2007/08 Break year	£0			60	35%	£21,000
	2008/09	£0			61	40%	£24,000
	2009/10	£0			62	40%	£24,000
	2010/11	£0			63	40%	£24,000
	2011/12	£0			64	40%	£24,000
	2012/13	£0			65	n\a	£3,600

In this example, the individual can base the calculation of maximum contributions on their 2001/02 net relevant earnings throughout the period from 2001/02 to 2011/12.

After 2011/12, they are no longer within the cessation rules period, and can only contribute up to the earnings threshold of £3,600.

(This example assumes that there will be no change to the cessation rules through the period under review. In practice, the simplification proposals discussed in **Chapter 15: Simplification of Tax Treatment** are likely to abolish these rules from a future date yet to be determined.)

Note that subject to the individual not having reached their 75th birthday, contributions can continue after the qualifying post cessation years but would be restricted to the earnings threshold. (This assumes that the individual is otherwise eligible, but has no net relevant earnings).

Excess contributions   3.35

If contributions in excess of limits are paid, they must be refunded. The prior agreement of the Inland Revenue is not required and the refund can be made by the scheme administrator, though the administrator may require evidence that the limits have been exceeded.

If there are employer contributions as well as contributions paid by the individual, the latter should be refunded first, and the employer contributions can only be refunded if there are still excess contributions after returning those paid by the individual. The employer's excess contributions would be refunded to the employer in these circumstances.

If there are several personal pension schemes, it is up to the individual to select the scheme or schemes from which the excess will be refunded. However, no employer contributions can be returned unless all the contributions paid by the individual to all schemes have been refunded, and an excess still remains.

Refunds to the individual are paid after deduction of basic rate tax, which the scheme administrator will pay to the Inland Revenue.

Adjustments can also be made by the administrator to reflect interest, changes in investment values, and charges.

4 — Tax Relief

Introduction   4.1

One of the main advantages of making retirement planning provision through personal pensions is the favourable tax treatment that such arrangements enjoy, and a large part of this is in the fact that contributions qualify for tax relief.

Contributions by individuals to personal pension schemes are paid net of basic rate tax, irrespective of whether the individual is employed or self employed. (Before 6 April 2001, this treatment applied only to contributions by employees; the self employed had to pay contributions gross and claim tax relief from their Inspector of Taxes.)

Individuals who are non-taxpayers, or who are subject only to tax at the starting rate of 10%, retain the advantage of this basic rate tax relief, which will make personal pension provision particularly attractive for them. Non-taxpayers may not have sufficient resources to make contributions themselves, but this is relevant also where contributions are made on their behalf by others. For example, a parent or grandparent making contributions on behalf of a minor child, with no earnings or other income, would still pay the contribution net of basic rate tax.

Note that the rate of relief available is determined by the tax position of the member, not the payer of the contribution.

The amount of the basic rate relief is claimed by the product provider and this is added to the amount invested on behalf of the individual.

Higher rate relief   4.2

An individual who is a higher rate tax payer, will claim higher rate relief on contributions, generally by including details of them in their tax return. Tax relief is given by increasing the basic rate tax band available to the individual by the amount of the gross contribution to the personal pension. As the example below shows, this provides further tax relief equivalent to 18% of the gross contribution.

Example – Higher rate relief I

A higher rate taxpayer has net relevant earnings of £42,000. They have no income from any other source.

They wish to make a personal pension contribution of £5,000 gross.

The contribution they pay to the product provider is net of basic rate relief at 22%, so they pay £3,900, and the product provider reclaims £1,100 (22% of £5,000) from the Inland Revenue. The total amount invested is therefore £5,000.

The higher rate threshold for the individual is increased from £30,500 to £35,500. The effect on their tax position is shown below:

Before PP contribution		After PP contribution	
Earned income	£42,000	Earned income	£42,000
Personal Allowance	£ 4,615	Personal Allowance	£ 4,615
	£37,385		£37,385
Tax Liability		Tax Liability	
£1,960 @ 10%	£196.00	£1,960 @ 10%	£196.00
£28,540 @ 22%	£6278.80	£33,540 @ 22%	£7,378.80
(to fully utilise basic rate band up to total income of £30,500 after allowance)		(to fully utilise basic rate band up to total income of £35,500 after allowance)	
£6,885 @ 40%	£2,754.00	£ 1,885 @ 40%	£754.00
Total tax liability	£9,228.80	Total tax liability	£8,328.80
		Reduction in tax liability is £900 ie £5,000 @ 18%	

The total relief obtained is £1,100 reclaimed by the product provider and £900 reclaimed by the individual, giving a total of £2,000 (ie 40% of £5,000).

Some care is needed in quantifying the amount of tax relief available in various circumstances, particularly if the contribution is made from income which spans the higher rate threshold. The effect of higher rate relief will of course be restricted to removing from higher rate only the amount of income which otherwise would have been subject to it.

Example – Higher rate relief II

Suppose that, using the same details as in the previous example, the individual now wants to make a personal pension contribution of £7,000 gross rather than £5,000.

The contribution they pay to the product provider is again net of basic rate relief at 22%, so they pay £5,460, and the product provider reclaims £1,540 (22% of £7,000) from the Inland Revenue. The total amount invested is therefore £7,000.

The higher rate threshold for the individual is increased from £30,500 to £37,500. As a result, they are no longer liable to higher rate tax and their tax position is as follows:

Before PP contribution		After PP contribution	
Earned income	£42,000	Earned income	£42,000
Personal Allowance	£ 4,615	Personal Allowance	£ 4,615
	£37,385		£37,385
Tax Liability		Tax Liability	
£1,960 @ 10%	£196.00	£1,960 @ 10%	£196.00
£28,540 @ 22%	£6,278.80	£35,425 @ 22%	£7,793.50
(to fully utilise basic rate band up to total income of £30,500 after allowance)		(which is within the enlarged basic rate band of £37,500 after allowance)	
£6,885 @ 40%	£2,754.00		
Total tax liability	£9,228.80	Total tax liability	£7,989.50
		Reduction in tax liability is £1,239.30 ie £6,885 @ 18%	

The higher rate relief is therefore limited to a contribution of £6,885, which is the amount of the individual's income on which they would otherwise have been liable to higher rate tax.

Interaction with other types of income   4.3

Complications also arise where the individual is in receipt of more than one type of income, because of the differential tax rates that can apply. The only reliable way to determine the amount of relief available is to carry out the tax calculation before and after the payment of the personal pension contribution.

The example below illustrates a situation where the individual is in receipt of earned income which does not fully utilise the basic rate tax band. However the individual is also in receipt of dividend income which takes their total income into higher rate.

Paying a personal pension contribution will again widen the basic rate tax band, and this therefore has the effect of bringing some dividend income which was previously taxed at higher rate into the basic rate band. (Income is always taxed in the same order, with non-savings income, including earnings, treated as the first part of income, savings income such as interest taken second and dividends treated as the top part of income.)

Example – Dividend income falling into higher rate

An individual has earned income of £30,000 from non-pensionable employment and dividend income (gross) of £20,000. They want to make a personal pension contribution of £2,000 gross. They will therefore pay the product provider £1,560, and the product provider will reclaim £440 from the Inland Revenue.

Their higher rate threshold will increase from £30,500 to £32,500 as a result of the contribution.

Before PP contribution		After PP contribution	
Earned income	£30,000	Earned income	£30,000
Dividend income	£20,000	Dividend income	£20,000
	£50,000		£50,000
Personal Allowance	£ 4,615	Personal Allowance	£ 4,615
	£45,385		£45,385
Tax liability – Earned income		Tax liability – Earned income	
£1,960 @ 10%	£196.00	£1,960 @ 10%	£196.00
£23,425 @ 22%	£5,153.50	£23,405 @ 22%	£5,153.50
Tax liability – Dividends		Tax liability – Dividends	
£5,115 @ 10%	£511.50	£7,115 @ 10%	£711.50
(to fully utilise basic rate band up to total income of £30,500 after allowance)		(to fully utilise basic rate band up to total income of £32,500 after allowance)	
£14,885 @ 32.5%	£ 4,837.63	£12,885 @ 32.5%	£ 4,187.63
Total tax liability	£10,698.63	Total tax liability	£10,248.63

The reduction in tax liability is £450. In addition, the product provider reclaims tax relief at basic rate of £440. The total relief obtained is therefore £450 + £440 = £890 (ie 44.5% of £2,000).

The effective rate of relief on the contribution in this example is 44.5%. This rather peculiar, and in some ways unexpected, rate of relief arises because 22% relief is obtained through payment of the contribution net of basic rate tax. In addition, the widening of the basic rate band means that the rate of tax on £2,000 of the dividend income has reduced from 32.5% to 10%, in other words a reduction of 22.5%. The total rate of relief is therefore 22% + 22.5% = 44.5%.

The payment of a personal pension contribution by an individual who would otherwise be a higher rate taxpayer can also affect the position on surrender of a non-qualifying life policy such as an investment bond. This effect would occur if, after the widening of the basic rate band to reflect the personal pension contribution, but before allowing for the encashment of the policy, there is insufficient income to fully utilise the total basic rate band.

The widening of the basic rate band will reduce (or could eliminate) the tax liability on any chargeable gain on the policy. In addition, the normal top-slicing procedures will increase the effect of this if the policy has been held for some years.

Example – Interaction with top-slicing relief

An individual has an investment bond, which they have held for just over five years. They now intend to surrender it, and this will result in a chargeable gain of £20,000.

Their income (all of which is net relevant earnings) before allowing for the gain is currently £34,115. After deducting the personal allowance of £4,615, their income uses the starting rate band and all but £1,000 of the basic rate band.

On surrender of the investment bond, the gain is divided by the number of complete years it has been in force, to give a 'slice' of £20,000/5 = £4,000. This is added to income, to calculate the higher rate tax on the slice.

Of the slice of £4,000, the first £1,000 uses the remainder of the basic rate tax band, so the liability on the slice is £3,000 @ 18% = £540. The tax on the gain as a whole is therefore £540 × 5 (the number of slices) = £2,700.

If the individual makes a personal pension contribution of £2,000 (gross), this will widen their basic rate tax band by £2,000. When calculating the tax liability on the surrender of the bond, this will reduce the tax on the slice because now the extent of the basic rate tax band remaining is £3,000. The tax on the slice is therefore only £1,000 @ 18% = £180, and the tax on the gain as a whole is therefore £180 × 5 = £900.

The tax saving in relation to the surrender of the bond is therefore £1,800. In addition, they will have received tax relief on the personal pension contribution of £440, by payment of a net contribution. The total tax saving in this example exceeds the contribution itself.

The payment of a personal pension contribution can also reduce income for age allowance purposes, and can reduce income for the purposes of calculating child tax credit.

By concession, the widening of the basic rate tax band to allow for a contribution can also affect the taxation of capital gains. This would occur where the effect is to bring all or part of a capital gain which otherwise would have been taxed at higher rate into basic rate. Strictly the legislation does not allow for this, but the situation is covered in *Inland Revenue Extra-Statutory Concession Number A101*.

Timing of tax relief   4.4

The current system for giving tax relief, which requires payment of contributions net of basic rate relief by individuals, means that relief at this level is given automatically and immediately. The system also avoids individuals who are not subject to higher rate tax having to make individual repayment claims to the Inland Revenue. (Indeed the system is intended to cut down individual claims in as many cases as possible.)

Higher rate taxpayers must claim higher rate relief from the Inland Revenue, and will generally do so through their tax return. Alternatively, the relief can be claimed by completing form PP120 and submitting this to the local Inspector of Taxes.

Where the individual is self-employed, he will usually pay tax in three instalments. The first falls due on 31 January in the tax year concerned, the second on the following 31 July, and the third and final payment on the following 31 January.

The first two payments are the payments on account (each of which is generally equal to one half of the tax liability for the previous tax year). The final payment is the balance payment, which brings the total tax paid up to the required level. Higher rate tax relief on the personal pension contribution is generally given against the balance payment.

This means that if a self-employed higher rate taxpayer pays a personal pension contribution and claims relief against 2003/04, although basic rate relief is available immediately through the payment of a net contribution, higher rate relief will only be available when the balance instalment of tax becomes due on 31 January 2005.

If the higher rate taxpayer is employed, income tax in relation to their earned income will be dealt with through the PAYE system. Nevertheless, generally further payments of tax will be made direct to the Inland Revenue in respect of the higher rate tax liability on other income. This would apply where income is received without deduction of tax, or with only part of the tax liability dealt with at source, for example as would be the case with interest, with basic rate tax deducted, or dividends received net of a 10% tax credit.

Unless the amounts involved are small, these payments are also dealt with through the same process of two on account payments and a final balance payment. Where this is so, higher rate relief will again be dealt with by reducing the balance payment.

Where however the individual has submitted their tax return, and paid all the tax which is due in respect of the year in which the contribution was paid, it may be possible to obtain a repayment of tax from the Inland Revenue. Such a repayment will only be made if the Inland Revenue agrees that there is no outstanding liability, and if no further payment of tax is due within the following 35 days (if further payment is due, higher rate relief would be given by an offset against the further payment).

It is possible to speed up the timing of higher rate tax relief by means of a carry back election. This is dealt with in section **4.13** below.

Contributions by employers   4.5

An employer is permitted to pay contributions to a personal pension for the benefit of an employee. The employer will be able to treat the contributions paid in this way as a deductible business expense (with the agreement of the Inspector of Taxes, as for all deductions) and so will obtain tax relief on them.

The employee will have no tax liability in respect of the contributions, nor will any National Insurance liability arise.

Overall, therefore, the treatment of these contributions is very favourable, and in line with the treatment of employer contributions to occupational pension schemes. This allows group personal pensions to be seen as a realistic alternative to occupational schemes (see section **1.22**).

The employee can also pay contributions to the same personal pension, but there is no requirement for this in tax law. This means that it is perfectly possible for a personal pension arrangement to be funded entirely by the employer.

Note however that many employers will require employees to contribute as a condition of the payment of the employer contributions. This is a matter relating to the contract of employment rather than in any way being a consequence of the tax law relating to pensions.

Contribution limits   4.6

Employer contributions, when aggregated with any paid by the employee (whether to the same or a separate arrangement) must lie within normal personal pension contribution limits, as discussed in **Chapter 3: Contribution Limits**. Employer contributions therefore could be said to reduce the scope for contributions by the employee themself.

The basis year rules can be used in the normal way, so there can be circumstances where the contribution limit is calculated in relation to earnings which derive from an earlier, unrelated, employment.

In some cases, the employee may also have earnings from a separate source, at the same time as those from the employment. If contributions above the earnings threshold are being paid, the contribution limit will reflect earnings from all sources. There is no objection to the employer paying contributions up to the maximum level even though this takes into account those earnings from the separate source.

Where earnings levels are low, contributions up to the earnings threshold of £3,600 can be paid in the usual way, and this amount can all be paid by the employer if the employee is paying nothing personally.

Similarly if the employee is eligible to make personal pension contributions under the concurrency rules (see section **2.20**) it is possible for the employer to pay all or part of these contributions (which are limited by the earnings threshold).

Example – Personal pension contributions under the concurrency rules

A member of an employer's approved occupational pension scheme is also eligible for a personal pension under the concurrency rules.

Their employer could pay a contribution to the personal pension (as well as funding all or part of the cost of the occupational scheme).

The contribution limit would be £3,600, and this would cover the total of the contributions which could be paid by the individual and their employer.

Note that employer contributions are always paid gross with relief claimed as a deductible business expense.

Deduction of employee contributions through payroll   4.7

Employers will sometimes deduct the employee's own contributions to personal pensions through payroll, and indeed under the stakeholder pension rules (see section **1.25**) will often be obliged to do so if the employee so wishes. The contributions which are deducted in this way will be paid over to the product provider by the employer, but they nevertheless constitute contributions by the individual rather than by the employer.

The deduction made from pay will therefore be equal to the employee contribution net of basic rate tax, irrespective of the tax position of the employee. The deduction is made from net pay, after deduction of tax and National Insurance, so that the effect is equivalent to the employee paying the contribution themself. Higher rate relief, where applicable, can be claimed by the employee in the normal way (see section **4.2** above).

It is not possible for the employer to operate the net pay arrangement as would apply if the contributions were being made by the employee to an approved occupational pension scheme. Under the net pay arrangement, contributions would be deducted from pay before calculation of tax liability, and for a higher rate taxpayer the effect would be to give 40% relief on the contribution at source. This basis is not available for personal pension contributions.

Group personal pensions 4.8

Many employers arrange with product providers to facilitate membership of, and entry to, personal pension arrangements for their employees. Sometimes these arrangements cover very large groups of employees, sometimes very modest numbers. A group personal pension arrangement provides a genuine alternative to an occupational pension scheme, but involves less responsibility on the part of the employer, and less administration.

Although often presented as a group scheme, in reality the arrangements are individual, between each member and the product provider. Even if the employer pays all or part of the cost, the employee remains in complete control of the arrangement, and can freely decide where and how it should be invested, and can decide when, and in what form, to take retirement benefits (subject to Inland Revenue requirements).

There is no special tax treatment for these arrangements, and the normal tax relief rules, as described in this chapter, apply.

Salary sacrifice 4.9

Where employees make contributions to personal pension arrangements, the earnings from which the contributions are made will have been taxed through PAYE, though this tax is balanced by the relief available on the contribution. The earnings will however also have been subject to

National Insurance liability (assuming that the employee's income is above the National Insurance threshold, which is £89 per week in 2003/04).

Employer National Insurance Contributions are at the rate of 11.8% of earnings above the threshold, and employee contributions are at the rate of 10% of earnings between the threshold and the upper earnings limit. In addition, from 6 April 2003, a further 1% is payable by both employers and employees, based on all earnings above the threshold (not limited, even in the case of employees, by the Upper Earnings Limit).

Salary sacrifice involves the employee giving up part of their salary and this then enables the employer to make a contribution to a personal pension on the employee's behalf. Because the employer contribution does not attract National Insurance liability, the resulting savings can be used to increase the amount of the contribution, and/or provide additional net income to the individual. The effect can be extremely advantageous, as the example below illustrates.

Example – Salary sacrifice

An individual earns £20,000 in 2003/04 from their employment with SDF Ltd. The employment is non pensionable.

The employee is considering making a contribution to a personal pension of £1,000 gross. If they do so, the net cost to them will be £780, because they will pay the contribution net of basic rate tax relief.

Suppose that instead, with the individual's agreement, SDF Ltd reduces the employee's gross salary by £1,000, down to £19,000, and agrees to pay a personal pension contribution for the individual. The reduction in salary would reduce the employee's tax liability through PAYE by £220, since the income sacrificed would have been subject to basic rate tax. In addition, the individual's National Insurance Contributions would reduce by 11% of £1,000 = £110.

Overall therefore, net pay would fall by £670 (£1,000 − £220 − £110). The employee would therefore be £110 better off than if they had paid the personal pension contribution themself.

SDF Ltd would have reduced their salary costs by £1,000, but also their National Insurance Contributions would reduce by £128 (12.8% × £1,000). They could therefore make a personal pension contribution of £1,128 for the employee's benefit, without any change to their net costs.

For a higher rate taxpayer, there is the added advantage that there is no need to claim higher rate relief from the Inland Revenue. Because salary is reduced, the tax collected through PAYE is reduced and this gives effect to tax relief at higher rate immediately. Generally however, higher rate taxpayers will not save employee National Insurance Contributions other than the new 1% addition, because their earnings are likely to be more than the upper earnings limit.

Care is needed in documenting the salary sacrifice and large sacrifices (in excess of £5,000 *per annum*) must be notified to the Inspector of Taxes who will rule on their effectiveness. The Inland Revenue does not offer guidance on how salary sacrifice arrangements should be constructed, but does issue guidance on the tax implications of the sacrifice and the issues with which they are concerned when they check effectiveness.

The two conditions which need to be met in order for the sacrifice to be effective are:

(*a*)   the potential future remuneration must be given up before it is treated as received for tax or National Insurance purposes; and

(*b*)   the true construction of the revised contractual arrangement between employer and employee must be that the employee is entitled to lower cash remuneration and an additional benefit.

This last point reflects the fact that the Inland Revenue is seeking to ensure that the arrangement is not merely one under which the employer is meeting an obligation of the employee.

If the sacrifice is not effective, the amount paid into the personal pension will be regarded as a diversion of the employee's own money (ie the employer is simply paying direct something which would otherwise have been paid by the employee from the money received from the employer). This will not be effective in reducing National Insurance liability.

An example of a possible sacrifice letter is given below. However, because any salary sacrifice alters the contractual relationship between the employer and employee, it is generally advisable to take legal advice in relation to it, and on the employment law implications in particular.

Example – Possible salary sacrifice letter

Dear Mr Employee,

As discussed today, this letter confirms our agreement that your salary will be reduced from £xxx to £yyy with effect from (future date).

Please sign and return a copy of this letter to me, to confirm your agreement.

Yours etc

Signed for employer

....

Signed by employee

....

Although salary sacrifice can be extremely advantageous from a tax and National Insurance Contribution point of view, there are disadvantages which need to be considered, and which can be significant if the sacrifice is of a substantial amount. The sacrifice must necessarily be made for all purposes, and some of the factors to be considered are:

(*a*)   the scope for personal pension contributions under the age and earnings related scale will be reduced because earnings are reduced (though the effect of this may be diminished by the use of basis years);

(*b*)   whether the employer provides salary related benefits, for example life assurance cover or permanent health assurance, as these are also likely to be reduced as a result of the salary sacrifice;

(*c*)   entitlement to some State benefits, for example, pensions under the State Second Pension Scheme (S2P) may be affected;

(*d*)   if earnings fall below the Lower Earnings Limit as a result of the sacrifice, entitlement to basic pension may also be affected;

(*e*)   a married woman paying reduced rate contributions will lose this right if earnings are below the Lower Earnings Limit for two consecutive tax years, even if this occurs only as a result of a sacrifice; and

(*f*)   the individual may be affected personally in that their credit rating may be eroded by the reduction in earnings, and this could reduce their scope for (amongst other things) mortgage borrowing where maximum levels are set as a multiple of earnings.

It is also important to ensure that the sacrifice does not result in the individual's earnings falling below the level of the National Minimum Wage in the case of those to whom this applies, since this would be unlawful. Note however that directors are not covered by the National Minimum Wage requirements, unless they are subject to a written contract of employment.

Bonus sacrifice   4.10

Bonuses can also be sacrificed in the same way as salary to provide an employer contribution. As with salary sacrifice, it is important that the sacrifice be made before the employee is regarded as having received the bonus for tax and National Insurance purposes, otherwise it will not be regarded as effective. Generally this point is when the bonus is actually paid.

Once again, a bonus sacrifice is an alteration to the contractual relationship between employer and employee, and it may be appropriate to take legal advice in relation to the employment law aspects of the exercise.

Dividend sacrifice 4.11

It is possible for shareholders to give up the right to receive dividends in a similar way to employees giving up salary or bonus payments, although the timing of this can be more difficult. It will generally be appropriate for the company to seek advice from the company accountant and/or legal adviser regarding the effectiveness of any dividend sacrifice.

Contributions for shareholding directors 4.12

Shareholding directors of private companies are often in a position to decide the way in which they will draw income and benefits from the company. In particular, it is likely to be possible for them to decide whether the company will make contributions to a personal pension on their behalf, or whether income should be drawn and contributions paid personally.

It is likely to be more attractive for the company to pay contributions direct than for the director to draw salary, which would be subject to National Insurance Contribution liability, and then make personal contributions. The reasoning is essentially the same as that which applies to salary sacrifice as discussed in section **4.9** above.

In some cases, however, it can be attractive for the company to pay an increased dividend to the director and for the personal pension contribution to be paid by the individual from this additional dividend income. The example below illustrates the effectiveness of this.

Example – Dividends and shareholding directors

A 62-year-old shareholding director of STU Ltd draws an annual salary of £20,000 and dividends of £50,000 per year (gross). The director wants to make a personal pension contribution, funded by the company, and there is £5,000 available in the company for this purpose.

STU Ltd is liable for corporation tax at the small companies rate of 19%.

If the company pays the contribution direct, corporation tax relief would be available and the gross contribution would be £5,000.

Alternatively, if the company used the £5,000 to pay a dividend, it would first need to allow for corporation tax of £950 (ie 19% of £5,000) and could then distribute a net dividend of £4,050. (From the shareholding director's point of view, this would be regarded for income tax purposes as a gross dividend of £4,500, paid net of a tax credit of £450.)

The director could use the net dividend to pay a contribution net of basic rate tax. The product provider would reclaim basic rate relief as follows:

Net contribution	£4,050
Basic rate relief	£1,142
Gross contribution	£5,192

There would be no additional higher rate liability as a result of the extra dividend, because the basic rate band would be widened by the amount of the gross personal pension contribution. Indeed, because the gross contribution exceeds the amount of the gross dividend, there would be a further small saving here.

The income tax position is as follows:

Before dividend and PP contribution		After dividend and PP contribution	
Earned income	£20,000	Earned income	£20,000
Dividend income	£50,000	Dividend income	£54,500
	£70,000		£74,500
Personal Allowance	£ 4,615	Personal Allowance	£ 4,615
	£65,385		£69,885
Tax liability – Earned income		Tax liability – Earned income	
£1,960 @ 10%	£196.00	£1,960 @ 10%	£196.00
£13,425 @ 22%	£2,953.50	£13,425 @ 22%	£2,953.50
Tax liability – Dividends		Tax liability – Dividends	
£15,115 @ 10%	£1411.50	£20,307 @ 10%	£2,030.70
(to fully utilise basic rate band up to total income of £30,500 after allowance)		(to fully utilise basic rate band up to total income of £35,692 after allowance)	
£34,885 @ 32.5%	£11,337.63	£34,193 @ 32.5%	£11,112.73
Total tax liability	£15,898.63	Total tax liability	£16,292.93
Tax credit	£5,000.00	Tax credit	£5,450.00
To be paid	£10,898.63	To be paid	£10,842.93

Overall, the effect of paying the dividend and the director using this to pay the personal pension contribution is to increase the gross amount invested by £192 (3.8%) and to reduce personal tax liability by over £50.

The advantage is dependent on the company's corporation tax rate – the lower the better. The advantage would therefore be greatest if the company was subject to the zero starting rate of tax. The approach would not be advantageous if the company was subject to the standard rate (30%) or to one of the marginal rate bands where the effective rate of tax is 23.75% (profits between £10,000 and £50,000) or 32.75% (profits between £300,000 and £1.5m).

There may be other factors to take into account in deciding whether an additional dividend payment is appropriate, not the least of which will be the distribution of shareholdings, given that a dividend entitlement will arise in respect of all shares of the same class.

In addition, there must be sufficient accumulated profit within the company to allow declaration of the proposed dividend.

Contributions must lie within normal limits too, and the dividend payment would not itself be regarded as relevant earnings.

The decision regarding the pension contribution cannot therefore be taken in isolation.

Carry back of contributions 4.13

The carry back facility has been available in respect of contributions to personal pensions since their introduction in 1988. However the facility has been amended with effect from 6 April 2001, and has in general become more restrictive.

The essential idea behind the facility remains unchanged. It allows a contribution to be paid during one tax year, yet be treated for tax purposes as if it was paid during the immediately preceding year. For example, a contribution paid during 2003/04 can be carried back and treated for tax purposes as if it was paid during 2002/03.

Note that the carry back facility is available to both the employed and self-employed, but that contributions paid by employers for the benefit of employees cannot be carried back.

There are a number of conditions which must be met in order to allow a contribution to be carried back. These are:

(a) the contribution must be paid on or before 31 January in any tax year (contributions paid between 1 February and 5 April inclusive cannot therefore be carried back in any circumstances);

(b) an election to carry back must be made at or before the time the contribution is paid; and (*c*)   the contribution to be carried back must be within the contribution limits applicable to the year in which the contribution is carried back, taking account of any contributions paid in the year itself.

Making the election   4.14

The election to carry back should be made on form PP43, a copy of which is reproduced at the end of this chapter. This form can be obtained from the product provider or from any tax office.

Generally this form must be completed and must be given to the scheme administrator. It will be held as part of their records, and may be subject to Inland Revenue audit.

For a higher rate taxpayer, details of the contribution carried back will generally be included in their tax return for the year to which the contribution is carried back and relief will be obtained through the normal self-assessment procedure. (The deadline for payment of contributions to be carried back is 31 January, which is the same as the date by which an individual's tax return for the preceding tax year must have been fully completed and returned to the tax office.)

There will be some situations where the higher rate taxpayer will already have completed their tax return by the time the personal pension contribution is paid. In such cases, the PP43 must be completed and must be sent to the individual's tax office, with a copy being given to the scheme administrator. Again the scheme administrator would keep this copy with its own records for Inland Revenue audit purposes.

Age restriction   4.15

Although carry back has the advantage of allowing a contribution to be treated for tax purposes as if paid in the previous tax year, it remains a requirement that the contribution must physically be paid before the individual reaches the age of 75. It is not for example possible to pay a contribution just after an individual's 75th birthday with the intention of carrying it back to the previous tax year when the individual was only 74.

Timing of tax relief   4.16

One of the major advantages of carrying back a contribution is that it can accelerate any claim for higher rate relief. Generally tax relief on personal pension contributions will be available against the balance payment for the year against which relief is claimed. If a contribution is paid during

2003/04 and is not carried back, then the balance payment will fall due on 31 January 2005, so relief will usually be delayed until then.

If on the other hand the contribution is carried back to 2002/03, the balance payment for that year falls due on 31 January 2004, and relief would be available then. Potentially therefore, for a higher rate taxpayer, there is a twelve month cash flow advantage to be had by carrying the contribution back.

Note that a contribution which is carried back does not amend the tax assessment for the year to which it is carried back. This means that it will have no effect on future payments on account.

Why carry back? 4.17

There are various advantages which can make it attractive to carry back a personal pension contribution. The most obvious arises where the individual was liable to a higher rate of tax in the previous year than will be the case in the current year. This may be because their earnings were high enough in the previous year to take them into higher rate tax, but in the current year their liability is limited to basic rate. If a contribution is carried back to the previous year, relief will be available at higher rate.

A similar situation arises if there is a general reduction in tax rates. For example, when the basic rate of income tax was reduced from 23% to 22% in 2000/01, a contribution carried back from 2000/01 to 1999/2000 by a basic rate taxpayer would have benefited from relief at 23% rather than 22%.

Even if there is no difference in tax rates, but the individual is a higher rate taxpayer, carry back should still be considered in order to accelerate the availability of higher rate relief from a cashflow point of view. This means that carry back is always worth considering for higher rate taxpayers. (There is no timing advantage for basic rate taxpayers, because basic rate relief is given immediately for all individual contributors, by payment of net contributions).

In some cases, the contribution which an individual intends to pay may be greater than the amount of income on which they have a higher rate liability. If, in the previous tax year, some income was subject to higher rate tax, it is likely to be worth carrying back part of the contribution in order to maximise relief. The example below illustrates this.

Example – Partial carry back

An individual has income in 2003/04 which (after allowances) is sufficient to use the whole of the starting and basic rate bands, and leave £2,000 falling into higher rate tax.

> In 2002/03, they were in a similar situation, but with £1,500 falling into higher rate.
>
> If they make a personal pension contribution of £3,000 (gross) in 2003/04, and make no carry back election, they will benefit from higher rate relief on only £2,000.
>
> If instead, they carry back £1,500 of the contribution to 2002/03, leaving the remaining £1,500 in 2003/04, they will obtain higher rate relief on the whole of the £3,000.

A further point to consider is the effective use of the allowable contribution limit over the long term. If contributions are being paid in 2003/04 but contributions in the preceding year, 2002/03, were not up to the limit, it may be advisable to carry back contributions to the maximum extent possible to 2002/03.

The point here is that the allowance for personal pension contributions in respect of 2002/03 will be lost if not used, whereas the allowance for 2003/04 remains available until 31 January 2005 under the carry back facility. Even if at the time of payment of contributions, it is not envisaged that the full allowance for 2003/04 will be utilised, circumstances may change, and it always makes sense to retain the option of using allowances for as long as possible.

Miscellaneous points 4.18

For the avoidance of doubt, it is possible to carry back a part of a contribution made to a single arrangement, with the remainder left for relief purposes in the year of payment. It is not necessary for the carried back contribution to be housed in a different personal pension arrangement.

There are no circumstances where a personal pension contribution can be carried back any further than the tax year preceding that in which it is actually paid. For contributions paid prior to 6 April 2001, it was possible to carry a contribution back two years in the relatively unusual circumstances where there were no net relevant earnings in the immediately preceding year. This facility is no longer available under personal pensions, though it remains under retirement annuity legislation (see section **14.18**).

Similarly, at one time it was possible for Lloyds underwriters to carry back contributions for three tax years, which reflected the rather unusual way in which underwriting profits were taxed at the time. The taxation basis of Lloyds underwriters has since been revised, so it is no longer appropriate for a three year carry back option to be available, and it has therefore been withdrawn.

Checklist – Personal pension carry back

- The contribution carried back is treated as paid in the tax year preceding the tax year of payment.
- The contribution must be paid by 31 January.
- The election must be made at or before the time the contribution is paid.
- The election on form PP43 is given to the scheme administrator in most cases.
- The form PP43 is sent to Inland Revenue if the individual is a higher rate taxpayer and has already submitted their tax return.
- A copy PP43 is given to the scheme administrator if the original is sent to the Inland Revenue.
- The contribution must be within limits for the preceding tax year, after taking account of contributions actually paid in that year.
- Employer contributions cannot be carried back.

Personal Pension Schemes

Your reference	
Inland Revenue reference	

Inland Revenue office Date stamp

Election to carry back contributions paid on or after 6 April 2001
Tax year ending 5 April _____

Name of client _____
(where form issued to an agent)

Please read the notes over the page before you fill in this form. These will tell you where to send the form once you have filled in Section A and B and signed the declaration.

Section A	*Membership details*			
Full name of Scheme member	Date of birth	Name of Personal Pension Scheme		Contract No

Section B	*Details of carry back*
Amount to be carried back to previous year	Date of payment (if it is part of a larger sum please give details)
£	

Declaration

It is a serious offence to make a false declaration

To the best of my knowledge and belief the details I have given above are correct.

I am attaching form PP120 ☐ *(✓ if appropriate)*

I claim the relief to which I am entitled

If you want to amend your tax return and self-assessment tick this box ☐✓ *(See Note 4 overleaf)*

Signature		Date	/ /

National Insurance number ☐☐ ☐☐ ☐☐ ☐

PP43 (New) (Substitute)(LexisNexis UK)

Carry back of contributions paid on or after 6 April 2001

Notes

1   You can elect for the contribution you pay between 6 April and the following 31 January in a year of assessment to be carried back to the previous year of assessment.

    You must make this election at or before the time of payment of the contribution which you want to carry back.

2   All contributions paid to personal pension contracts on or after 6 April 2001 are paid net of tax at basic rate. Your scheme administrator will make any adjustment where the basic rate of the year to which your payment is being carried back differs from the basic rate for the current (payment) year. You need only fill in this form and send it to your scheme administrator. Unless you are liable to tax at a higher rate no further relief will be given by your Inland Revenue office.

3   If you are liable to tax at a higher rate the additional tax relief due (the difference between the higher rate and basic rate) will be given by your Inland Revenue office. You can claim your relief by either including it in your tax return or by completing this form and sending it to your Inland Revenue office with a claim form PP120. You can get form PP120 from your scheme administrator or from any Inland Revenue office.

    Whichever route is chosen to make your claim for relief at the higher rate, you will also have to give your scheme administrator a copy of this form so that the necessary adjustments for the basic rate tax can be made.

    There is no need to send any Contribution Payment Certificate (CPC) or contribution receipts with your election but these should be retained as the Revenue may call for these in selected cases under Self Assessment. If you would like more information ask your Inland Revenue office for Help Sheet IR 330 "Pension payments".

4   If you have already sent in your tax return for the year to which you are now carrying back your personal pension payment, your tax return will now need to be amended to reflect this carry back. You should tick the box in the declaration overleaf and that will be sufficient to amend your tax return and self-assessment.

5 — Retirement Benefits

Introduction   5.1

The main purpose of personal pension arrangements is to provide financial resources for a person in their retirement, and this therefore is an area where important decisions must be made. Over the years, the range of alternatives available has increased markedly, but this has also increased the degree of complexity involved.

Timing   5.2

Retirement benefits must normally be accessed no earlier than the member's fiftieth birthday, and no later than their 75th birthday.

It is possible to take benefits earlier than the age of 50 if the member becomes incapacitated, and details of this are given in **Chapter 9: Incapacity**. There is no minimum age at which benefits can be accessed in this circumstance.

There are also certain special occupations, largely involving professional sport, where the Inland Revenue has agreed that benefits may be taken at an earlier age. Details of these occupations are given in **Chapter 13: Special Occupations**.

Protected rights   5.3

Where the member has protected rights benefits as a result of contracting out, it is a requirement of the contracting out legislation that these benefits cannot be accessed until age 60, at the earliest. It is not possible for them to be taken earlier, even in cases of incapacity, and the early retirement ages permitted for those in special occupations do not apply to protected rights benefits. This is discussed in detail in **Chapter 12: Contracting Out**.

Retirement   5.4

Apart from cases of incapacity, the ability to access benefits under personal pensions is purely dependent on age. Although it is not unreasonable to describe the benefits discussed in this chapter as 'retirement benefits', there is actually no link to the retirement of the individual concerned.

It is possible for a member of a personal pension scheme to take their retirement benefits at age 50, even though they may be continuing to work. Where they are working on in a full-time capacity, this may not be an appropriate option, because they probably have no need of the benefits whilst still in receipt of an income from their job. In these circumstances taking benefits which are largely taxable may aggravate the member's income tax position. However, if they have reduced their work activity and, as a result, their income has declined, it may be appropriate to take all or part of the benefits available.

There is also no requirement that an individual draw benefits when they finish working. Although this may be the most likely time when benefits are required, there will be many situations where individuals draw on other resources for a period, prior to taking their personal pension benefits. These other resources may be in the form of capital, or the individual might seek lower paid work for a period.

Given the tax-advantaged nature of pension fund investment, this can be a very attractive option.

Example – Deferring benefits

An individual has been in non–pensionable employment for a number of years, and has built up a substantial personal pension fund. They are now 57 years old.

They have taken voluntary redundancy, and received a generous golden handshake from their employer. The individual plans to work part–time for another employer, at least for a few years, and to supplement their reduced income from the golden handshake payment.

They therefore choose not to draw any personal pension benefits for the moment, but will allow the pension fund to remain invested, to provide increased benefits when they do choose to draw them.

If they were to die in the meantime, the fund built up under the personal pension could be paid out, generally as a tax free lump sum (see section **8.10**).

Even if the individual has no further source of earned income, pension contributions can continue whilst they remain under the age of 75, at a level up to the earnings threshold (currently £3,600 per year), and higher contributions may be permitted for a period under the basis year rules (see section **3.30**).

Phased retirement 5.5

It is also possible to start to draw different tranches of personal pension benefits at different times, in order to gradually build up retirement benefits, particularly those in income form. This approach is generally called 'phased retirement', or sometimes 'staggered vesting'.

The concept is not a new one, and indeed it is a very natural approach to retirement planning. It is easy, at least in advance, to view retirement as occurring at a specific single point in time, when work activity stops and the related income therefore falls to nothing. This may be the case for employees, though there is an increasing tendency for individuals to retire from one job and take up lower paid, and less onerous work elsewhere (as in the example discussed in section **5.4** above).

For those who are self-employed, it is much less likely that the expected point of retirement can be precisely identified in this way. Instead, the individual may gradually take on less work, reduce their hours, and see a gradual decline in earned income as a result. In these circumstances, it can be very attractive to encash personal pension benefits on a gradual basis so that they build up as earned income declines.

In the meantime, the remainder of the personal pension fund remains invested and continues to grow within the tax-advantaged pensions environment. Further tranches of benefits can be taken as the individual requires, subject to the overriding requirement that all benefits must commence by the 75th birthday at the latest.

Mechanics of phased retirement 5.6

The concept of phased retirement was first used in connection with retirement annuity contracts. These were the forerunners of personal pensions and are discussed in detail in **Chapter 14: Retirement Annuity Contracts**. They were available until 30 June 1988.

At that time, many product providers offered retirement annuity contracts which did not allow for contributions to be increased. Strangely enough, the intention behind this was to increase, rather than to reduce, flexibility for the individual. If the individual wished to increase contributions, they simply started a new retirement annuity contract.

By the time the individual reached an age when they wanted to draw benefits, they would have a range of different contracts, which could be with a single product provider or with a range of different providers. Although the individual could choose to cash in all of the contracts at the same time, it was possible to phase retirement, simply by cashing in some contracts immediately, and holding some in reserve for later.

Gradually the design of contracts became more sophisticated, and in particular 'clustered' or 'segmented' plans were introduced in the early 1980s. Although the individual simply had to complete one application form, this application related not to one retirement annuity contract but to a number of contracts, (often as many as 100 or 1,000) from a legal point of view. This concept was also applied (and still applies) under many personal pension schemes. A single personal pension application form has the effect of establishing a number of legally separate arrangements for the member.

Generally only one set of documentation is issued, and this evidences all the arrangements. From an administrative point of view, the arrangements are often handled as a single entity so that, if there were 1,000 arrangements, each would be regarded as precisely one thousandth of the total. Each therefore would be invested in the same way and would have the same value at all times.

Example – Segmented personal pension

An individual contributes £10,000 to a unit-linked personal pension, which is segmented into 1,000 arrangements. They sign a single application form, and choose to invest 75% in a UK equity fund, and 25% in a property fund.

They receive only one set of documentation, and one statement of unit allocation, showing that a total of £7,500 has been invested in the UK equity fund, and £2,500 in the property fund, divided in each case across the 1,000 arrangements.

Each arrangement is a precisely equal division of the whole by 1,000. Each arrangement has therefore received a contribution of £10, of which £7.50 has been invested in the UK equity fund, and £2.50 in the property fund.

A segmented personal pension allows the individual to phase their retirement by encashing different arrangements at different times, but without complicating the administrative arrangements in the meantime. Because each arrangement is identical to all other arrangements, the total can be administered as one.

Until 5 April 2001, it was not possible to partially encash a single personal pension arrangement, and this is what led to the development of segmented contracts. However, the *Finance Act 2000* inserted a new *section 638ZA* into the *Income and Corporation Taxes Act 1988 (ICTA 1988)*, and this took effect from 6 April 2001. The effect is that it is now possible to take partial encashments from a single arrangement. This change can be applied to existing arrangements as well as those arrangements entered into on or after 6 April 2001, and so greatly increases flexibility. (Note however that this provision applies only to personal pension arrangements, not retirement annuity contracts, where partial encashment is still not available.)

Each encashment, whether of a number of distinct arrangements, or a partial encashment under a single arrangement, is treated in the same way for benefit purposes, and the conditions regarding the form of benefits will apply to each encashment.

Form of benefits 5.7

Although contributions to personal pensions are limited as described in **Chapter 3: Contribution Limits**, there is no limit on the overall value of the fund which can be built up to provide benefits at retirement. (As discussed in **Chapter 15: Simplification of Tax Treatment** which deals with the Inland Revenue's current proposals for simplifying the tax treatment of pensions, this position may change in the future.)

There are however restrictions on the form in which benefits can be taken, and in particular on the extent to which benefits can be taken in cash. Nevertheless, the availability of benefits in this form is an important aspect of the advantages of personal pensions overall.

Tax free cash 5.8

A tax free cash sum is permitted to be paid to the member on his pension date under *s 635, ICTA 1988*. The maximum amount that can be taken in the form of cash is generally 25% of the total fund.

If the individual is using phased retirement, the calculation is based only on the fund built up under those arrangements which are being encashed to provide benefits at that time.

Example – Calculation of maximum tax free cash

A 62-year-old has a personal pension which is segmented into 100 identical arrangements. The total value of the fund is £80,000.

They now want to encash 30 of the arrangements, and take the maximum possible amount in the form of tax free cash.

The total value of the fund encashed is 30/100 × £80,000 = £24,000.

The maximum cash sum is therefore 25% of £24,000 = £6,000.

Where a partial encashment is being taken from a single arrangement, the part being encashed is treated as a separate arrangement for this purpose.

Immediate vesting 5.9

There is no minimum term for which a personal pension must run in order to retain the associated tax advantages. An eligible individual could therefore start a personal pension arrangement one day and encash it the next, at least in theory.

Although such an exercise does not allow time for the fund to grow, and so to benefit from the tax advantaged treatment of the investment return the results can be attractive, particularly for a higher rate taxpayer. The tax relief on contributions is a major benefit, and the tax free cash sum can effectively reduce the individual's outlay.

Example – Immediate vesting

A higher rate taxpayer is aged 65. They have made little pension provision in the past, but now want to increase their available pension income, though they intend to draw benefits immediately.

Suppose they invest £10,000 (gross) in a personal pension. After allowing for basic rate relief given by payment of net contributions, and for their ability to claim higher rate relief, the net cost will be 60% of £10,000 = £6,000.

They can take benefits immediately, and 25% of the fund will be available in the form of tax free cash. Assuming there are no initial charges, this will be 25% of £10,000 = £2,500. This reduces their effective outlay from £6,000 to £3,500.

However, at a cost of £3,500, they have £7,500 in their pension fund, which is available to provide income.

If they buy an annuity at a rate of say 8%, the income would be £600 per year.

As a percentage of his effective outlay of £3,500, this is just over 17%.

It remains a better use of pension tax advantages to invest early, but immediate vesting can provide a useful last minute boost to benefits.

In practice, the individual would need to allow a sufficient length of time for the product provider to deal with both setting up the arrangement in the first place, and then set up the payment of benefits.

A conservative fund choice, probably deposit, would be suitable in the meantime.

Protected rights and cash   5.10

Where the arrangement includes protected rights (see section **12.14**), no part of these can be taken in the form of cash.

Generally too, the protected rights must be excluded from the calculation of the cash available from the rest of the personal pension fund, under *s 635(3), ICTA 1988.*

Example – Effect of protected rights on calculation of maximum tax free cash

A 64-year-old has a personal pension, which they started in 1990. The total fund value is £210,000, and of this, £30,000 is protected rights. The individual wants to take all of their benefits now.

The non-protected rights fund is £210,000–£30,000 = £180,000.

The maximum cash sum is therefore 25% of £180,000 = £45,000.

Pre-Royal Assent arrangements   5.11

The exclusion of protected rights from the calculation of tax free cash was introduced by the *Finance Act 1989 (FA 1989)*. As a result, different rules apply to arrangements entered into before 27 July 1989, which was the date on which the *FA 1989* received Royal Assent. Under these arrangements, although it is still not possible to take any part of the protected rights themselves in the form of cash, it is possible to include their value in the calculation of cash available from the rest of the fund.

Example – Pre-Royal Assent arrangement I

Suppose in the previous example, the individual had started the personal pension in January 1989. It is therefore a pre-Royal Assent arrangement.

The maximum tax free cash sum is now 25% of the total fund, provided this amount does not exceed the non-protected rights fund.

25% of the total fund of £210,000 is £52,500. This is less than the non-protected rights fund of £180,000.

The maximum tax free cash sum is therefore £52,500.

In some circumstances, though relatively rare, it may therefore be possible under pre-Royal Assent arrangements to take the whole of the non-protected rights fund in the form of cash.

Example – Pre-Royal Assent arrangement II

An individual started a personal pension in September 1998 and the total fund is now £48,000. Of this, £40,000 is protected rights. The individual is 66 and wants to take all of their benefits.

25% of the total fund of £48,000 is £12,000. However, this exceeds the non-protected rights fund, which is only £8,000.

The maximum tax free cash is therefore £8,000 (ie the whole of the non-protected rights fund).

The effect of transfers   5.12

Where a transfer value has been received, there may be further restrictions on the availability of tax free cash from the personal pension. This will only be the case where the transfer is from:

(*a*)   an occupational pension scheme in respect of which the individual is a regulated individual;

(*b*)   an occupational pension scheme where all or part of the benefits on transfer are regarded as being protected rights;

(*c*)   a free-standing AVC scheme;

(*d*)   a personal pension scheme where all or part of the rights are already regarded as protected rights; or

(*e*)   a personal pension under which tax free cash benefits would have been restricted as the result of the receipt of an earlier transfer.

Where the transfer is from a free-standing AVC scheme, because these schemes themselves cannot provide any benefits in the form of cash, any transfer must be accompanied by a 'nil-cash certificate'. The effect of this is to prohibit any tax free cash being taken from the part of the fund built up as a result of the receipt of the transfer value. This part of the fund must also be excluded from the calculation of tax free cash on the rest of the fund.

Regulated individuals   5.13

In some cases, transfers from occupational pension schemes to personal pensions are subject to restrictions on tax free cash benefits, generally referred to as the certification requirements.

For transfers which are made on or after 6 April 2001, these requirements apply only apply to 'regulated individuals'.

The definition of this term covers anyone who is or was a controlling director of the company from whose occupational scheme the transfer is made, either at the time of the transfer or at any time within the preceding 10 years.

It also covers individuals who are aged 45 or over at the date of transfer, but only if they are 'high earners'. An individual is regarded as a high earner for this purpose if their annual remuneration for any tax year falling wholly or partly within a period of six years before the date of the transfer exceeds the earnings cap for the tax year in which the transfer is made.

Examples – Regulated individuals

1 An individual was a controlling director of KJH Ltd, but now works for RFG Ltd, having left KJH seven years ago. If they transfer their pension rights from the KJH Ltd occupational scheme to a personal pension, the certification requirements would apply, because they were a controlling director of KJH Ltd within the last ten years, which makes them therefore a regulated individual.

If they wait until the expiry of a ten year period since leaving KJH Ltd, they would no longer be a regulated individual and the certification requirements would no longer apply.

Whether or not they are a controlling director of RFG Ltd is not relevant.

2 Another individual is 48, and currently earns £120,000 from RFG Ltd. They also used to work for KJH Ltd, but they were not a controlling director. Their highest earnings from KJH Ltd arose in the 1999/2000 tax year and were £100,000.

If they now transfer their pension rights from the KJH Ltd occupational scheme to a personal pension, they would be a regulated individual. This is because they are over 45 and 1999/2000 falls within the six years prior to the date of transfer, and their earnings in that year exceed the earnings cap for 2003/04 (£99,000).

If the individual waits until 6 April 2006, or later, they will no longer be a regulated individual, because 1999/2000 no longer falls (wholly or partly) within the six years preceding the transfer.

They may cease to be a regulated individual earlier than this, if the earnings cap rises to a level in excess of £100,000. Note that it is the figure at the time of the transfer which is applied, not that relevant to the year in which the earnings arose.

Note that prior to 6 April 2001, the group affected by the certification requirements was wider than that covered by the current definition of regulated individuals. However, if an individual was subject to certification of the maximum cash benefit at the time they transferred, the limitation will remain in force. This applies even if they would not have been within the current definition of a regulated individual either at the time of transfer or now.

Application of the certification requirements   5.14

The effect of the certification requirements is to place a limit on the tax free cash which can be provided under the personal pension in respect of the fund derived from the transfer value. This restriction is that the tax free cash sum cannot exceed the amount certified by the trustees of the occupational pension scheme as being available from the occupational pension scheme (referred to as the certified amount), indexed in line with the RPI from the date of the transfer to the point where benefits are taken.

This restriction does not replace the normal 25% restriction under personal pension rules, but is an additional restriction. The tax free cash sum available is therefore the lesser of 25% of the fund (generally excluding protected rights) or the certified amount, with indexation.

Example – Effect of certification on tax free cash

A 56-year-old has a personal pension with a total fund size of £220,000 (none of which is protected rights).

The fund derives from a transfer value received from an occupational scheme, relating to a previous employment. At the time the transfer was made, the certification requirements applied to the individual and the maximum tax free cash sum was certified as £40,000.

The RPI has increased by 10% since the transfer took place.

If they take their retirement benefits now, the maximum tax free cash limit would be the lesser of:

(a)   the normal personal pension limit of 25% of the fund ie 25% of £220,000 = £55,000; and

(b)   the certified amount with indexation, ie £40,000 increased by 10% in line with the RPI index = £44,000.

The maximum available is therefore £44,000.

Transfers of protected rights 5.15

If protected rights are transferred from an occupational scheme or from another personal pension scheme, they will continue to be regarded as protected rights, and will therefore be subject to the restrictions discussed in section **5.10** above.

Transfers of post-6 April 1997 COSR rights 5.16

If an individual was a member of an occupational pension scheme which was contracted out on a defined benefit basis (ie a COSR – Contracted Out Salary Related Scheme), and their rights are transferred to a personal pension, the whole of the benefits corresponding to service on or after 6 April 1997 must be treated as protected rights under the personal pension. As a result, no tax free cash will be available from this portion of the personal pension at retirement.

Where it applies, this restriction is likely to be more onerous in many cases than the certification requirements (even if also applicable).

Note that the restrictions on post–6 April 1997 COSR rights apply to all transfers, not just those in respect of regulated individuals.

Timing of tax free cash 5.17

It is often said that tax free cash benefits can only be taken at the time when the personal pension income commences. Strictly the requirement is that the tax free cash is taken at the pension date.

Pension date is the date on which the member elects to take retirement benefits. It is possible (see section **5.21** below) for income to be taken in the form of an annuity payable annually in arrears, in which case the first annuity payment will be made at the end of a period of a year from pension date.

Similarly if income benefits are taken by means of income withdrawals (see **Chapter 6: Income Withdrawals**) the first withdrawal may also be delayed until the end of the first year.

Income benefits 5.18

To the extent that the member cannot take all of their benefits in the form of a tax fee cash sum, or indeed to the extent that they elect not to do so, the remaining fund must be used to provide income benefits.

These income benefits will be taxed as earned income under PAYE (though note that they do not constitute relevant earnings) and – once started – must continue at least for the individual's lifetime.

Traditionally, the income has been provided by the purchase of an annuity at the member's pension date. However since 1 May 1995, it has been possible under *s 634A, ICTA 1988* to defer the purchase of the annuity beyond pension date, to a point no later than the member's 75th birthday, and in the meantime take income withdrawals from the personal pension fund.

These two alternatives are considered in detail below.

Annuity purchase   5.19

An annuity is essentially an arrangement under which the insurance company accepts a lump sum, and agrees in return to provide regular payments to the annuitant. With a conventional annuity, the amount of these payments will be guaranteed, either on a level basis or with increases, for example at a fixed annual rate. In order to match its investments and its liabilities, the insurance company will back the annuities primarily through investments in gilts, and perhaps to some extent in corporate bonds, which provide a higher yield than gilts, but with slightly higher risk.

The advantage of investing in gilts and bonds is that the income produced from the investment is fixed and known. This allows the insurance company to calculate its annuity rates, that is the amount of income it can provide in return for a given purchase price, with a reasonable degree of certainty.

The insurance company does however take some risk with its annuity business. The most important of these is the mortality risk. Because the annuity payments will continue for the life of the annuitant, assumptions must be made as to their life expectancy. Over the years, life expectancy has tended to increase, particularly as standards of medical diagnosis and treatment have improved, but also because the living standards enjoyed by individuals have risen. When an individual purchases an annuity, calculations and projections can be made based on existing mortality experience, but some assumption has to be made as to the extent to which this will change in the future.

There is also an investment risk, even though the terms of a particular gilt are fixed in the sense that the income level is known and the redemption value and date is also known. When that gilt reaches its redemption date, the resulting cash must be reinvested, and there can be no guarantee in advance of the terms upon which such reinvestment will be possible. The insurance company therefore runs the risk that those terms will be less favourable than it assumed when setting the annuity rate.

From the annuitant's point of view, purchasing an annuity essentially means committing to a long term investment in gilts. Historically, investment returns on gilts (and bonds) have been lower than the returns available through equity based investment. This is not unexpected in the light of the lower level of risk involved. It may therefore be that the investment return available by means of annuity purchase is at a lower level than the individual would ideally wish. (This is one of the reasons why income withdrawals have become popular – see section **6.16**.)

Some of the developments in annuity design over recent years, in particular the emergence of investment linked and with profits annuities, involve the annuitant taking a larger share in the risk, and in particular the investment risk involved. On the other hand, this allows more volatile, but potentially more rewarding investments such as equities to be used to back the annuity.

It remains important that the level of risk involved in the annuity is reasonable in the light of the individual's circumstances, and in particular the extent to which they are reliant on the income from the annuity to maintain their living standards.

CPAs and PLAs   5.20

If income is provided by means of an annuity, the annuity must be purchased from an authorised insurance company. This does not necessarily have to be the provider of the personal pension arrangement under which the fund was built up. Instead, it is possible at pension date for the member to choose that the annuity be purchased from any authorised insurance company which is prepared to provide it.

This ability to transfer, which is generally known as the open market option, does not require the receiving insurer to establish, and obtain approval for, a personal pension scheme in order to provide the annuity. Any tax free cash payment is made by the original provider before the transfer is made, and the residual fund is then paid over to the insurer who will provide the annuity. It is then the responsibility of the annuity provider to operate a PAYE system to collect the tax which is due.

The annuity will be a compulsory purchase annuity (CPA). As a result, the whole of each income payment is taxable as earned income. Purchased life annuities (PLAs), which are annuities purchased with an individual's own money, are subject to a more favourable tax treatment of the annuity instalments. This involves the separation of the PLA instalments into capital content and interest.

In principle, the capital content is the purchase price of the annuity divided by the individual's life expectancy, based on standard mortality tables set by the Inland Revenue (and which cannot be adjusted, even if the member is in poor health). This part of each instalment is paid free of tax (even if the individual lives beyond their initial assumed life expectancy).

The balance of each annuity instalment is regarded as interest, and is taxed as savings income, with basic rate tax (20% in 2003/04) generally deduced at source by the annuity provider. A higher rate taxpayer must pay a further 20% tax, but non-taxpayers, and those liable to tax only at the starting rate of 10%, can reclaim the excess tax deducted.

A non-taxpayer has no tax liability on the interest and can reclaim any tax deducted, or alternatively can arrange for gross payment of the annuity instalments.

The result of this is that if a member of a personal pension arrangement does not require a lump sum, but instead wishes to receive all benefits in the form of annuity payments, it is likely to be advantageous, if they are a taxpayer, to nevertheless elect benefits in the form of cash to the maximum extent possible, and then utilise the cash to buy a purchased life annuity.

Example – PLA treatment for higher rate taxpayer

A higher rate taxpayer is taking retirement benefits from their personal pension, under which they have built up a fund of £200,000, none of which is protected rights.

They have been told that they could receive either a pension of £13,600 per year, or a tax free cash sum of £50,000 and a reduced income of £10,200 per year. Their wish is to maximise their net income.

If they take the full annuity from the personal pension, it will be a CPA, and they will pay 40% tax on the whole of each instalment. Their net income is therefore 60% of £13,600 = £8,160 per year.

Alternatively, they could take their tax free cash sum, and buy a PLA with it. Suppose the annuity available in return for the purchase price of £50,000 was £3,000 per year, of which £2,000 per year was the capital content.

The net annual income from this would be:

Capital content	£2,000 (tax free)
Interest content	60% of £1,000 = £600
Total	£2,000 + £600 = £2,600

The total net income the individual would receive is therefore £2,600 from the PLA plus a further £6,120 (60% of the reduced CPA of £10,200) ie a total of £8,720 per year.

This is considerably better than if they used the whole fund to purchase a CPA.

In general, gross PLA rates are less favourable than CPA rates (because of the internal taxation of the life insurance company), but for taxpayers, the net effect is that the PLA is more favourable.

For basic rate taxpayers, a further minor advantage derives from the fact that interest income is taxed at 20%, compared to the 22% rate which applies to earned income.

Example – PLA treatment for basic rate taxpayer

If the individual from our previous example had been a basic rate taxpayer, the comparison would have been as follows:

If a CPA is purchased with the whole fund:

Gross income	£13,600
Tax @ 22%	£2,992
Net income	£10,608 per year

If maximum cash is taken and a PLA is purchased:

Gross CPA income	£10,200
Tax @ 22%	£2,244
Net CPA income	£7,956
PLA Interest content	£1,000
Tax @ 20%	£200
	£800
Capital content	£2,000
Net PLA income	£2,800
Total net income	£10,756 per year

Clearly the individual could use the tax free cash sum to provide income in other ways, for example by purchase of equities, unit trusts or OEICs, gilts or any other investment. Certainly an individual should not simply allow the whole of the personal pension fund to be used to purchase a compulsory purchase annuity without giving serious consideration to the alternatives.

Legislative requirements   5.21

There are a number of requirements which the compulsory purchase annuity must meet, and these are contained in *s 634, ICTA 1988*. The main provisions are:

(a)   the annuity must be payable at least for the individual's life;

(b)   however, it is possible to arrange for a minimum guaranteed payment period to apply, or for the annuity to continue on the member's death to, for example, a spouse;

(c)   the annuity must generally be non-assignable and non-surrenderable;

(d)   however, it can be assigned or surrendered where required under a pension sharing order, as discussed in section **9.11**; and

(e)   the right to payments under the terms of a guaranteed payment provision can be assigned by will or in the distribution of an estate.

Instalments of the annuity must be payable at least once a year, although they may be paid at more frequent intervals, and may be paid either in advance or in arrears.

These requirements must be met, but then the member will have a wide range of additional options from which they can choose, and these are discussed in the following sections.

The choice of annuity is made at the time of purchase, and can therefore reflect the individual's circumstances at the time. For example, whether they make provision for the annuity to continue to a spouse will depend on whether they are married at the time, and the extent of the spouse's dependency on the individual's pension income.

Where benefits are taken on a phased retirement basis, the circumstances of the individual may change during the phasing period. Each annuity purchase is regarded separately however, and it is often the case that the type of annuity purchased on the various occasions when arrangements are encashed, will differ.

Types of annuity   5.22

When an annuity is purchased with the fund arising from a personal pension, the individual is faced with a wide range of choices, which provides flexibility, but inevitably adds some complexity.

Some of the choices affect the basis of the income which the individual themself will receive, and for example, the extent to which it will increase to counteract the effects of inflation, or to reflect investment returns. Other choices relate to the position on the member's death, and whether the annuity continues in some form, for example to a surviving spouse.

These decisions must be made in the light of the circumstances, including both the individual's personal situation and their other assets and sources of income. The choices affect the cost of the annuity, and therefore the initial level of income which can be generated for any particular fund size. For example, for a 60 year old male, the level of initial income might be perhaps 20% less if the income is to increase at 3% *per annum* as compared to a level annuity.

Historically, given an unfettered choice, individuals have tended to opt for a level annuity to provide themselves with the highest possible initial income, perhaps on the basis that the future will look after itself. Given the fact that life expectancy has increased markedly over recent years, and appears still to be increasing, this may not be a wise decision.

The table below shows the effect of different rates of inflation on the purchasing power of a level annuity over 10, 20 and 30 years, at different levels of inflation.

Table – Effect of inflation on the purchasing power of a level £10,000 per annum annuity

Period	Inflation rate			
	2% *per annum*	4% *per annum*	6% *per annum*	8% *per annum*
5 years	£9057	£8219	£7473	£6806
10 years	£8203	£6756	£5584	£4632
15 years	£7430	£5553	£4173	£3152
20 years	£6730	£4564	£3118	£2145
25 years	£6095	£3751	£2330	£1460
30 years	£5521	£3083	£1741	£994

Although inflation is currently at a low level, and appears to be settled, it is worth remembering that the annualised rate of increase in the Retail Prices Index has been close to 10% within the last 15 years, and within the last 30 years has at times been over 20%. The life expectancy for a male retiring at 65 is now around 15 years, and for a female of the same age is around 18 years, according to the Government Actuary in his most recent Quinquennial Review of National Insurance Fund expenditure (prepared in February 2000).

This review also indicates that these life expectancies are expected to increase to almost 18 years and over 21 years respectively for those reaching age 65 in 2030.

Escalating annuities   5.23

Although a level annuity may be attractive in terms of its starting level, an annuity which provides for escalation, in other words one which increases during payment, provides a far greater level of security for the future. There is no limitation on the extent to which an annuity can escalate under either the legislation or under Inland Revenue practice. Given that there is no limitation on the overall level of benefits provided by a personal pension scheme, it would be illogical to impose any limitation on escalation.

Having said that, from a commercial point of view, it is unlikely that insurance companies would offer high levels of escalation whilst inflation rates are relatively low. There would simply not be sufficient demand to make this worthwhile.

In the current environment therefore escalation at perhaps 3% *per annum* or 2.5% *per annum* might be an attractive choice.

If escalation is included on fixed basis, the level of income will increase each year by the agreed percentage, irrespective of what happens in the economy, for example in terms of inflation rates.

Index-linked annuities   5.24

As an alternative, a number of insurers offer annuities where the payments are increased each year in line with movements in the Retail Prices Index (RPI). If inflation is low, this may provide a lower level of benefits than would be the case if a fixed and higher rate of escalation had been included. However this approach does provide protection of the purchasing power of the annuity income, even if inflation returns to very high levels.

Often increases in the level of annuity income will occur annually, on the anniversary of the start date, so in this situation, there remains something of an inflation risk over the twelve months between the increase dates.

In addition, although full RPI indexation maintains the level of annuity income in line with prices, this may still mean that the recipients tend to fall behind general increases in living standards over the period of their retirement. This simply reflects the fact that the incomes – and therefore the living standards – of those who are working tend to increase faster than the RPI.

Index linked annuities are often regarded as being expensive, though much depends upon the individual's view of possible future inflation trends. It is true that index linked gilts, which are used by insurance companies to back these annuities, can be in short supply, which may mean that they are relatively highly priced in the market, so reducing the investment returns available to the insurer.

Many insurers also offer a combination of indexation with a fixed rate increase, for example, an annuity which increases at the lesser of 3% *per annum* or the RPI increase, which can be a useful compromise.

Investment linked annuities 5.25

For many years, some insurers have offered annuities where the income level varies according to the value of investments. This is generally done in relation to the movement in the price of units in a particular fund.

Originally these annuities provided income which moved directly in line with unit prices month by month, with no features to smooth out any fluctuations, large or small. Although the potential for growth in income with such an annuity is high, particularly if the fund chosen is an equity based fund, the volatility of income is difficult for many people to accept.

In addition, the starting level of the income on this basis is generally much lower than would be the case for a level annuity, or even an annuity with fixed escalation increases built in. This reflects the fact that with a conventional annuity, the insurance company makes assumptions about the growth which it can achieve by investing the purchase price. It then sets the annuity income so that, after allowing for costs and profits, the individual will receive back through the annuity payments the amount of the purchase price plus the assumed growth over his life expectancy.

Where the annuity payments are linked directly to unit prices, the basic concept is that the purchase price, again allowing for costs and profits, is invested in units of the fund concerned. The number of units represented by each annuity instalment is calculated so that over life expectancy, the total number of units available is paid out to the recipient. This in effect means that there is no assumed growth allowed for in the initial income level, which is therefore low.

All of the growth achieved will be reflected in increases in future annuity instalments, and the hope is that these will outstrip the levels of increase which would have been available with, for example, an annuity with fixed escalation increases.

There is however a clear risk with an annuity of this type, and those who have been in receipt of income linked to the value of units in an equity based fund over recent years will have seen that income reduce substantially over the period. It is important therefore that those who are attracted to an investment linked annuity fully understand the risks involved, and are in a position where they are not entirely reliant on the income from this source being maintained at least a minimum level.

The design of investment linked annuities has moved on considerably in recent years. In particular, most providers of these annuities will now allow the annuitant to choose (generally within limits set by the provider) an assumed rate of growth which is then built in to the calculation of the starting level of income. This brings the basis more into line conceptually with that underlying the more traditional, gilt backed annuity, where an assumed level of future growth is taken into account in setting rates.

The actual growth achieved is checked from time to time (often annually), and if the assumed rate has been precisely matched, then the income level will be unchanged. If the actual growth has been more than that assumed, the future level of income will increase, but conversely if the assumed growth rate has not been achieved, future annuity instalments will reduce.

The effect of this approach is first of all to increase the starting level of income so that investment linked annuities become a realistic choice for more people. The potential volatility of the annuity is also reduced, provided the assumed growth level is set at a realistic figure.

However, the risk of equity linked investment remains, and indeed the potential for a reduction in future income levels is greater, simply because a positive growth rate has been assumed in setting the initial income level. Essentially, the higher the growth rate assumed, the higher the initial level of income, but the greater the risk of a future reduction.

In some circumstances, it may be appropriate for a member to use part of the total personal pension fund to provide a guaranteed level of income, whilst the rest is used to provide an investment linked or with profit annuity. This might allow a member to be certain that their basic income requirements are met, while still enjoying the possibility of high level investment related increases on the remainder of the annuity income.

With profit annuities 5.26

With profit annuities are similar in construction to investment linked annuities, but the assumption that needs to be made at outset is of the level of bonuses which will accrue to the with profits fund of the insurer. As with investment linked annuities, the higher the bonus rate assumed, the higher the starting level of income, but the greater the risk of subsequent reductions.

However, a with profit annuity has the advantage that bonus rates should not fluctuate to the same extent as the growth rate of a unit linked fund might fluctuate.

One of the features of with profit investment generally is that the value of the investment cannot fall, and that bonuses once added cannot be taken away. Whilst this remains true of the underlying with profit fund to which the annuity is linked, it is important to realise that the amount of annuity payments is dependent not simply on the addition of bonuses to the fund, but on the level of those bonuses. It is therefore possible for the payments to reduce if the assumed bonus rate is not achieved in reality, and this may seem strange to individuals more used to other forms of with profit investment. (The operation of with profits funds is discussed in section **7.33**.)

There are variations in the detailed design of with profit annuities, and, for example, some include a guaranteed minimum income level, which may appeal to some individuals. Generally however it is not possible after the annuity starts to change its nature, for example from being a with profit annuity to one linked to the performance of an equity based fund, or a conventional annuity with fixed increases.

Annuity features   5.27

Whatever the type of annuity the individual chooses, it may be appropriate to add in features designed to protect people other than the member who may be dependent on the income which it produces.

These features include the possible provision for the annuity to continue following the member's death in some circumstances. Because the result is to increase the potential period for which the annuity is paid, inevitably the annuity rate will be affected and the starting level of income will be reduced.

Guarantees   5.28

One of the most straightforward ways in which this can be done is to include a minimum period for which the annuity is guaranteed to be paid, irrespective of whether the member survives.

Section 634(5), ICTA 1988 makes provision for such a guarantee, but limits it to a maximum of ten years.

If the member dies during the guarantee period, the annuity will continue to be paid as each instalment falls due. Note that the legislation does not allow the outstanding instalments to be commuted for a lump sum in any circumstances. (Under occupational schemes, provided the initial guarantee period was no longer than five years, outstanding instalments can be commuted for a lump sum, but this is not permitted where the annuity arises from a personal pension arrangement.)

The right to the annuity can be assigned by will or in accordance with the intestacy rules, or by the legal personal representatives as part of the disposal of the original annuitant's estate.

As a broad indication of cost, the inclusion of a five year guarantee on an annuity for a male aged 65 might reduce the starting level of the income by around 2%. The inclusion of a ten year guarantee is more costly, because it is far more likely to have a practical impact, and this might reduce the starting level by around 6% compared to an annuity with no guarantee. Where guarantees are included, a five year guarantee is generally most popular, and probably represents a reasonable compromise between building in some certainty that the annuity provides fair value for money, and the need to ensure that the initial starting level of income is not too dramatically affected.

Mortality gain 5.29

Many individuals buying an annuity will be concerned that the insurance company might make an excessive level of profit if the annuity has no guarantee and the individual dies, perhaps within a few months of starting to receive payments. In reality, the possible 'mortality gain' to the annuity fund where this occurs is factored into the calculation of annuity rates in the first place, and in effect subsidises the rates available to annuitants in general, rather than providing a large profit for the insurer. There will clearly be a gain to the fund if the annuitant dies early, but similarly there will be a loss if the annuitant lives longer than anticipated. The rates are set so that on average, the overall effect is neutral.

Whether a guarantee is appropriate will depend on the circumstances of the case, and particularly whether there is anyone that the annuitant would wish to continue to receive income in the event of their early death. If there are no dependants, then it may be most appropriate to choose an annuity with no guarantee, in order to secure the highest possible income for the annuitant themself, during their lifetime.

Survivor pensions 5.30

It is possible when setting up the annuity to build in provision for the annuity to continue, wholly or partly, to one or more individuals who survive the member.

The group for whom such continuing income can be provided is limited by the Inland Revenue to what are termed 'survivors'. The definition of this term is given below. Essentially the group consists of the member's spouse and dependants.

Definition of survivor

'Survivor' means a widow, widower or dependant of a member who has died.

'Dependant' means a person who is financially dependent on the member or dependent on the member because of disability or who was so dependent at the time of the member's death or retirement.

An ex-spouse of the member who was in receipt of payments from the member up to his or her death in respect of, for example, a financial provision order under the *Matrimonial Causes Act 1973* may be regarded as financially dependent on the member. An adult relative who is not or was not supported by the member is not that member's dependant.

Subject to the following paragraphs a pension paid to an adult dependant who qualifies on grounds of financial dependency or disability may continue indefinitely.

Natural or adopted children of the member may automatically be regarded as dependent on the member if at the time of his or her death they were:

1. under 18;
2. over 18 but continuing to receive full-time education or vocational training;
3. dependent on the member because of disability.

Any pensions paid by reason of 1. and 2. should cease when age 18 is reached or full-time education or vocational training ceases* whichever is the later. A pension paid by reason of 3. may continue indefinitely.

Other children (ie neither natural nor adopted children of the member) may qualify as dependants only if they were financially dependent on the member, or dependent on the member by reason of disability. Any pensions paid to such children on grounds of financial dependence should cease when age 18 is reached or full-time education or vocational training ceases* whichever is the later. This ensures parity of treatment between offspring and other minor dependants.

A pension paid because of dependency by reason of disability may continue indefinitely. It is not necessary to show financial dependency for a person dependent on the member because of disability or in the case of widows or widowers. The latter automatically qualify for survivors' benefits on the basis that partners in a legal marriage may always be assumed to be financially dependent on one another. But an unmarried partner, whether of the same or opposite sex, can qualify for a survivor's pension only if he or she were financially dependent on the member. Financial interdependence of the member and his or her partner would be an acceptable criterion, e.g. where the partner relied upon a second income to maintain a standard of living which had depended on joint income prior to the member's death.

Whether or not a person is a dependant is a matter for scheme administrators to decide. The Inland Revenue SPSS (Nottingham) would not challenge their judgement provided they had acted in accordance with the scheme rules.

★ A break of not more than an academic year between leaving school and taking up a confirmed place in full-time further education or vocational training will not be regarded as a cessation for this purpose, but it is for trustees to decide whether the pension should be paid during the break.

Source: *Inland Revenue Guidance Notes IR76*

Note in particular that a legally married spouse will automatically be included in the definition of survivors, but that an unmarried partner will be included only if regarded as a dependant. In practice, because financial interdependence is sufficient to meet this criterion, it would be very unlikely that a common law or same sex partner would fail to qualify.

The person or persons to whom the annuity will be paid following the member's death must be determined at the point when the annuity is purchased. Where however annuities are purchased at different times by an individual who is phasing retirement (see section **5.5** above) a different choice may be made on each occasion, reflecting the member's circumstances at the time.

Under *s 636(3), ICTA 1988*, it is required that the total amount of annual income provided for survivors must not exceed the amount in payment to the member at the time of their death (or where the annuity payments have fluctuated, the highest annual amount that has been paid).

Practical application   5.31

It has been common to provide survivor pensions, particularly for a spouse or partner, often either for the full amount of the member's own annuity, or at two thirds or half that level.

The cost of the inclusion of a survivor pension will be influenced by a number of factors, but in particular by the relative ages of the member themself and the nominated survivor. The younger the survivor, the more likely it is that the member will die first and that the survivor's provision will come into effect. Also, the younger the age, the longer the payments to the survivor are likely to continue. This effect is increased where the annuity escalates, because the real value of the later payments is increased.

Based on a male aged 60 at retirement, with a wife five years younger, the inclusion of a two thirds widow's pension might reduce the starting level of income by some 25%, whereas if the annuity escalates at 5% *per annum*, the difference might be around 30%.

Where the couple have been wholly or largely dependent on the member's income during his working life, and subsequently on his pension, it makes natural sense to include provision for the survivor when purchasing an annuity. However increasingly, both partners in a relationship may have had a full and active working career, and each may have built up their own pension entitlement. In these circumstances, there may be far less justification for including survivor benefits, since each has an independent income.

Where the pension income of each partner varies substantially, it could be wise to include a survivor pension provision in the larger annuity, but this may be unnecessary for the smaller. As always in such situations, the decision should be made on the basis of anticipating the circumstances that would arise on the death of either partner.

Terms of survivor's annuity 5.32

Generally the survivor's pension must be payable from the time of the member's death, throughout the survivor's life. There is an exception to this where the survivor is a minor child, in which case, unless the child is dependent because of incapacity, the survivor pension income can only continue until the later of the child's 18th birthday or the cessation of full time education or vocational training.

It is also possible, though in practice unusual, to include a provision whereby the income would cease on the remarriage of a spouse.

Where the member's own annuity was subject to a guarantee, it is possible to arrange that the annuity for the survivor starts immediately, or that it starts only at the end of the guarantee period. This is sometimes referred to as 'with overlap' or 'without overlap' respectively. Clearly the provision for a survivor's pension with overlap will be more expensive than without overlap.

Special annuity terms 5.33

Increasingly, the market is recognising that different individuals have different life expectancies, depending on the circumstances of their health, or their lifestyle. Accordingly, better annuity rates can be offered to reflect this.

Impaired life annuities 5.34

Where the individual's health is such that their life expectancy is reduced, then it may be possible to obtain preferential annuity rates, generally known as impaired life annuity rates.

The terms offered will reflect the precise circumstances of the individual, and medical evidence will invariably be obtained. It would be unusual for a medical examination to be required however, since generally the state of health of the individual is such that there would already be a considerable amount of evidence on record.

Not all companies offer impaired life rates, and those that do may differ in their opinion of different cases, so it will often be worth shopping around to find the most favourable terms.

If however the individual wishes to include a minimum guarantee period or a survivor pension within the annuity, this would substantially reduce or eliminate the advantage which would otherwise be obtainable from the use of these preferential rates, since the relevance of the individual's own life expectancy is diminished.

Market segmentation annuities 5.35

In many cases, it will be the individual's lifestyle rather than their personal medical position which affects their life expectancy. In such cases, some insurance companies offer special rates to defined groups, and these are known as market segmentation annuity rates.

Probably the most familiar situation in which market segmentation rates apply is for smokers. This reflects the statistical evidence that the life expectancy of smokers is less than that of non-smokers, assuming all other factors to be equal.

Note that the definition of a smoker may vary from insurance company to insurance company, and the individual will be required to sign a declaration that they are within the terms of the appropriate definition.

Restrictions on protected rights 5.36

Members of personal pension schemes generally have a free choice regarding the inclusion of features such as escalation or survivor pensions within their annuity, subject to the legislative requirements mentioned in section **5.21** above. However, protected rights are subject to a number of specific requirements which are discussed in this section.

Survivor's benefit 5.37

If the member is married at the time of retirement, the annuity must include provision for 50% of the protected rights income to continue to a surviving spouse. At one time, provision had to be included for such a benefit even if the member was not married, but this provision has now been withdrawn.

Escalation 5.38

The annuity provided from the protected rights fund must always include escalation. For benefits which accrued in respect of periods of employment on or after 6 April 1997, the rate of escalation required is the lesser of 5% *per annum* or the increase in the Retail Prices Index.

For earlier periods of service, the required rate is the lesser of 3% *per annum* and the increase in the Retail Prices Index.

Increases at this rate must apply to the member's own annuity and also the annuity payable to a qualifying survivor.

Other provisions 5.39

As already mentioned, protected rights benefits cannot be accessed before the age of 60. There are no exceptions to this rule, even where the member becomes incapacitated, or works in a special occupation.

In addition, insurance companies offering protected rights annuities must not differentiate between men and women in setting annuity rates. These rates are therefore often referred to as unisex annuity rates.

Advantages and disadvantages of annuities 5.40

Annuities have attracted a great deal of negative publicity in recent years, as the level of income which can be purchased by any given fund size has reduced. This has reflected dramatic reductions in gilt yields over recent years.

Certainty of income 5.41

The main advantage of annuity purchase is in the certainty of the income which is provided. A pension fund is intended to provide income in retirement. If the fund is of a sufficient size to purchase an annuity which would provide at least the required level of income, together with a reasonable level of inflation protection, there needs to be a strong case in order for an alternative to be chosen.

The purchase of an annuity effectively represents a significant investment commitment to gilts. Many people would however take the view that it is possible to achieve a much higher potential investment return by investing elsewhere, though at the price of having to accept a higher level of risk. Nevertheless, if income needs can be met with certainty by means of an annuity purchase, there may be little point in taking a greater risk in order to have the opportunity to achieve a level of income greater than the individual's requirement.

The options available in respect of annuities are also wide, as already illustrated by the range covered in this chapter. An annuity can be tailored to the individual circumstances, in particular the potential needs of the member's dependants. Again the certainty of making such provision through an annuity will be attractive in some circumstances, for example where the survivor is wholly dependent on the prospective income, perhaps because of incapacity.

Disadvantages 5.42

There are also a number of disadvantages of annuity purchase. One of these is the link to gilts already mentioned, and the resultant need to accept lower potential investment returns than equity related investment might produce.

Also, although the annuity can be tailored to the individual's circumstances at the time of purchase, these circumstances may subsequently change. The annuity terms are however fixed, and cannot generally be altered once the purchase is made. For example, at the point of annuity purchase, allowance may be built in for the annuity to continue on the member's death to a surviving spouse. In the event that the spouse predeceases the member, the provision for a continuing annuity is, in a sense, wasted.

Neither can changes be made to reflect different investment conditions. The terms of a traditional annuity will be fixed in relation to gilt yields available at the time of purchase. At the present time, these are at a level which looks low historically, but if gilt yields increase in the future, even though annuity rates for new purchases will improve, there will be no improvement in payments under annuities already purchased. This reflects the fact that the insurance company has already accepted the risk and backed the annuity with suitable investments.

Similarly a decision might have been made regarding the inclusion of escalation. This will have reflected the inflation level at the time of purchase and the individual's view of future trends. This decision cannot be changed even if the level of inflation in the economy, and the individual's view of the future change dramatically.

A further difficulty is that no allowance can be made for any future change in the individual's state of health.

Example – Deterioration in health

A member uses their personal pension fund to purchase an annuity when they retire at the age of 60, and the annuity is arranged on standard annuity rates. The individual opts to include index-linked increases in their annuity, and accepts that this means a relatively low initial income.

As they have no dependants, they do not include a minimum guarantee period, nor any provision for survivors' pensions.

Two months later, the individual is diagnosed as having a terminal illness, and is told that they only have a few months to live.

They cannot change the basis of the annuity in any way, and so cannot opt for a higher level of income with no increases, or for a minimum guaranteed payment period.

The potential disadvantage relating to changes in health is an unavoidable aspect of the way in which annuities are currently structured, and indeed is a feature of insurance generally. The concept is that the experience of individuals is averaged out over a large group. In the case of annuities, those who die relatively early will not have achieved value for money in terms of the annuity payments received, but those who live much longer than the average life expectancy will have achieved extremely good value for money.

Similarly, with a traditional annuity, the intention is that the income level is guaranteed irrespective of economic conditions. The insurance company therefore needs to make investments which reflect this, and will purchase gilts to back the annuity at the time it is purchased. The terms of this investment must therefore be fixed at the time.

The more modern annuity options, for example those which are investment linked, can assist in some ways. However, they do so by passing some of the risk back to the annuitant, and in return for the possibility of sharing in improved investment conditions, the annuitant must also take the risk that income levels may reduce if investment conditions are poor.

More recently, and to some extent in recognition of the increased sophistication of investors, more flexible options have been developed, in particular through the increasing availability and use of income withdrawals. Whilst these remove some of the disadvantages mentioned above, they also remove some of the advantages, and annuities will continue to have a place for many people at retirement. Under current legislation, income withdrawals cannot persist beyond age 75 in any event, and an annuity must be purchased at that date. For further information see **Chapter 6: Income Withdrawals**.

6 — Income Withdrawals

Features of income withdrawals   6.1

The concept of income withdrawals is that instead of the fund at retirement being used (after taking any tax free cash) to purchase an annuity, it is instead left invested, and income is provided for the individual by means of withdrawals taken directly from the fund itself.

Because the fund remains invested, the opportunity arises to continue to invest in equities and related investments such as unit linked funds, unit trusts, OEICs and investment trusts. Whilst this provides the potential of a higher level of return than could be achieved by the gilt based investment underlying an annuity, it also carries a degree of risk.

As a result, the income withdrawal option is generally seen as appropriate only for those with large personal pension funds (perhaps £100,000 or more). Perhaps more logically, it should be regarded as an option for those with significant assets overall, of which their pension fund forms a part. Certainly income withdrawals should only be taken up by those who understand not only the advantages of the option, but also the risks involved, and who feel that those advantages outweigh the risks.

Deferment of annuity purchase   6.2

Income withdrawals are provided for in *section 634(A)* of the *Income and Corporation Taxes Act 1988 (ICTA 1988),* which was inserted by the *Finance Act 1995.* This allowed income withdrawals as an alternative to immediate annuity purchase with effect from 1 May 1995.

The income withdrawal option is however merely a deferment of the requirement to purchase an annuity, and under *s 634A(3), ICTA 1988* cannot continue beyond the age of 75, by which time, at the latest, an annuity must be purchased.

Basic requirements   6.3

Income withdrawals therefore offer a temporary alternative to annuity purchase. Many of the same basic requirements apply, however, as would apply to an annuity. In particular, income withdrawals must be taken at least annually, and once started cannot be stopped, other than in order for an annuity to be purchased.

If the member wishes to take a tax free cash sum, this must be taken at pension date (ie the date when the member elected to take income withdrawals), and cannot be deferred until a later date. Note in particular that it is not possible to delay taking the cash sum until the point of annuity purchase.

Just as an annuity can be payable annually in arrears, it is possible for the first income withdrawal to be made at the end of the year starting on pension date. This allows a limited delay between taking the cash and starting to receive the income benefit, which is taxable in the same way as payments received under an annuity.

Example – Timing of withdrawals

A 65-year-old has a personal pension, and is currently a higher rate tax-payer.

They wish to take their tax free cash at 1 July 2003, but ideally would like to delay the start of their income until the tax year 2004/05, when they will only be liable to tax at basic rate. They have decided to take income withdrawals, rather than buy an annuity immediately.

The individual can take their tax free cash at 1 July 2003, but they do not need to take income withdrawals until (at the latest) 30 June 2004.

Limits   6.4

Section 634A(4) of the *ICTA 1988* sets limits within which the level of income withdrawals taken from the personal pension arrangement each year must lie. These limits are based on hypothetical annuity rates which are set by the Government Actuary's Department (GAD) and which reflect the current gross redemption yield on UK gilts (15 years) as determined for the FT-Actuaries Fixed Interest Indices.

GAD rates for non-protected rights are intended to be a reasonable reflection of market rates for a level annuity with no provision for survivor benefits. Where protected rights are taken in this way, separate GAD rates are used which make allowance for escalation and survivor benefits.

The limits are initially calculated at pension date and are based on the gilt yield as published in the *Financial Times* on the 15th of the calendar month preceding that in which pension date falls. If the 15th is not a business day, the rate taken is that for the immediately preceding business day.

The GAD publishes a table of rates which vary by sex, and age. The rates reflect the gilt yield in steps of 0.25%, and if the actual yield published in the *Financial Times* is not an exact multiple of 0.25%, the published figure must be rounded down for this purpose to the next lower multiple. Thus for example, if the published yield is 5.7%, the GAD rates would be those relating to a yield of 5.5%.

The maximum level of withdrawals in each annual period (usually twelve month periods measured from pension date) is 100% of the annuity calculated on the appropriate GAD rates. The minimum level is 35% of the maximum level.

Example – Application of withdrawal limits

Taking the same details as in the last example, the income withdrawal limits would be set at the pension date under the individual's personal pension arrangement ie 1 July 2003.

Suppose that, based on their fund, after taking cash, the maximum level of withdrawals is £10,000 for each annual period, and the minimum is therefore £3,500.

If they delay the start of their withdrawals to (say) 1 May 2004, they must still have taken at least £3,500 by 30 June 2004.

The difference between the minimum and maximum levels is great enough to allow those taking withdrawals a significant amount of flexibility. Essentially the difference is intended to reflect a similar range to that which might apply to annuity income, based on the rates applicable to a level annuity with no guarantee or survivor's benefit as compared to an escalating annuity including spouse's benefit.

However, once the basis of an annuity is fixed, the individual has no control over the level of income. With income withdrawals, subject only to any requirements of the product provider, the level of income drawn can vary freely within the GAD limits from year to year.

Example – Calculation of withdrawal limits

A 66-year-old male has a total personal pension fund of £240,000, none of which is protected rights.

They intend to take their retirement benefits on 22 August 2003. The individual wants to take the maximum possible tax free cash sum, and then to start income withdrawals. The gilt yield as published in the *Financial Times* on the 15th of July is 5.45%.

The figure from the GAD tables for non-protected rights, for a male aged 66, and a gilt index yield of 5.25% (ie 5.45% rounded down) is £95 *per annum* per £1,000 of purchase price.

The maximum tax free cash sum is £60,000, leaving a fund for income withdrawals of £180,000.

The maximum level of withdrawals for each annual period is therefore £180,000 x 95/1000 = £17,100.

The minimum level is 35% of £17,100 = £5,985.

This ability to vary withdrawals within the GAD limits can be of great advantage to those whose income needs fluctuate, whether because of fluctuating expenditure requirements, or because of fluctuating levels of income from other sources.

There is no requirement regarding the frequency of withdrawals provided they lie within the GAD related limits for each annual period. It is possible for income withdrawals to be taken on a regular basis, for example monthly, or annually. However it is also possible for withdrawals to be made on demand, though product providers are likely to impose some constraints on this.

Tax planning   6.5

There can also be clear advantages from a tax planning point of view. For example, an individual who is taking income withdrawals might have income from another source (perhaps continuing self-employment) and may vary the amount of the income withdrawals they take to remain below the higher rate threshold.

Example – Variability of income

Using the details from the last example, suppose that in addition to the income from his personal pension, he has self-employed earnings, the level of which varies from year to year. He has no other income.

In 2003/04, his taxable income from self-employment is quite low, at only £10,000. He decides to take the maximum withdrawal of £17,100 just before the end of the tax year, because this will all fall below the higher rate income tax threshold.

In the following tax year, 2004/05, his self-employed earnings are higher and as a result, he is only £6,000 below the higher rate threshold, before allowing for the income withdrawals from his personal pension. He therefore decides to limit his withdrawals to £6,000, so as to avoid having a higher rate liability.

The following year, earnings are lower once again, and he is £12,500 below the higher rate threshold. He therefore decides to withdraw £12,500 in 2005/06, to fully utilise his basic rate tax band, but not create any higher rate liability.

There might also be situations where an individual wishes to avoid any taxable income from a personal pension falling into a particular tax year. Although income, once started, cannot be suspended, careful timing can often achieve the required result.

The requirement is simply that within each annual period, the total withdrawn must lie between the 35% and 100% GAD limits.

Example – Tax year planning

An individual starts taking income withdrawals on their pension date of 15 December 2003. The maximum level permitted is £24,000 per year, and the minimum is therefore £8,400 per year. They decide to take withdrawals starting at the level of £1,500 per month.

In February, the individual hears that they will receive a substantial taxable income payment in the tax year 2004/05, so would like to avoid having other taxable income, such as income withdrawals, falling in the same tax year, if possible.

The individual needs to draw at least £8,400 in the first year of withdrawals, so they increase their March 2004 withdrawal to £3,900. They then take no further withdrawals until 15 April 2005, when they restart withdrawals at the rate of £1,500 per month.

In the annual period 15 December 2003 to 14 December 2004, the withdrawals are:

15 December 2003	£1,500
15 January 2004	£1,500
15 February 2004	£1,500
15 March 2004	£3,900
Total	£8,400

In the annual period 15 December 2004 to 14 December 2005, the withdrawals are:

15 April 2005	£1,500
15 May 2005	£1,500

15 June 2005	£1,500
15 July 2005	£1,500
15 August 2005	£1,500
15 September 2005	£1,500
15 October 2005	£1,500
15 November 2005	£1,500
Total	£12,000

The total of the withdrawals in each annual period is within the limits of £8,400 to £24,000. However, no withdrawals have been made in the tax year 2004/05.

Reviewing limits 6.6

Limits are initially set on the pension date, but must then be reviewed, generally at three year intervals. The dates on which limits are set (including the pension date) are referred to as relevant reference dates, and the three year period is known as a valuation period.

The review of limits on each relevant reference date takes account of the position at that time, and therefore reflects the then age of the individual, the value of the fund and the gilt yield at that time.

In the past, the review of limits had to reflect the position precisely on the relevant reference date, but it is now possible to carry out the calculation as at any date within a 60 day window ending on the relevant reference date. This both simplifies the administration of these arrangements, and also provides some element of choice if conditions, particularly as regards fund value, are volatile.

The new limits will however still be effective from the relevant reference date, and not the date at which the calculation is carried out, if different.

Example – Relevant reference dates

An individual has a personal pension and is taking income withdrawals from it. The pension date was 13 September 2001. Limits were set at this date, which was the first relevant review date.

The limits must be reviewed after three years, and the new limits will come into effect from 13 September 2004, the three year anniversary of the pension date. This is the first relevant reference date.

The review can be carried out at any date between 16 July 2004 and 13 September 2004 inclusive (ie the 60 days ending on the three year anniversary), but will always be effective from the relevant reference date.

The next relevant reference date will be 13 September 2007.

Combining relevant reference dates 6.7

Although it is generally true that the limits on income withdrawals must be reviewed at three year intervals, where an individual is taking retirement benefits on a phased basis, it would be unduly cumbersome if it was necessary for each tranche to be reviewed separately. There are therefore provisions to allow the combination of relevant reference dates under different arrangements with the same provider.

This is carried out based on the pension date of the first arrangement from which income withdrawals were selected. Relevant reference dates under this arrangement will fall on each third anniversary of the pension date in the normal way.

Where income withdrawals are selected from a second arrangement, and the relevant reference dates are to be combined, the first valuation period will be reduced to less than three years, so that it ends on a relevant reference date under the first arrangement.

The shortened valuation period under the second arrangement may consist of one, two or three 'annual' periods. The last of these periods is the one which is shortened to bring the relevant reference dates into line.

Example – Combining relevant reference dates

An individual decided to take income withdrawals from some arrangements under their personal pension. The pension date was 1 November 2002.

In the following year, the individual decides to take income withdrawals from some further arrangements with the same provider, and wants to combine the date on which limits will be reviewed. The pension date under these arrangements is 1 December 2003.

Under the first set of arrangements, the annual periods for the application of limits will be:

First annual period	1 November 2002 to 31 October 2003
Second annual period	1 November 2003 to 31 October 2004
Third annual period	1 November 2004 to 31 October 2005

Under the second set of arrangements, the annual periods will be:

First annual period	1 December 2003 to 30 November 2004
Second annual period	1 December 2004 to 31 October 2005

The relevant reference date at which the first review of limits will take place is 1 November 2005 for both sets of arrangements.

However short the final annual period may be, the normal minimum and maximum limits on the income withdrawals still apply. They are not reduced proportionately or in any other way. This means in effect an acceleration of the income withdrawal requirement.

Example – Shortened annual period

Suppose that in the last example, instead of starting to take benefits from the second set of arrangements at 1 December 2003, the individual delayed this until 1 October 2004. The annual periods for the application of limits would then be:

First annual period   1 October 2004 to 30 September 2005
Second annual period   1 October 2005 to 31 October 2005

Suppose that the limits calculated at 1 October 2004 in respect of the second set of arrangements give a maximum of £10,000 per year and a minimum of £3,500.

Even though the second 'annual' period is only one month in length, the individual can withdraw £10,000 in this period, and must withdraw at least £3,500.

This aspect should be considered in determining the timing of encashment of each tranche of benefits where phased retirement is in operation.

Once a link has been established between arrangements, it cannot subsequently be broken. Future relevant reference dates will remain linked to the pension date under the first arrangement from which income withdrawals were taken, irrespective of subsequent events. For example, the whole of the fund under the first arrangement may be used to purchase an annuity, but this will have no effect on relevant reference dates under subsequent arrangements (even if the first valuation period has not ended).

Example – Constant relevant reference date

Using again the same individual as the last example, suppose they decide to use the whole of the residual fund under their first set of arrangements to purchase an annuity on 1 February 2004, but continue to take income withdrawals from the second set.

The annual periods, and the relevant reference date under the second set of arrangements are not changed, even though withdrawals are no longer being taken from the first set. The first relevant reference date remains 1 November 2005.

Annuity purchase   6.8

Income withdrawals cannot continue beyond the age of 75 and by this time the individual (assuming they have survived) must have used the residual fund to buy an annuity. If the whole fund is utilised in this way, the normal minimum and maximum limits will not apply to the part of the annual period prior to the date of annuity purchase.

This can allow a considerable gap between income payments if the individual so wishes.

Example – Buying an annuity

An individual has been taking income withdrawals from their personal pension arrangement, on an annual basis. They last took a withdrawal in January 2002, close to the start of the annual period, which runs from 1 January to 31 December each year. The withdrawal was sufficient to meet the minimum requirement for the 2002 annual period.

They do not take any withdrawals from the arrangement during 2003, because they have sufficient income from other sources during the year, but they buy an annuity with the whole of the residual fund in mid-December 2003. No minimum requirement for income withdrawals therefore applies in the uncompleted annual period running up to the date of annuity purchase.

If the individual wishes to delay income as long as possible, they could choose an annuity payable annually in arrears, in which case the next income payment would not fall due until mid-December 2004.

Annuitisation   6.9

Where however only part of the fund is used to purchase an annuity (this is known as an 'annuitisation'), more complex provisions apply.

First of all, there will be no effect on limits in the annual period during which an annuitisation occurs. If however there are further annual periods within the same valuation period, the limits applicable to those subsequent annual periods will be affected.

In this situation, the limits on income withdrawals must be recalculated on the day when the annuitisation occurs, taking into account the remaining fund after the annuitisation, the member's age and the gilt yield at the date of the annuitisation.

The new limits will then be applied to the remaining annual periods (other than that in which the annuitisation occurred) within the valuation period. In relation to those remaining annual periods, the annuitisation is known as a 'qualifying annuitisation'.

Example – Qualifying annuitisation

An individual has been taking income withdrawals from their personal pension, which consists of a single arrangement. The pension date was 1 November 2002 and the maximum withdrawal limit is £15,000 per year. The minimum is therefore £5,250.

They decide to use part (but not all) of their fund to purchase an annuity at 1 July 2003.

The limits for the first annual period (1 November 2002 to 31 October 2003) are unchanged, and they must withdraw a total amount between £5,250 and £15,000 during this period.

Limits must be recalculated at 1 July 2003, taking into account the residual fund, the individual's age, sex and GAD rate details at that time. Suppose the recalculation produces a maximum limit of £8,000 per year and a minimum of £2,800. These limits apply to the annual periods 1 November 2003 to 31 October 2004 and 1 November 2004 to 31 October 2005.

The limits must be reviewed at the relevant reference date falling on 1 November 2005, in the normal way.

Note that where the annuitisation occurs within the last annual period of any valuation period, no special action is required. The normal review of limits at the relevant reference date at the end of the valuation period will take place and will be based on the fund at the relevant reference date. Such an annuitisation is never a qualifying annuitisation therefore.

Checklist – Useful terminology for income withdrawals

Terminology is an important aspect of understanding the way in which limits and reviews of limits operate under income withdrawal arrangements. The following are amongst the most important terms.

Annual period	Generally a twelve month period measured from the pension date, or a subsequent anniversary. The annual period may be shortened when phased retirement is used and relevant reference dates under different arrangements are combined (see section **6.7** above).
Annuitisation	Using part of the fund under an income withdrawal arrangement to purchase an annuity.
Pension date	The date on which the member elects to take income withdrawals, and on which tax free cash becomes available.
Qualifying annuitisation	In relation to any annual period a qualifying annuitisation is an annuitisation which occurred in an earlier annual period within the current valuation period.
Relevant reference date	The date on which newly calculated income withdrawal limits are put into effect. The first relevant reference date is always pension date, and subsequent relevant reference dates are usually each three year anniversary of pension date. However, the date may be combined with that under other arrangements where phased retirement is in operation (see section **6.7** above).
Review	A recalculation of income withdrawal limits based on GAD rates.
Valuation period	The period between relevant reference dates. The valuation period is generally three years, but can be less where relevant reference dates are combined (see section **6.7** above).

Transfers between income withdrawal providers   6.10

At one time, it was not permitted for a transfer to be made between providers after income withdrawals had started, except at the time when an annuity was purchased. This limitation was removed by the *Personal Pension Schemes (Transfer Payments) Regulations 2001 (SI 2001/119)* with effect from 14 February 2001, and transfers during the income withdrawal period are now permitted. This could be appropriate if the individual wishes to change the investment links available.

When a transfer is made, the scheme administrator of the receiving arrangement must recalculate income withdrawal limits at the date of transfer and a new three year valuation period commences at that time. Importantly, the normal minimum and maximum limits on withdrawals will not be applied to the part-annual period prior to the transfer. This is also a situation in which a substantial gap can occur between withdrawals.

Example – Transfer whilst taking income withdrawals

An individual has been taking income withdrawals from their personal pension for five years, but has been disappointed by the investment performance achieved, and wants to transfer to a new product provider.

The current annual period runs from 1 April 2003 to 31 March 2004, and they intend to transfer on 15 March 2004. They want to minimise income withdrawals, because investment values are low, and the individual feels they will recover shortly.

They are not required to take any income in the period 1 April 2003 to the date of transfer (assuming this is 15 March 2004, and so before the end of the annual period).

Under the new arrangement, 15 March 2004 is the pension date and the new provider calculates the income withdrawal limits in the usual way. The individual can then delay their first withdrawal from the new arrangement until 14 March 2005 if they wish, though they would then need to take an amount equal to at least the minimum annual limit.

There are however a number of restrictions which apply in this situation. The whole of the fund under the arrangement(s) in question must be transferred (though if withdrawals are occurring from a number of arrangements, it is not necessary for them all to be transferred).

In addition, the new provider must have established the receiving arrangement(s) solely to receive the transfer, and these arrangements cannot receive new contributions direct from the member.

Regulations 14(2)(b) and *14(3)(c)* of the *Personal Pension Schemes (Transfer Payments) Regulations 2001 (SI 2001/119)* require that income withdrawals must be taking place under the transferring scheme before the transfer is made. This means that if a transfer is requested during the first annual period, it cannot take place unless withdrawals have actually started. In these circumstances the Inland Revenue *Guidance Notes (IR76) para 12.50* state that:

'It is not intended to specify a maximum amount to be taken in the period up to the date of transfer, but the amount withdrawn should be no less than the proportion of the minimum income withdrawal limit that the pre-transfer period bears to a full year.'

Death during income withdrawals   6.11

Where death occurs whilst income withdrawals are being taken, there will be a residual fund, and this is available to provide benefits. There are a number of options available.

The residual fund can be used to provide benefits in lump sum form, in which case the scheme administrator must deduct tax at the rate of 35% before payment. This amount must be paid to the Inland Revenue by the scheme administrator and is, from a technical point of view, a tax charge on the administrator under *s 648B, ICTA 1988*. There is no further tax liability on the recipient of the lump sum, but neither can any part of the 35% deducted by the scheme administrator be reclaimed, even if the recipient is a non-taxpayer.

Alternatively, the survivor can choose to take income withdrawals from the residual fund. In this case, the minimum and maximum limits will be calculated at the date of death, based on the survivor's age and sex, the current level of gilt yield and the residual fund at the time. The income withdrawal limits are consistent in style with those applying to the member themself, and are a maximum of 100% of the annuity which would be available on GAD rates, and a minimum of 35% of the maximum.

The income withdrawals will be taxed as earned income under PAYE in the same way as income withdrawals received by the member, though based on the survivor's tax position.

Note that income withdrawals can only continue until the earlier of:

(*a*)   the date that would have been the member's 75th birthday; and
(*b*)   the survivor's 75th birthday.

The remaining fund must be used to purchase an annuity no later than this date.

Where the survivor is a minor child, income payments must end by the later of the child's 18th birthday or the cessation of full-time education, unless the child was dependent on grounds of disability.

Where the survivor initially chooses to take income withdrawals, they can, within a period of two years, choose to take the balance of the fund as a lump sum, subject to the 35% tax charge as discussed above.

Alternatively, the survivor can choose to utilise the residual fund at the date of death to purchase an annuity. Generally, the annuity will be payable for the survivor's life, but it can be guaranteed payable for a minimum period of up to ten years. It is also possible (though unusual) to arrange for the annuity to cease in the event of remarriage where the survivor was the member's spouse. The annuity can be level, escalating, index-linked or investment-linked, and would be taxable as earned income under PAYE.

It is also possible where the survivor is a spouse, and if the date of the member's death is under 60, to defer the purchase of an annuity for the survivor until a date no later than the survivor's 60th birthday. Note that in the event that the spouse dies before the annuity comes into payment, there is no provision under the legislation for a death benefit to be payable, and so the fund would create a windfall profit for the insurance company concerned.

If there is more than one survivor entitled to benefits on the member's death, each may choose independently the way in which death benefits will be paid. So for example, if there are three such survivors, one might choose to receive a lump sum, one to take income withdrawals, and the third to purchase an annuity.

There are usually no inheritance tax implications where an individual dies whilst taking income withdrawals, but some care is needed. If the Inland Revenue believes that income withdrawals have been taken, or that the level of withdrawals has been reduced for estate planning reasons, rather than from the point of view of the individual's income needs, it can seek to establish that a liability exists.

This would be on the basis that there is a loss to the estate, as a result of the individual not opting for an annuity with a ten year guarantee, the residual value of which on death would have formed part of the estate.

The Inland Revenue has indicated that it would not expect to take this line unless death occurs within two years of the decision to take income withdrawals, or to reduce their level, and the individual was aware of their declining health at the time of making the decision.

Impact of death benefits 6.12

The availability of the remainder of the fund to provide death benefits where a member of a personal pension scheme dies whilst taking income withdrawals is a very powerful advantage of income withdrawals. Where the member's income is provided by means of an annuity, it is possible to build in a minimum guarantee period and/or survivor pension benefits. However, it will generally be the case that the value of these death benefits is less than what would have been the residual fund under an income withdrawal arrangement.

This may mean that in situations where death benefits are particularly important, for example if the member is in ill-health at the time of retirement, or if they have a spouse or partner who is considerably younger, income withdrawals are particularly attractive.

However, there are negative as well as positive aspects to consider in relation to death benefits. When an annuity is purchased, the insurance company calculates annuity rates taking into account the fact that some annuitants will not live as long as their theoretical life expectancy at the point of annuity purchase, whilst others will live longer.

The release to the annuity fund where an individual dies early is known as mortality gain, and this concept is discussed in section **5.29**. This gain in effect subsidises the annuity payments which are made to individuals who live longer, so there is a cross-subsidy from those who die early to those who live longest.

Where income withdrawals are taken, the fund provides benefits for the individual and their survivors, and no one else. If the individual dies early, the residual fund will be used to provide survivor benefits so there is no cross-subsidy to those who live longer, and therefore no 'loss'.

However, if the individual lives long, then their fund alone must provide their benefits, and there will be no cross-subsidy from those who live less long, and therefore no mortality gain.

Mortality drag 6.13

The income provided under an annuity therefore consists of three parts, namely:

(*a*) payments from the capital represented by the purchase price;
(*b*) investment returns achieved on the capital by the insurance company; and
(*c*) mortality gain arising from earlier deaths.

Under an income withdrawal arrangement, only the capital and the investment return is available.

It follows from this that if the investment performance of an income withdrawal fund merely matches that of an annuity fund, the income available will, over the long term, be less than the annuity would have provided. This simply reflects the absence of mortality gain, and could reasonably be regarded as the cost of the enhanced death benefit.

If the individual wishes to match, through income withdrawals, the level of income which could be provided by an annuity, the investment return on the income withdrawal fund must not merely match, but must exceed the investment return which could be achieved by an annuity fund.

It is this effect which is referred to as mortality drag.

The impact of mortality drag increases with age, simply because at older ages a higher proportion of annuitants will die during any given period, and therefore the extent of the mortality gain released for the benefit of the surviving annuitants is greater.

Purely in income terms, therefore, it becomes increasingly difficult as age advances for an income withdrawal arrangement to match the income level which could be provided by annuity purchase. This is sometimes used as an argument to support the legislative requirement for an annuity to be purchased by age 75 at the latest. However for those for whom the provision of death benefits for dependants is a high priority, a lower level of income may be acceptable if the overall package of benefits is seen as attractive.

Investment issues 6.14

Investment issues are covered in detail in **Chapter 7: Investment Considerations**. However in principle, as discussed above, if an individual wishes to use income withdrawals to match or exceed the income which would have been available from annuity purchase, they must invest in a manner which is capable of counteracting mortality drag. This means that they will need to use investments which provide the potential of a higher return than gilts, and therefore are likely to carry a higher risk. Generally, a significant proportion of the fund under income withdrawal arrangements will be invested directly or indirectly in equities.

This in turn creates risk, but not just in the sense that investment values can go down as well as up, and can fluctuate significantly from time to time. It is also necessary to consider the effect that this has when withdrawals are taken.

Where investments are made outside pension arrangements, equity based holdings are likely to be regarded as suitable only when the investment period is at least five years, or perhaps longer. Although an investor might choose to take money out of his overall portfolio if investment returns are strong, he probably will not do so from the equity based holdings if their value is weak. With an income withdrawal portfolio, the existence of a minimum as well as a maximum limit on withdrawals means that the individual lacks the flexibility to stop taking withdrawals when market conditions are poor.

If investments are wholly in equities, the need to make withdrawals at a time when investment values are low may have a disproportionate effect on the overall fund.

The effect of this is discussed further, with an example, in section **7.16**.

Alternatively, to avoid this particular problem, and reduce risk, it may be appropriate to diversify the income withdrawal portfolio to include lower risk investments, for example deposits, at least to cover the level of withdrawals required in the immediate future. However, the lower investment returns available on more secure investments will dampen down the performance of the income withdrawal portfolio as a whole, making it more difficult to outperform an annuity fund by a sufficient margin to allow income to be matched.

Other influences on investment 6.15

Where income withdrawals are chosen largely because of the increased death benefits, perhaps in circumstances where the member themself is terminally ill, the investment decisions will need to reflect this. In particular, if the intention is that the residual fund (after tax) is to be taken as a lump sum by the survivors, it may be appropriate to hold the fund in cash form in the interim.

Advantages and disadvantages of income withdrawals 6.16

The availability of income withdrawals has considerably widened the choice available for members of personal pension schemes. It makes personal pensions once again an attractive option, even for those who do not want to be locked into an annuity immediately at the point of retirement. The facility offers considerable advantages in terms of flexibility of income, and the ability to plan the levels of taxable income taken from tax year to tax year can be immensely attractive.

In addition, the ability to leave the pension fund invested until age 75 opens up the possibility of achieving high investment returns in equity related investments over long periods.

The enhanced death benefits can also remove the fear which some individuals have that a considerable part of their pension fund would be lost in the event of their death should this occur soon after annuity purchase, even if they build in a minimum guaranteed period and/or survivor benefits.

Taking income withdrawals can also allow the individual to choose the moment when he purchases an annuity, subject always to the overriding requirement to do so by the age of 75. So if, for example, the individual feels that annuity rates are currently at a low level, but that annuity rates will become less expensive in future, he can take income withdrawals for a temporary period until annuity rates recover. In the meantime, the fact that withdrawals can be restricted to 35% of the maximum calculated according to GAD rates means that they should not significantly erode the fund. In addition, annuity rates become less expensive as age increases (to reflect reduced life expectancy).

There are however a number of disadvantages and risks which need to be taken into account. These certainly include the investment risks discussed in section **6.14** above, particularly in the light of the effect of mortality drag, which places the emphasis firmly on equity related investment.

There is also the chance that investment performance will turn out to be below what was hoped, and in addition, when the time comes to buy an annuity, it may be that annuity rates have worsened from their initial position. This would mean that the individual's long term retirement income could be severely and permanently damaged.

The timing of annuity purchase is a further area of difficulty. An individual might start taking income withdrawals at, say, 60, when there is a 15 year period within which to make the decision to buy an annuity. This gives a great deal of flexibility. However if annuity purchase is delayed, the window of time within which the purchase must take place reduces in size, and the decision can become increasingly difficult. This will be particularly so if the individual is waiting for either a recovery in investment markets or an improvement in annuity rates, which seems slow to materialise.

Overall then the individual will need to consider whether income withdrawals are appropriate, and in making this decision will need to take account of all of these factors. Having decided to follow this route, the individual must continue to monitor the changing situation and keep their decision under review so that they can opt for annuity purchase at the most auspicious moment.

Checklist – Main advantages and disadvantages of income withdrawals

Advantages

- Opportunity to continue to invest the pension fund in equities or related investments.
- Flexibility to alter income levels.
- Ability to control, within limits, the taxable income falling in each tax year.
- Residual fund available on death to provide benefits for dependants.
- Control of the timing of annuity purchase up to age 75.
- Annuity, when purchased, can reflect circumstances and needs at the time.

Disadvantages

- Risk of investment performance not matching expectations.
- Possibility of a decline in annuity rates.
- Need to outperform investment returns assumed by annuity rates in order to match income level (mortality drag), and resulting equity bias.
- No guaranteed income level.
- Requirement to take minimum withdrawals even if market values are depressed.
- Reducing period until age by which an annuity must be purchased.

7 — Investment Considerations

Introduction   7.1

The underlying function of any pension arrangement is to provide a means whereby an individual can accumulate a fund from which to provide for all or part of their financial needs in retirement. Whilst the limitations and tax advantages of pension arrangements are very important, the approach to investment will also have a major effect on the ultimate value of the accumulated fund.

There is an extremely wide range of options available to assist in the implementation of the investment strategy adopted. These will be considered later in this chapter, but initially we consider the influences on strategy, before and after retirement benefits are taken.

Personal aspects   7.2

An overarching consideration is the attitude of the individual. Attitude to risk is a key factor in determining the investment choices, because however appropriate a particular strategy might be in theory, if the individual is unhappy with it, then an alternative will need to be found.

This will also have an influence in determining future changes in strategy, for example as retirement approaches. The lifestyle approach to investment is considered later in this chapter (see section **7.11** below), but essentially involves a gradual shift of focus towards lower risk areas prior to purchasing an annuity. How long before retirement such a process should start, and the speed with which the change of focus occurs, will need to reflect individual preferences.

Similarly, some individuals will seek to avoid insurance company products, whether for sound reasons or simply prejudice, whilst others actively seek out the familiarity of this approach to investment.

Advisers need to ensure that the individual is aware of the alternatives open to them, and has access to sufficient information to make reasonable decisions. This will include not only an awareness of risk, but also of the investment potential of the various choices, and of the need to diversify.

Other investments   7.3

Pension related investment strategy should not be considered in isolation, but should always take account of the individual's other assets. For example, an individual with considerable assets overall should probably have a degree of geographical diversification within his portfolio. However, the extent to which an individual's pension portfolio is diversified in this way should be considered in the light of the make up of their investments overall.

The extent to which other assets are liquid will also affect strategy. For example, suppose an individual has not yet started to take retirement benefits, and has a lot of cash outside their pension arrangement. Even though they might be planning to retire in two years, they might choose to remain invested in equities, because, in the event of a fall in the market, they hope to ride out the downturn by delaying pension benefits and living instead on their cash.

Other income 7.4

Similarly, other sources of income may allow the individual greater scope to control the timing of encashment of their pension arrangements. This in turn might enable them to accept a higher level of risk in an attempt to maximise the returns achieved.

Conversely, the more reliant an individual is on their pension planning, the greater the need for security is likely to be.

Pre-retirement strategy 7.5

An individual investing for retirement will generally do so over a considerable period, and can therefore take a long term view of investment prospects. This will usually mean a strong bias towards investment in equities, or related collective investments such as unit trusts or insurance company equity funds. Historically, equities have outperformed most other types of investment over periods of ten years or more, though in the short term, prices can fluctuate dramatically.

If the term is relatively short, the risk of equities performing poorly increases, and other investment areas, such as gilts or even cash deposits would need to be considered.

Investors must be aware that equity investment is not guaranteed to produce favourable returns, and indeed experience over the last two or three years has been poor. In addition, where investment is made in shares in any particular company, it is possible that the value of those shares may fall to nothing if the company fails.

Nevertheless, on the assumption that the objective is to achieve a high potential return over a long period, most commentators would agree that a fundamentally equity based strategy is most appropriate.

Investment term 7.6

Identifying the likely investment term is important, but may be less than straightforward in practice. Most people will have an expectation of when they would like to retire, but it is unlikely that this will be certain, particularly whilst the individual is relatively young. Plans may change significantly over the years, and may be influenced by, for example, a move to a new job, or perhaps something less positive, such as an enforced redundancy.

Given that the age range within which retirement benefits can be accessed is very wide – anywhere between the ages of 50 and 75 – the range of possible investment terms is similarly wide.

Example – Investment term

An individual starts contributing to a personal pension when they are 40, and their intention is to retire at 65, so the expected investment term is 25 years.

They can however draw benefits anytime between the ages of 50 and 75, so the investment term could be anywhere between 10 and 35 years.

Phased retirement can complicate the issue still further, since this will mean that different tranches of benefit will be accessed at different times. This may therefore mean arranging the overall investment portfolio so that some investments are focused on the relatively short term, whilst others reflect the longer term view.

Example – Phased retirement

A 52-year-old self-employed individual has been contributing to a personal pension for a number of years, and initially intended to retire at 60.

They have now decided that they want to start reducing the hours they work from their 55th birthday, and would like to take some of their pension benefits then. They will continue working indefinitely, on a reduced basis, gradually lessening their hours and replacing lost income by phasing in more of their personal pension benefits.

The investment strategy of their pension fund will need to be adjusted to reflect the need to draw some benefits in about three years time, but also the fact that other benefits will be drawn gradually over a period of up to 23 years from the present time.

An individual may also access benefits earlier than expected if they become incapacitated, and given that such circumstances may arise suddenly and unexpectedly, this may further complicate consideration of the term. There is no minimum age at which benefits can be accessed in these circumstances.

Diversification and risk 7.7

The importance of diversification is familiar and well established. An individual who, at the extreme, chooses to invest the whole of their pension fund in the shares of a single company stands the chance of achieving a spectacularly good investment return if the company is successful. However there is also the possibility that the company will do poorly, or even fail entirely, with disastrous effects on the investment fund. This is a high risk strategy, essentially because it is extremely difficult to predict the outcome, and the probability that the actual outcome will differ from expectation is very high.

The idea of diversification is to reduce the extent to which performance is likely to differ from expectation, and therefore give more certainty to the portfolio as a whole. There are many ways of achieving diversification, the most important of which are shown in the checklist below.

Examples of methods of achieving investment diversification

(*a*)   Investing in the shares of different companies within the same stock market sector.

(*b*)   Investing in different stock market sectors.

(*c*)   Investing in stock markets in different countries.

(*d*)   Investing in different asset classes, for example, equities, property, fixed interest securities and cash.

(*e*)   Investing at different times.

It must be accepted that diversification reduces the risk of unexpected performance in both directions. As discussed earlier, the individual who invests in the shares of a particular company may do extremely well, but runs the risk of doing poorly. Diversification reduces the risk of extremely poor performance, but also of extremely positive performance.

In most situations, pensions related portfolios will be diversified in a number of ways. For example, it is likely to be appropriate to invest in different asset classes, so that the whole of the portfolio is not exposed to, for example, equities. Even though equities may be predominant in the portfolio as a whole, having investments in assets such as fixed interest securities, will protect the portfolio from situations where equity investments perform poorly over a relatively long period in a bear market.

Within the equity portion of the portfolio, diversifying across different market sectors will tend to reduce the risk that the portfolio will perform in a significantly different way than the market as a whole. If the investor's belief is that equities in general are likely to outperform other types of investment in the long term, this should ensure that the portfolio participates in this overall success.

Different investment sectors do perform differently from time to time, and sometimes may perform significantly at variance with the market as a whole. For example, the boom in technology stocks at the end of the twentieth century provided, for a period, much better performance than the rest of the market as a whole. This was followed by a period of virtual collapse within this sector, during which it significantly underperformed the market.

Within any particular sector, there will also be variations between the performance of the shares of different companies. This will reflect largely the management decisions made within any particular company, which in turn will flow through to an effect on both short term and expected long term profit.

Correlation 7.8

If two assets were influenced in the same way, and the same extent by particular events, they would be said to be positively correlated. Holding assets which are positively correlated will not therefore provide effective diversification because the value of those assets would fluctuate in the same way. The effect is the same way as if only one asset was held.

The art of diversification is therefore to invest across assets which are not positively correlated. This may in some cases involve choosing assets which are negatively correlated (that is that the value of one asset tends to move upwards when the value of the other moves downwards, and vice versa) or those which are not correlated (that is there is no relationship between the movement in the value of the assets concerned).

Example – Positive and negative correlation

Suppose an investor buys a shareholding in Company A which specialises in arranging holidays in the UK. The performance of this sector of the stock market might be adversely affected if the UK suffered a series of poor summers.

Company B specialises in providing soft drinks and ice cream for the UK market, and so might be similarly affected. It would show positive correlation with Company A.

On the other hand, Company C, specialising in Caribbean holidays, would probably be helped by poor UK weather conditions, which might encourage more people to holiday abroad, and so would show negative correlation to both Company A and Company B.

Holding shares in Companies A and B would mean that the investor was exposed to significant risk if UK weather was poor, but should do well if UK weather was good. They could diversify by investing in Company C, which would reduce the impact of weather on their portfolio.

Weather is only one influence on the share prices of these three companies. There are many other factors, and perfect positive or negative correlation is unlikely to arise in practice.

Commercial property and equities are generally not correlated. In some circumstances where the value of equities has increased, so have property prices, but on other occasions when equity prices have increased, the value of commercial property has fallen. One reason to include commercial property in an overall portfolio is therefore to provide a means of effective diversification.

Contribution frequency 7.9

As mentioned in the checklist at **7.7** above, another aspect of diversification is that which is achieved by timing. With a one off contribution, or a switch of assets from one investment to another, the timing (as distinct from the remaining term of the investment) can be crucial. Timing is far less important with regular investments, or with those which, although not precisely regular, are repeated, for example through a series of one off contributions.

The concept of pound cost averaging can also be relevant where regular investments are made to purchase assets which fluctuate in value, such as units in a unit linked fund. When unit prices are low, the regular contribution will purchase a large number of units, whilst far fewer units will be purchased when the price is high.

Overall, the effect is that the average price paid for the units is less than the average price at which units have been valued.

Although the effect is most marked where units fluctuate in price significantly, it is still present where growth is more consistent, as the example below shows.

Example – Pound cost averaging

An individual contributes £1,000 per year to their personal pension. The arrangement is unit-linked, and they invest in a UK Equity fund.

The units purchased with the first five years' contributions are shown below:

Year	Contribution	Unit price	Units purchased	Total units to date
1	£1,000	£1.00	1,000	1,000
2	£1,000	£1.10	909	1,909
3	£1,000	£1.20	833	2,742
4	£1,000	£1.30	769	3,511
5	£1,000	£1.40	714	4,225

The average price which units achieved over this period was £1.20.

The total units purchased were 4,225, at a total cost of £5,000. The average price paid by the individual was therefore £5,000/4,225 = £1.18.

Investing on a regular or repeated basis reduces risk as a result of the diversification by time. It may therefore be acceptable to choose a more volatile fund where regular contributions are being made than would be appropriate for a one off contribution, where the importance of timing is much greater. Where an individual is making both regular and occasional one off contributions, different investment strategies might be adopted in respect of each type of contribution.

However, it is important to consider the effect of the build up of a fund as a result of regular contributions. For example, if an individual starts to make regular contributions to a unit linked personal pension, and initially the value of units falls, although this will reduce the value of units already purchased, the effect is modest, and – in the long term – should be outweighed by later increases in the unit price. On the other hand, once a substantial fund has built up, any fall in unit prices will result in a substantial reduction in the value of the existing fund, and the attraction of purchasing additional units at the depressed price may be much less of a compensation.

Example – Effect of existing fund

An individual invests £3,000 per year into a relatively volatile fund within their personal pension.

Suppose the unit purchased with the first two year's contributions are as follows:

Year	Contribution	Unit price	Units purchased	Total units to date
1	£3,000	£1.00	3,000	3,000
2	£3,000	£0.60	5,000	8,000

If the unit price recovers to £0.80 over the next few months, the individual's total investment will be valued at £6,400. So, even though the fund price has fallen over the period since the start of the personal pension, they have still achieved a positive return on the £6,000 invested.

However, if the personal pension arrangement had been started some years before, and the individual had already built up a holding of 10,000 units, the position would be as follows:

Year	Contribution	Unit price	Units purchased	Total units to date
			Already built up	10,000
1	£3,000	£1.00	3,000	13,000
2	£3,000	£0.60	5,000	18,000

The value of the investment already built up was 10,000 × £1.00 = £10,000 at the time of the first contribution shown above, and a further £6,000 has since been contributed, giving a total of £16,000

If the unit price is now £0.80, the total value is now only 18,000 × £0.80 = £14,400.

Where an individual chooses a volatile fund for regular investments, it may therefore be wise to consider moving some of the accumulated fund to more secure areas from time to time.

Transfers   7.10

Where a personal pension receives a transfer value from another arrangement, this will be, by definition, a one off payment, and investment decisions should be approached with care. Investment in a volatile fund may be attractive if the investor believes that current prices are low, and provide significant scope for recovery. However, there is inevitably a risk that the investor's view will prove incorrect in practice and that values will continue to slide.

One approach might therefore be to choose a less volatile, more secure fund for the investment of the transfer value. However, often one of the major attractions of the transfer is to achieve a high level of investment performance, so as to achieve enhanced benefits at retirement. This is likely to orientate against a conservative fund choice.

An alternative approach might be to hold the transfer value initially in a secure investment area, possibly cash, and then to transfer to a more volatile investment on a gradual basis. This approach would certainly take some pressure off the decision regarding the timing of investment, and therefore reduces risk. However it can mean that there may be a loss of growth during the period over which the investment is being gradually transferred.

If the transfer is being made from a money purchase arrangement, and the style of investment is being maintained, for example with the transfer being from one UK equity related fund to another, timing will be less of an issue. However, where the transfer is from a defined benefit occupational scheme and where the objective is to outperform a critical yield in order to provide improved benefits at retirement, timing may be of crucial importance.

Lifestyle approach   7.11

One fairly stylised approach to the investment of a pension fund portfolio prior to retirement is the 'lifestyle' approach.

At its simplest, the intention is to transfer investments from relatively high risk areas such as equities to more secure areas over a period as retirement approaches. The intention is to consolidate gains which may have been made over a possibly long period of investment in equities or other assets, and to reduce or avoid the risk of a fall in available benefits shortly before retirement.

At one time, it was common for individuals to use a cash deposit account as the secure investment within this strategy. This consolidates gains, but does not insulate the individual from adverse movements in annuity rates.

In fact, it will generally be more appropriate to transfer into gilt-edged securities, or a fund which itself invests in gilts (or similar fixed interest securities). The price of gilts fluctuates, but in general, it will increase if interest rates fall, and decrease if interest rates rise. Because annuity rates reflect interest rates generally, and in particular gilt yields, annuity rates become more expensive when gilt yields fall, but the individual would be protected to an extent by the associated increase in the value of their investment in gilts.

Overall the effect is to limit, from the point that the investment is switched to gilts, the potential variation in the amount of the annuity which the individual could purchase at retirement.

> *Example – Lifestyle approach*
>
> An individual has a personal pension fund of £100,000, currently invested in an equity fund. They intend to retire in five years' time, and they will use the whole of their fund to purchase an annuity. They decide to switch 20% of the fund to gilts each year over the remaining five years.
>
> They therefore retain some opportunity to benefit from the continuing, but gradually reducing, exposure to equities, but at the same time, lock into current gilt prices and therefore annuity rate levels with an increasing proportion of the fund.

Tax free cash   7.12

In most cases, the individual will wish to take part of their benefits in the form of tax free cash at retirement. It may be appropriate to switch part of the investment fund to cash to provide for this requirement, since insulation from changes in annuity rates is not required on this part of the fund.

This cannot be an exact science, because the way in which the value of the gilt related investment and the cash element changes will in turn alter the relationship between the two elements. However, the general strategy is a reasonable one to adopt in appropriate cases.

Application of lifestyle approach   7.13

Because the prime objective of the lifestyle approach to investment is to avoid the individual being adversely affected by changes in annuity rates, it follows that this approach will only be relevant where the intention is to purchase an annuity at a reasonably predictable future date.

Where the intention is to provide for income through income withdrawals, as discussed below, it will generally be appropriate for the fund to remain invested largely in equities, to provide the best prospects of long term growth. A gradual move away from equities into more secure environments would be counter-productive in these circumstances.

There may however still remain a case for moving part of the total fund into deposit in order to provide for any tax free cash requirement.

Where the individual intends to take benefits on a phased retirement basis, and will provide income by annuity purchase, the lifestyle approach is only likely to be practical if a large proportion of the overall fund is intended to be encashed at any one time. If phasing is to be more gradual, it would be difficult to operate in practice, because of the variations in the term for different portions of the fund.

A lifestyle approach is sometimes adopted on an automatic, or default basis, particularly under group personal pensions. In reality, its application should be tailored to the circumstances of each individual involved if it is to be truly effective.

Post-retirement investment 7.14

When retirement benefits are taken, income can be provided either by means of annuity purchase or through income withdrawals. If annuity purchase is selected, the annuity rates on offer from the insurance company will reflect the current level of gilt yields, and the insurance company will primarily back its liability to pay the guaranteed income by investment in gilts.

From an investor's point of view, the decision to buy an annuity is in effect a decision to invest in a gilt related environment.

The choice of an annuity is not however usually a positive investment decision, but is more commonly driven by other factors, for example the need for a secure income. This aspect is considered in section **5.41**. To defer annuity purchase and instead take income withdrawals is a decision which generally requires much greater investment awareness.

Income withdrawals 7.15

The income withdrawal option provides the individual with the opportunity to continue to control the manner in which the pension fund is invested. If the individual feels they can achieve a high investment return, then this will ultimately be reflected in the level of income they can draw.

However the investment issues associated with an income withdrawal portfolio are difficult, and the individual must accept that a significant degree of risk is involved. If receiving a guaranteed income is important, then the purchase of an annuity would be the right route to take.

For much the same reasons that equities tend to dominate the investment of pre-retirement pension portfolios, this will also be the case after retirement if income withdrawals are being taken. In order to achieve a higher level of income, the fund from which the income withdrawals are being taken must outperform the return the insurance company assumed to be available from gilts when setting its annuity rates. Otherwise, the income withdrawal option will produce a lower income.

In fact, because of the effect of mortality drag (see section **6.13**), just to match the annuity income, it is necessary for the income withdrawal fund to outperform. This is because of the need to compensate for the fact that no mortality gain is available. In addition, the cost of administering an income withdrawal arrangement is generally higher than the cost of administering an annuity, so charges will be higher, and this must also be compensated for by investment outperformance.

Critical yield 7.16

A critical yield will generally be calculated in connection with an income withdrawal arrangement, and this will indicate the level of investment return required from the portfolio in order to match the income which would have been available from annuity purchase. This then provides an important benchmark against which the performance of the income withdrawal portfolio can be judged.

The investment strategy adopted for the portfolio must be determined in the light of the critical yield. If the chosen investment mix is unlikely to produce a return at this level, then the individual would be better off from an income point of view if they purchased an annuity.

Given that the critical yield when income withdrawals are selected is likely to be slightly in excess of gilt yields (to allow for mortality drag and charges) it is unlikely to be appropriate for the individual to invest to any large extent in gilts. Similarly, the relatively low expectations of returns from deposit investment are likely to make this type of investment inappropriate for any substantial part of the portfolio.

Property might have attractions, but is generally too illiquid. Thus equities will usually be the favoured option.

However, the long term nature of equity investment does not always sit comfortably with the way in which income withdrawals operate. There are a number of factors which contribute to this position, for example:

(a) income withdrawals cannot continue beyond the individual's 75th birthday, and as a result the maximum term of the investment is limited;

(b) in the event of a market decline, the requirement to purchase an annuity by age 75 at the latest may mean that the individual does not have the opportunity to wait for the market to recover;

(c) as age 75 approaches, and the maximum remaining term declines, it may become increasingly difficult to justify continued equity related investment, because of the risk of a fall in value; and

(d) because of the imposition of a minimum level of income withdrawals which must be taken each year, it is not possible to entirely avoid encashment of part of the portfolio each year, and therefore it will usually be attractive to hold some investments in a more secure form, to cater for short term withdrawal requirements.

Taking a regular income from a fund which is invested wholly in assets and which can therefore fluctuate in value can be problematic. If asset values are weak, the effect of a regular withdrawal will be exaggerated. The effect is much like pound cost averaging (see section **7.9** above), but working against the investor.

Example – Effect of regular withdrawals

An individual has an income withdrawal fund of £200,000 invested entirely in an equity fund. They hold 200,000 units at an initial price of £1.00. They want to take regular withdrawals at the rate of £10,000 at the end of each year. This is within the limits calculated according to GAD rates.

Unit prices fluctuate as follows:

Period	Withdrawal	Unit price	Units encashed	Units left
			Brought forward	200,000
1	£10,000	£0.90	11,111	188,889
2	£10,000	£0.80	12,500	176,389
3	£10,000	£0.80	12,500	163,889
4	£10,000	£0.90	11,111	152,778
5	£10,000	£1.00	10,000	142,778

Although the unit price has recovered, the fund has reduced by almost 29% in this example, though total withdrawals represent only 25% of the initial fund value.

The average price of units over the five encashment points is £0.88.

However, a total of 57,222 units have been encashed, for a total realised of £50,000. The average price realised is therefore only just over £0.87. Although this is a modest difference, over a long period, the effect can be damaging.

Effect of deposit investment   7.17

If the result of the need to allow for short term withdrawals is that part of the portfolio is held, for example, in cash, this will mean that the level of return required on the remainder of the portfolio must be that much higher if the critical yield is to be exceeded overall.

> ### Example – Deposits and the critical yield
>
> An individual is considering taking income withdrawals and has been told that the critical yield they must achieve in order to match the income which could be provided by annuity purchase is 7% per year. They believe that they can do this with an equity portfolio.
>
> However, to allow for withdrawals in the short term, the individual decides they must keep 15% of the portfolio in cash, and the expected return on this is only 4% per year.
>
> In order to achieve an average return of 7% on the portfolio as a whole, the return on the equity portion would need to be over 7.5% per year.

This may make it much more difficult to achieve higher levels of income through income withdrawals.

Decision to purchase an annuity   7.18

The timing of annuity purchase may also be a difficult area in which to reach a decision. Interest rates and annuity rates are not easily predictable, and the option is one way – once the decision is made it cannot be reversed. It is also difficult to justify taking a more cautious approach to the investment of an income withdrawal portfolio in the period leading up to annuity purchase, since the purchase itself represents a switch to a more secure investment basis. To move funds from equities into more secure investment environments before purchasing an annuity is more likely to damage the eventual income rather than improve it, compared to purchasing an annuity straight away.

It is however possible to use a phased approach to annuity purchase by using the fund under some arrangements to buy an annuity whilst maintaining income withdrawals with the remaining arrangements. This gradually increases the level of security attaching to the individual's income as a whole, whilst retaining an element of investment control on the remainder of the portfolio.

Phased retirement   7.19

Where the individual is phasing retirement, in conjunction with income withdrawals, then different investment strategies are likely to be appropriate for those arrangements from which withdrawals are being taken, as opposed to those which are not yet providing benefits. In particular, the difficulties arising from the need to provide for short term withdrawals will not apply to the arrangements which are not yet providing benefits.

Investing for death benefits 7.20

Where an individual is aware of having a reduced life expectancy, it may be that a significant driving force in relation to investment decisions is a consideration of the position that would arise on their death. Where the individual has not yet started to draw retirement benefits, and plans not to do so, it will generally be the case that the whole of the fund, (excluding any protected rights if they are married), can be paid as a tax free lump sum. In such circumstances, the individual may choose to switch the investment into a secure environment in order to safeguard the amount of the fund which would be available.

Although this seems a natural approach, the investment decision should more properly be taken having regard to what will happen to the eventual lump sum death benefit. If its destination is known (subject to the various discretions which may apply – see section **8.10**) then the intentions of the likely recipient may be relevant. For example, if the recipient intends to use the money to purchase an annuity, then a switch to gilts would again be more logical than a switch to cash.

If the individual intends to invest in equities, then there may be little point in moving money which is currently invested in this way into a cash environment on a temporary basis, unless there is a strong investment justification for doing so.

There may of course be too many uncertainties to allow a judgement to be made with certainty, and in these distressing circumstances, the wishes of the personal pension scheme member should always remain paramount.

Note that in some circumstances, there may also be inheritance tax considerations and these may also influence decisions, both about investment and about the level of withdrawals an individual takes. These aspects are considered in section **6.11**.

Insured schemes 7.21

One of the advantages of an insured personal pension scheme is the wide range of professionally managed funds which are usually available. The checklist below lists the main types of fund available within unit-linked arrangements, and we discuss these in more detail below.

Checklist – Main fund types commonly available under insured personal pension arrangements

The range of funds available varies widely, but the most common are:

(*a*)   UK equity;
(*b*)   Overseas equity;
(*c*)   Worldwide equity;
(*d*)   Specialist equity (eg technology);
(*e*)   Ethical;
(*f*)   Tracker;
(*g*)   Property;
(*h*)   Gilt & fixed interest;
(*j*)   Deposit;
(*k*)   Derivative based;
(*l*)   Managed; and
(*m*)   With profit.

In the past, the range offered by any particular provider has often been quite limited, and the management of the available funds has been handled by an in-house team. One of the most important developments in recent years has been a general tendency to widen the range, to give maximum investment choice, and also to include funds managed by outside specialist organisations.

Some personal pension providers now offer a very comprehensive range, including in some cases similar funds (for example UK equity funds) managed by a choice of different external investment management groups. This allows the individual to move out of an underperforming fund into a similar fund which they believe to have better prospects, without changing the overall investment strategy, and without needing to transfer between product providers.

Although charging structures within insured personal pension arrangements vary, it is usually the case that fund switches take place at either no cost or a very small cost, but without the imposition of a new initial charge. This can be a very attractive feature for those with an active interest in investment.

UK equity funds 7.22

Most insurers offer a UK equity fund, and this will often be a major constituent of the overall investment portfolio of many members. Equities probably provide the best long term growth prospects, and investing in the UK market means that there is no additional currency risk to consider.

There are many different investment strategies underlying these funds, and many different levels of risk. Some funds concentrate on shares in large companies, which may be amongst the constituents of a major stock index, and this will usually mean that the performance of the fund will not vary markedly from that of the index. However this would not be guaranteed.

Others cast their net more widely, and may have a larger proportion of the fund invested in smaller companies or new companies, which will generally provide prospects for greater reward, but at the same time would carry increased risk.

Overseas equity funds 7.23

Similar considerations in general apply to these funds, though some overseas markets are distinctly different from the UK, and this would need to be taken into account in considering such an investment. For example, the Japanese market tends to offer relatively low income yields, so the emphasis of the total return will be towards capital growth, which is likely to carry greater risk.

In addition, there will usually be a currency risk involved with an investment which is based on one or more overseas stock markets.

Example – Currency risk

An individual invests in a unit-linked personal pension, and chooses to invest their contributions in units in a Japanese equity fund.

Over a year, the value of assets per unit increases 5% in terms of Japanese yen, from 400 yen to 420 yen. However, over the same period, the yen depreciates against sterling and the exchange rate moves from 180 yen to the pound, to 200 yen.

The unit price in sterling at the start of the year was $400/180 = £2.22$.

At the end of the year, it would be $420/200 = £2.10$.

In spite of the positive performance of the assets on the Japanese stock market, the sterling investor faces a loss of around 5%, because of the decline in the value of the yen.

Clearly the impact of currency fluctuation can be positive as well as negative, and if the currency appreciates rather than depreciates, this will increase any gains, and reduce any losses, for sterling investors.

Some funds hedge the currency risk through the purchase of suitable currency related derivatives, and this will reduce or eliminate the additional currency risk. Equally it removes or reduces the possibility of increased returns which could result from positive currency movements.

Investors considering investing in overseas equity funds must take a view on the prospects of the particular market(s) involved. They must also consider possible currency movements, and must decide whether or not to select a fund which hedges the currency risk.

Many investors shy away from funds linked to overseas equity markets, and this is understandable enough in terms of the potential additional risk. They may also feel a lack of familiarity with overseas investment conditions. However, the size and influence of overseas markets, particularly the United States, can be very substantial, and may dwarf the UK market. Effective diversification is likely to mean diversifying geographically as well as in other ways, and it may prove unwise to ignore the opportunity to share in the performance of the world economy as distinct from merely that of the UK.

Worldwide equity funds   7.24

Some insurers offer an equity fund which invests in various markets worldwide, either directly, or by investing in specialist funds, with the manager determining the geographical spread. This can be convenient, but strategies vary widely from fund to fund and can vary from time to time. This could include the extent to which the geographical spread is changed as market conditions alter, and whether the currency risk is hedged.

The particular approach adopted by a fund being considered by an individual investor therefore needs to be identified and considered in the light of that individual's needs.

Whilst convenient, investing in such a fund means that the individual is not in control of the geographical distribution. This may make it difficult to take a holistic approach to the individual's investments overall, as opposed to those simply within the pension arrangement.

Specialist equity funds   7.25

Specialist equity funds tend to be higher risk than other equity funds, since by definition, they are less diversified. Often they are launched to reflect, to an extent, fashion at the time, and they may suffer considerable outflows of cash if fashion changes.

Specialist funds may concentrate in particular stock market sectors, for example technology or health care, or might reflect particular criteria, for example a smaller companies fund, investing only in companies with a market capitalisation below a defined figure.

These funds can add considerable interest to a portfolio as a whole, and may accelerate performance. Because of their undiversified nature however, they should generally not form too large a proportion of an individual's overall investment strategy.

Ethical funds   7.26

Ethical investment (also known as Socially Responsible Investment or SRI) has become very topical in recent years. Increasing numbers of investors, whilst still seeking to achieve good levels of investment return, are prepared to limit the ways in which they invest in line with their ethical principles. For example, an individual might wish not to invest in the shares of companies who are active in the armaments trade, or who manufacture or sell alcoholic beverages. Various ethical funds are available which apply negative criteria, ie they define a list of criteria (such as those mentioned above) which would debar any particular share from being included.

Other funds operate on the basis of positive criteria, where the managers actively seek out companies which meet specific requirements. These might be companies with a commitment to support the community within which they work, or who have a major commitment to recycling.

The criteria applicable to individual funds vary widely, and investors therefore will wish to ensure that the fund selected applies criteria which are as close as possible to their own beliefs, and which would exclude any particular types of business with which they would not wish to be associated.

In principle, a fund which limits its ability to invest according to non-investment criteria might be expected to underperform a fund which does not do so, simply because the manager has constraints on their ability to invest freely. There are however counter-arguments in the case of ethical funds.

Many people take the view that companies which meet the kind of requirements which are applied by ethical fund managers are those which are likely to be most modern in outlook generally. They may also be amongst the best equipped to deal with the increasing levels of regulation that apply in the modern world. In addition, because the manager of an ethical fund inevitably has to carry out more in depth research into the companies in which they plan to invest than would be the case for a manager of a more conventional fund, this may improve their ability to find those companies with the best investment potential.

The evidence regarding investment performance is, at least for the moment, inconclusive, however it does seem that the possible investment downside is at most small.

Tracker funds 7.27

Tracker funds have proved popular over recent years, and look set to become an increasingly prominent permanent feature of investment choice. These funds are designed to produce performance which remains as closely as possible in line with the performance of a particular index, for example the FTSE 100 index.

The argument in favour of tracker funds reflects the view that many funds which are actively managed end up underperforming the market generally. In such cases, investors would have been better off had they simply achieved performance in line with a relevant index. If the fund manager fails to outperform the index, the investor will not have seen value for the additional cost of the active management, including, for example, the research which has been undertaken, as well as the manager's own remuneration.

A tracker fund however does not require active management, but can be managed passively, to reflect the index. Some funds operate on a basis known as 'full replication', where the holdings of the fund are aligned as closely as possible to precisely reflect the index. Thus for example, if a particular share represents 3% of the relevant index, then 3% of the value of the fund will be held in those shares. Full replication requires a substantial fund in order to allow every holding which constitutes the index to be held within the fund in large enough quantities to keep dealing costs in check.

Even then, full replication will not necessarily produce a result which is precisely in line with the index. Adjustments to existing holdings will be made, but it may not always be practical, in terms of dealing costs, to maintain a precisely accurate reflection of the index. Nevertheless, the tracking error (ie the difference between actual performance and the performance of the index) is likely to be very small.

An alternative approach is known as 'stratified sampling'. With this technique the sectoral makeup of the fund will reflect the index, but individual shareholdings may not do so precisely. The result is more approximate, but dealing costs are smaller, and this can be reflected in performance. This approach is also possible with a smaller fund, under which full replication would not be feasible.

Various other approaches based on computer modelling techniques are used by some funds, but the overall objective of producing performance in line with an index remains unchanged.

The arguments against the use of tracker funds rest largely on the belief that a good active manager can outperform the index, at least in the long term, by making the right decisions based on research and their view of future trends in the market.

It is true that many managers have underperformed the market over recent years, but it is equally true that many have outperformed it. The problem confronting the investor and their advisers is to choose the right manager for the future, and this is never easy.

There is a case for investors to treat a tracker fund as a core holding within their portfolio, and to try to achieve outperformance overall by careful selection of specialist funds alongside. This can produce excellent results, with the underlying certainty of performance roughly matching the index from the tracker fund portion.

Property 7.28

Property funds may invest directly in property (generally commercial property) or may invest in the shares of property companies to achieve exposure to the property market. Holding some assets in property provides a good level of diversification because there is little or no correlation between commercial property prices and equity prices.

Few personal pension investors have sufficient funds to allow them to invest directly in property themselves (though see section **7.39** below for a discussion of self-invested personal pension schemes) and certainly few have the resources to be able to invest in a range of different properties to provide a spread of risk.

Some care is needed with property funds where they invest directly into property. Such funds will usually have a clause enabling the managers to delay any encashment of units for a specific period (often several months). The intention is to protect the fund as a whole by avoiding situations where a forced sale might be necessary to provide cash resources for redemptions in the short term. The use of a delay period would allow the managers time to sell property, where necessary, at a fair market price. Nevertheless, this could potentially be of considerable inconvenience if an individual needed to take retirement benefits.

It may therefore be wise to consider moving investment from property funds to an alternative fund six months or a year before benefits are likely to be required, if there is any possibility of such a delay clause operating.

Although in practice managers would not expect to apply the delay clause frequently, it could cause considerable inconvenience should it arise.

Gilt and fixed interest funds 7.29

Gilts and other fixed interest securities certainly have a place within a diversified investment portfolio. They represent an area which historically has seen considerably less volatility than equity investment, though long term returns have tended to be less good. Funds are available which invest only in gilt edged securities issued by the UK government. Other funds invest more widely, perhaps also using corporate bonds, or fixed interest securities issued by overseas governments.

Gilts issued by the UK government are regarded as being immensely secure, and there has never been a default in relation to any payment due in relation to them. This is not the case with corporate bonds, but to compensate for this, higher yields can be achieved in return for taking the slightly higher level of risk.

There is also risk involved with securities issued by overseas governments, particularly as far as currency is concerned, but again these securities might be attractive if, because of economic conditions in their country of origin, higher yields are available.

As always, individual investors need to ensure that the level of risk inherent in the strategy of any particular fund is acceptable to them.

As discussed in section **7.11** above, gilts and fixed interest securities generally, to an extent, provide protection from adverse changes in annuity rates. This means that, as well as figuring in a balanced portfolio over the long term, such an investment may also be useful as a means of consolidating gains made in, for example, equities, and avoiding any downturn in the period immediately before annuity purchase. The strategy adopted by any particular fund may make it more or less appropriate for use in this way. Annuity rates reflect yields on medium to long term gilts, and to provide insulation from changes in rates, the fund would need to invest in a similar manner.

Deposit funds   7.30

Within the range of funds offered by an insurer, there will almost invariably be a deposit fund. This is designed to provide a secure investment alternative, where the capital value is either guaranteed not to reduce, or would only do so in extreme circumstances, such as the default of a major banking institution.

However, deposit based investment is unlikely to be appropriate for the long term, because although capital values are secure in monetary terms, there is no guarantee that their value will not be eroded by inflation. In addition, there is an opportunity cost in the sense that the money held in the deposit fund could have been invested in other areas, such as equities, which are likely over the long term to produce a higher return.

Nevertheless, a deposit based investment might be appropriate for short term investment where the individual believes that equity prices are artificially high and will reduce over the forthcoming period. The individual might then choose to leave money on deposit until equity prices fall, and then switch to an equity based fund. The risk here is essentially that their view of the market will prove to be incorrect and that equity prices will increase whilst they have invested in the deposit fund. In this case a considerable growth opportunity will have been missed.

Deposit investment may also be useful to consolidate gains from other areas, particularly to the extent that benefits will be taken as a tax free cash sum. Deposit may also be used to house money required in the relatively short term for income withdrawals.

Derivative based funds 7.31

Various derivative funds have been put together at various times. The intention is to allow investors to benefit from most of the gains which would have arisen had they invested in equities, but with an underpinning guarantee of no loss, or a limited loss if the market declines. The terms of offer vary substantially from time to time, reflecting the cost and availability of derivatives in the marketplace. Since the decline in investment markets worldwide following the terrorist action in New York on 11 September 2001, derivatives have become more expensive, and the cost of investing in derivative based funds has also increased.

In some ways, these funds provide the best of all worlds, and they will certainly appeal to investors who wish to participate in asset backed growth, but who do not wish to take on the risk of doing so fully. It must be recognised however that there is a cost involved in the safety factor a derivative based fund can provide.

In order to finance the level of security involved, the effect will be that the investor will have a limited upside potential. Over the long term therefore if equities show a positive performance, investors in derivative based funds are likely to do less well than those who are fully committed to equities. Conversely, if equities decline, the derivative based fund will do much better.

Because of the nature of the derivatives involved, these funds will generally be open for new investment only for a specific time period, and the guarantees will only apply on a specified date or dates. Repeat investments may not be possible, or may be possible on different terms reflecting changes in market conditions.

While these funds are useful therefore, they may not fit with a particular investor's needs, particularly in relation to timing.

Example – Derivative based fund

A fund might offer growth of 90% of the increase in the FTSE 100 Index over a defined period of (say) two years, but with a guarantee that even if the market declines, the value of the investment will not be less than the amount invested.

The fund could be structured in various ways, for example, part could be invested in a fixed rate deposit to generate the capital guarantee, with the balance invested in derivatives to produce the FTSE 100 linked return.

It is not usually possible to switch out of these funds before the end of the period specified (or if switching is possible, the terms are likely to be poor). The investor needs therefore to commit their money for the whole term.

Managed funds   7.32

Most companies offer a managed fund where the asset distribution is determined by the fund manager. Often these are constituted as funds of funds, so the breadth and quality of choice available to the manager will depend on the range of funds available from that insurer.

Managed funds can be very useful for those who do not wish to, or do not have the expertise to decide the most suitable asset split for themselves. For those whose total investments within the personal pension arrangement are relatively modest, this may also be the most straightforward option to take.

Generally the managed fund will include a range of different investments, predominantly equity based, and predominantly in the UK, but with some diversification both in terms of asset classes and in geographical terms. Although therefore the use of such a fund can provide the investor who is building up the value of his fund before retirement with a similar spread to that which they might choose on their own, managed funds are much less suitable in relation to post–retirement investment for income withdrawal purposes.

Generally in such a situation a mix of assets is chosen, but with a view to taking withdrawals from secure investments should market conditions make encashment of asset backed investments inappropriate. Where the individual diversifies their portfolio across a range of the insurer's funds, this can be achieved, but a managed fund is a 'bundled' investment, which cannot be separated into its constituent parts. Encashment must therefore be of units in the managed fund as a whole, and the isolation of, for example, the deposit element is not possible.

The cost of investing in a managed fund is generally modest in that there may be no extra charges in addition to those on the underlying funds in which the managed fund invests. In these circumstances, there is in effect no additional charge for the manager's role in determining asset allocation.

With profit funds   7.33

Some insurance companies (but not all) offer a with profit fund as an alternative to a more straightforward managed fund as described above. The broad intention of such funds is to allow investors to share in the growth of a fund invested in a diversified range of asset classes, but to smooth out the fluctuations in value which assets such as equities inevitably display.

The underlying range of asset classes, and the proportions of the portfolio invested in each, vary widely. Generally there will be a substantial equity proportion, but also holdings of gilts, corporate bonds, cash deposits and, in many cases, commercial property.

Generally, the with profit arrangements currently available are based on a unitised with profit fund, where the individual's holding is expressed as a number of units, in much the same way as with a unit linked fund. However the price of units is determined by the insurance company, rather than directly by the value of the underlying assets. The insurance company smooths investment returns by holding back some of the growth achieved in positive investment conditions and placing this in its reserves. Whilst this is occurring, the unit price will increase, but will do so more slowly than the increase in value of the underlying assets.

In poor investment conditions, the insurance company is able to support the price of units by reducing reserves. In these circumstances, the unit price will continue to increase, even though the value of the underlying assets may be reducing.

The smoothing effect is underpinned by the insurance company guaranteeing that the price of units within the with profit fund will not reduce, so that growth once added cannot subsequently be lost. However though this is a desirable feature from the point of view of many investors, it means that the growth passed on through increases in the unit price must be pitched at a conservative level, which the insurance company feels comfortable in guaranteeing.

To bring overall returns to a level which relates more closely to the investment results actually achieved, it is normal practice to pay a terminal bonus when units are encashed. The level of terminal bonus will often be related to the length of time money has been invested in the fund, but where a lengthy term is involved, the terminal bonus can be very substantial. It is not however guaranteed in advance, and may be reduced or withdrawn at any time.

A with profit fund will have a natural appeal to the more cautious investor who wants to enjoy the prospect of a favourable return, but wishes to reduce the risk compared to investments in funds where the unit price is directly related to the value to the underlying assets.

However with profit funds also have their difficulties, and following the Myners and Sandler reviews of financial services and products, which criticised the basis of such funds, their operation is now being reconsidered. There are various problem areas, though their importance to individual investors will vary, for example:

(a) detailed information regarding the assets of the fund is often not available, making it difficult for investors and their advisers to judge the suitability of any particular fund, and its comparative position with other such funds;

(b) the rate of growth in unit values is determined by the insurance company at its discretion, and essentially reflects the extent to which the insurer is prepared to guarantee growth already achieved, but the basis for deciding this rate is generally not disclosed;

(c) the extent to which the expected total return to the investor relies on terminal bonuses may be very substantial, but terminal bonuses are not guaranteed in advance and can change at short notice, making the total return itself unpredictable; and

(d) the basis of determining the terminal bonus is generally also not disclosed, so changes may be unpredictable.

Market Value Reduction   7.34

A further difficulty in relation to with profit funds is that although the unit price is guaranteed not to reduce, the insurance company will generally have the discretion to encash units at a price lower than the normal (guaranteed) price if the encashment occurs earlier than expected, perhaps to switch to an alternative fund. Such an adjustment, often called a Market Value Reduction (MVR) can be applied where market conditions are poor, and the guaranteed unit price is being supported from reserves.

The intention of applying the MVR is to prevent investors taking advantage of such situations to encash units at the guaranteed price, in order to purchase units in an ordinary unit linked fund, whilst prices are low. If this were permitted without the application of an MVR, the encashment price would have been supported by other investors in the fund, because a disproportionate share in the reserves would have been used.

The MVR, if in operation, will generally be applied to switches, and to transfers to other providers, but will not apply on retirement or death. The interpretation of 'retirement' may vary from insurer to insurer, and for some will mean the date originally indicated at outset when the individual expected to retire, whilst for others it will mean any point at which retirement benefits are taken.

Investors will be made aware if an MVR is in operation at the time that they seek to encash, and will be able to reconsider their decision in the light of the MVR position. However the basis for the decision by the insurance company as to whether the MVR is to apply is another feature of with profit investment which is generally not disclosed.

Overall then, although the concept of with profit funds is reasonably straightforward, its detailed operation can be difficult for individual investors to understand. Although the concept will appeal to more cautious investors, the considerable discretion available to insurance companies can make ultimate performance very unpredictable.

In times of strong market performance, because of the need to build reserves against weaker investment conditions, it is likely that a with profit fund will underperform funds which are directly linked to the value of the underlying assets. Conversely in weak conditions, the ability of the with profit fund to draw on reserves will improve its performance relative to asset linked funds. It is nevertheless generally true that guarantees cost money, and investors who are not risk averse may be better choosing a normal unit linked fund, where unit prices directly reflect asset values.

With profit funds have been widely recommended and used in conjunction with income withdrawal portfolios and in some ways the concept helps to remove some of the risks involved, particularly the difficulty of taking withdrawals from an investment fund where values are fluctuating. However the view is widely held that the need to maintain reserves is likely to mean that, over the long term, the returns available from these funds are unlikely to reach the levels of critical yield commonly required to make income withdrawals a viable method of improving overall income levels.

In addition, as with unit-linked managed funds (see section **7.32** above), the with profit fund, although itself diversified, is bundled, and the individual constituents cannot be separately encashed.

Impact of financial strength 7.35

The financial strength of the insurance company concerned, which broadly means the extent of its reserves relative to its liabilities, is a further important influence on with profit performance. The extent of reserves is an indication of the ability of the insurance company to support future growth rates within the with profit fund, and therefore gives an indication of the likelihood that growth rates will be maintained. It is also true that when reserves fall, in order to back guarantees, the insurance company must move assets out of equities and into more secure investments, for example gilts and deposits. This can place a considerable constraint on its investment decisions, and its ability to achieve positive performance. This factor can also put long term pressure on the rate of return which can be passed on to investors.

In the past it has often been the case that investors and advisers have placed great reliance on reviewing the financial strength of the insurance company in deciding whether its with profit fund should be recommended. Whilst it remains true that financial strength is an important aspect of any with profit fund, there are many other factors which must be taken into account, including asset allocation, historic rates of growth in unit price, policy as regards the balance between unit growth and terminal bonus, and policy regarding the application of MVRs.

Unit trust and OEIC schemes 7.36

Personal pensions can also be provided by the managers of unit trusts and the ACDs of OEICs. These are often very flexible and useful arrangements offering the opportunity to invest in a wide range of funds, and sometimes with a greater number of specialist funds than would be available through an insurance company.

Some investors will be attracted to these arrangements by the investment management skills available, or by the specialist funds. However the availability of a with profit fund, as might be the case under an insurance company's personal pension scheme, cannot be matched, because there is no ability to build up reserves in the way that an insurance company can.

Unit trust and OEIC schemes are sometimes cheaper in terms of charges than insured schemes, particularly when contributions are paid on a regular basis. However, since the advent of stakeholder pensions, and the related CAT standards (see section **1.23**), there is much less difference in this area.

Similarly, whereas many insured arrangements in the past have had restrictions on the extent to which contribution levels could be changed or contributions could be missed, and also often penalties when benefits were drawn before anticipated retirement age, this is now much less common. Unit trust and OEIC related arrangements are generally very flexible however, with no constraints on changes in contribution levels (other than legislative limits) and no penalties on early retirement.

Investment trust schemes   7.37

Investment trust companies and groups may also market personal pension arrangements, though investment trust companies are not amongst the group of approved pension providers (see section **1.20**).

In general, these arrangements are established with a bank or insurance company acting as pension provider, but essentially providing the shell within which individuals can invest in the investment trust or range of investment trusts involved.

Investment trusts offer a further way in which individuals can access a collective investment linked to equities, with a number of differentiating features. Because investment trusts are constituted as companies, they can issue different classes of shares, each with different rights over the income and capital returns generated from the underlying investment portfolio. This can provide a useful addition set of options for investors seeking to structure their portfolio in relation to their specific needs and wishes.

These arrangements are often very competitive in terms of charges and also very flexible.

Investment trusts are also permitted to gear, in the sense of borrowing for investment purposes. This ability is not available to the managers of other collective investments. Borrowing provides the potential for a greatly enhanced investment return in positive market conditions, but carries significant risk if market conditions are poor.

Example – Effect of gearing

Suppose the total assets within an investment trust are £10 million. The fund manager believes that the equity market is about to rise dramatically, and feels confident that it will show a 20% increase in value over 12 months. They borrow to increase their exposure, at an interest rate of 10% over a year.

Suppose they borrow £5 million, and their prediction of a market rise is correct.

The asset value (including the loan) is initially £15 million, and given a 20% increase, this would rise to £18 million over the year. The loan, plus interest (£5.5 million) must be repaid, leaving net assets of £12.5 million.

The increase in asset value has been 25%, although the market has increased by only 20%. This should be reflected in the share price, and the effect may be enhanced if the outperformance relative to the market results in increased demand for shares in this investment trust relative to others.

However, if the market moves against the manager, the effect can be very damaging. Suppose, with the same level of gearing, the market falls by 20%.

The asset value (including the loan) will fall from £15 million to £12 million, and after repaying the loan and interest, the net assets amount to just £6.5 million. The reduction is 35%, though the market fall has been just 20%.

This could also affect market sentiment, and could mean that the share price fell by more than 35%, to reflect not only the reduction in asset values, but also a fall in demand for the shares.

There is no restriction on the extent to which investment trusts can gear, other than anything contained in the trust's own memorandum and articles. The greater the extent of gearing, the greater the potential reward becomes, but the greater the risk too.

Example – High levels of gearing

Suppose in our last example, the investment trust manager borrows £10 million, again at 10% interest.

Assuming an increase of 20% in the market, the asset value (including the loan) will increase from £20 million to £24 million. The net asset value (after repaying the loan of £10 million plus interest of £1 million) will therefore have increased from £10 million to £13 million, an increase of 30%.

However, if the market falls by 20%, the £20 million will reduce to £16 million, and after repayment of the loan, the net asset value will have fallen from £10 million to £5 million. The net asset value has therefore halved as a result of a 20% market fall.

Split capital trusts 7.38

Split capital investment trusts offer the opportunity to invest in different classes of share within the investment trust. Each class has different rights in relation to overall returns, and for example, some shares may have an increased entitlement to the income generated by the total assets of the trust, but a limited (or non-existent) right to benefit from capital growth. The structure of these trusts varies widely and the precise terms need to be considered with care.

In addition, there will be a specific order in which the shares are redeemed on the winding-up of the investment trust. A low priority on winding up will increase the level of risk involved in most cases.

Zero dividend preference shares (known as zeros) may be useful within an income withdrawal portfolio. These shares provide a return entirely in the form of capital growth, at the point when the investment trust winds up. No income is received in the meantime. These shares have a predetermined target redemption value, and this can provide a low risk, known return. The zero holders are paid out before holders of other share classes (but after borrowings), and the target redemption value will be paid in full provided the assets of the trust as a whole are sufficient.

They may therefore be suitable to provide for withdrawals in the short to medium term, subject to the precise timing of winding-up. Competitive levels of return can be achieved in some cases, though there is risk involved in that the target redemption value will not be paid in full if the assets of the trust are insufficient. A hurdle rate is calculated, which gives the annualised rate of return needed to redemption date in order to enable the trust to pay zeros out in full. The lower this is, the lower the risk involved. A negative hurdle rate means that the assets of the trust already exceed the value needed, and could fall at the hurdle rate without preventing a full pay out to zero holders.

However, if the trust employs gearing, this can affect the potential returns as discussed in section **7.37** above, so the risk still needs careful evaluation. Indeed, events over the last two or three years have highlighted the risk involved.

Self-invested personal pensions   7.39

The concept of self-invested personal pensions (SIPPs) is to allow the individual investor the opportunity to control the investment of their pension fund to a far greater extent than is possible when using insurance company funds or collective investments as described above.

There are a number of attractions in using this route, but the Inland Revenue also imposes a number of restrictions. These are particularly concerned with the type of investments which can be made, and these must conform with the requirements of the *Personal Pension Schemes (Restriction on Discretion to Approve) (Permitted Investments) Regulations 2001 (SI2001/117)*. These regulations came into force on 6 April 2001.

There must still be a personal pension provider, which must be amongst the normal permitted group (see section **1.20**). The distinguishing feature of SIPPS is that the member is in a position to control the individual investment decisions if he so wishes (as distinct from merely controlling the choice of fund). The Inland Revenue has published a list of the permitted and prohibited investments as part of its guidance notes (IR76) and these lists are reproduced below.

Permitted investments for SIPPS

(a) Stocks and shares listed or dealt in on any Inland Revenue recognised stock exchange (including the AIM), including:
  (i) equities;
  (ii) fixed interest securities issued by governments or other bodies;
  (iii) debenture stock and other loan stock;
  (iv) warrants (for equities);
  (v) permanent interest bearing shares; and
  (vi) convertible securities.

(b) Shares received by a SIPP as a contribution to the scheme (see section **3.4**).

(c) Futures and options, relating to stocks and shares traded on a recognised futures exchange.

(d) Authorised unit trusts resident in the UK and authorised under *Financial Services Act 1986 (FSA 1986)*.

(e) Tax exempt unauthorised unit trusts that do not hold residential property.

(f) Investment trusts.

(g) Stocks and shares in investment trusts purchased and held through investment trust savings schemes or investment plans operated by persons:
  (i) resident in the UK and authorised for that purpose under *FSA 1986*; or
  (ii) resident outside the UK but subject to regulation for that purpose in terms of the *FSA 1986*.

(h) UK based open ended investment companies (OEICs) or FSA recognised EEA member state equivalents (investments limited to stocks and shares or related warrants).

(j) Insurance company managed funds and unit-linked funds, investment policies or unit linked funds of a UK insurance company or an insurance company within the EEC authorised under *Article 6* of the (*First Life Insurance Directive 79/267/EEC*).

(k) Endowment policies traded by a FSA regulated person (TEPs).

(l) Deposit accounts held with any UK based deposit taker (as defined in *section 481(2), ICTA 1988*) in any currency.

(m) Commercial property (including land whether development land, farmland or forestry) in or outside the UK including:
  (i) hotels and motels;
  (ii) guest houses;

(iii)   nursing homes; and

(iv)   public houses.

(*n*)   Borrowing to finance the purchase or development of a commercial property, or to pay for VAT liability arising from the purchase or development of any such property.

(*o*)   Undertaking for Collective Investment in Transferable Securities (UCITS) that is either a recognised scheme or a designated scheme within the meaning of *section 86* or *87* of the *FSA 1986*.

(*p*)   Ground rents.

(*q*)   Depositary Interests (including CREST Depositary Interests).

(*r*)   Individual Pension Accounts (IPAs).

Source: *Inland Revenue Guidance Notes (IR76).*

Prohibited investments for SIPPS

Prohibited investments include:

(*a*)   Premium bonds.

(*b*)   Loans to any party.

(*c*)   Milk quotas.

(*d*)   Fishing quotas.

(*e*)   Residential property (except as an element of commercial property as specified in 11.17 of Part 11).

(*f*)   Gold bullion.

(*g*)   Shares traded on OFEX.

(*h*)   Unlisted shares (except in a site maintenance company, for the necessary extent needed to purchase a commercial property and those received as contributions in [certain circumstances – see section **3.4**]).

(*j*)   Personal chattels (e.g. paintings, antiques, fine wine and jewellery).

(*k*)   Borrowing other than [for specific purposes such as property purchase or development].

Source: *Inland Revenue Guidance Notes (IR76).*

These particular restrictions apply to investments which are 'member directed', in other words where they are directly decided upon by the member. They do not apply where the member chooses (as they can do) to invest wholly or partly in insured funds or collective investments, provided these arrangements are generally available and not funds developed solely for the use of that individual or by connected persons. This means that the restrictions would apply to an insured SIPP, if this is an arrangement where a personalised fund is established within a unit linked policy, such that the member determines the investments which will be held within the fund.

A connected person for this purpose is as defined in *section 839* of the *Income and Corporation Taxes Act 1988 (ICTA 1988)*, which is reproduced below.

Definition – Connected person

The following is the text of *s 839 of the ICTA 1988*:

'(1) For the purposes of, and subject to, the provisions of the Tax Acts which apply to this section, any question whether a person is connected with another shall be determined in accordance with the following provisions of this section (any provision that one person is connected with another being taken to mean that they are connected with one another).

(2) A person is connected with an individual if that person is the individual's wife or husband, or is a relative, or the wife or husband of a relative, of the individual or of the individual's wife or husband.

(3) A person, in his capacity as trustee of a settlement, is connected with—

   (a) any individual who in relation to the settlement is a settlor,
   (b) any person who is connected with such an individual, and
   (c) any body corporate which is connected with that settlement.

   In this subsection "settlement" and "settlor" have the same meaning as in *Chapter IA of Part XV* (see *Section 660G(1)* and *(2)*).

(3A) For the purpose of subsection *(3)* above a body corporate is connected with a settlement if:–

   (a) it is a close company (or only not a close company because it is not resident in the United Kingdom) and the participators include the trustees of the settlement; or
   (b) it is controlled (within the meaning of *Section 840*) by a company falling within paragraph (a) above.

(4) Except in relation to acquisitions or disposals of partnership assets pursuant to bona fide commercial arrangements, a person is connected with any person with whom he is in partnership, and with the wife or husband or relative of any individual with whom he is in partnership.

(5) A company is connected with another company –

   (a) if the same person has control of both, or a person has control of one and persons connected with him, or he and persons connected with him, have control of the other; or

---

(b) if a group of two or more persons has control of each company, and the groups either consist of the same persons or could be regarded as consisting of the same persons by treating (in one or more cases) a member of either group as replaced by a person with whom he is connected.

(6) A company is connected with another person if that person has control of it or if that person and persons connected with him together have control of it.

(7) Any two or more persons acting together to secure or exercise control of a company shall be treated in relation to that company as connected with one another and with any person acting on the directions of any of them to secure or exercise control of the company.

(8) In this section —

"company" includes any body corporate or unincorporated association, but does not include a partnership, and this section shall apply in relation to any unit trust scheme as if the scheme were a company and as if the rights of the unit holders were shares in the company;

"control" shall be construed in accordance with *Section 416*; and

"relative" means brother, sister, ancestor or lineal descendant.

In relation to any period during which *Section 470(2)* has effect the reference above to a unit trust scheme shall be construed as a reference to a unit trust scheme within the meaning of the *Prevention of Fraud (Investments) Act 1958* or the *Prevention of Fraud (Investments) Act (Northern Ireland) 1940.'*

Sole purpose 7.40

The basis of the Inland Revenue's concern is to ensure that the sole purpose of the SIPP remains the provision of retirement benefits rather than tax avoidance.

The Inland Revenue will therefore look very carefully at certain types of investment. Two examples are given in the *Personal Pension Schemes Guidance Notes (IR76)*. The first is where a SIPP acquires land which is adjacent to land or property owned by a member of the SIPP, or a connected person. The Inland Revenue will seek to ensure that no special advantage is gained as a result of the purchase by the SIPP.

The second is where the SIPP buys (as it can) a leisure property, such as a golf course, leisure centre or bowling alley. Here the Inland Revenue will seek to ensure that these facilities are not made available to members at anything other than a normal commercial rate.

For similar reasons, the SIPP is not permitted to buy investments from, nor sell them to, a member or connected person except in very particular circumstances. One exception is where the SIPP buys a commercial property, and it is then leased for business purposes to a member, or to a company connected with the member. Any such arrangement must be on normal commercial terms, and a commercial rent must be payable. The amount of the rent must be supported by an independent professional valuation.

Note that although the property can be leased to a member in this way, it cannot initially be purchased from the member, nor may it at any stage be sold to the member.

Advantages of property investment   7.41

Investment in a property in this way is an extremely attractive use of a SIPP, and is often the main driving force in the establishment of such an arrangement. The benefits largely flow from the tax advantages of pensions generally, including the fact that contributions to the scheme, which provide all or part of the finance for the property purchase, will have attracted full tax relief. In addition, any capital gain made on the property whilst within the SIPP will be free of tax.

The rent paid will be tax deductible for the member's business, and will be received without tax liability within the SIPP, and will further boost the fund. The rent is part of the investment return generated by the SIPP, and does not form part of the contribution limit for the member.

Care is necessary in the sense that property is a relatively illiquid investment, and there is clearly a lack of diversification where the property forms a major part of the fund as a whole. There can be further problems where the property is vital to the business, and would lose value if the business failed. The individual would need to consider whether too much of their current and future wealth is tied into the one business.

In addition, it may be necessary to sell the property at retirement in order to provide benefits. This may be difficult, both for commercial reasons and perhaps because of market conditions at the time. This is an event which needs to be planned for carefully in advance. Nevertheless, the tax advantages are substantial.

Residential property   7.42

Residential property is generally not permitted to be held within a SIPP, though when a commercial property includes a small residential element, for example a caretaker's flat, this would be acceptable. The Inland Revenue would require that the residential accommodation be an integral or associated part of the commercial property rather than something separate and free-standing.

Property such as a hotel or guest house, or a nursing home, would be permitted and would be regarded as a commercial property for this purpose. Once again however members or connected persons must not be permitted to use the facilities except on normal commercial terms.

It is not however permissible for the SIPP to purchase a residential property, even where there is planning permission for conversion to residential use.

Loans   7.43

SIPPS are not permitted to make loans in any circumstances. There is no equivalent to the facility which exists under small self-administered occupational pension schemes, which are permitted in limited circumstances to lend to the sponsoring employer.

The SIPP can however borrow money, and this will often be necessary to allow the SIPP to purchase property. Property purchase and development are the only purposes for which long term borrowing by a SIPP is permitted.

There is also a strict limit on the amount of any such borrowing. This limit is 75% of the purchase price (which can include related costs such as legal fees) or the cost of the development. Where the ownership of the property is shared with another party (which cannot be a member or a connected person) the borrowing limit for the SIPP will be 75% of the appropriate share of the cost.

It is permitted to replace a loan originally taken for one of these purposes, though the amount of the loan cannot be increased, even if the value of the property has risen. The loan must be repaid if the property is sold.

Restrictions on property investment   7.44

Note that it is not permitted for any new investment in land or property to be made once the member has reached the age of 65, or, if later, the pension date, ie the date on which they elect to commence retirement benefits.

Transitional arrangements   7.45

The 75% limitation on loans was introduced with effect from 6 April 2001, and there will be some arrangements which were then already in force and where larger loans had already been taken before the limitation was applied. Prior to this date there were no limits other than those applied by lenders, and it was also possible to borrow for purposes other than property purchase and development.

Such loans are permitted by the Inland Revenue to stand, notwithstanding the change in practice resulting from the regulations referred to above.

Other investments 7.46

Often the attraction of a SIPP is to give the investor control over the fund, but for this to be used to determine the choice of more conventional investments, such as equities, gilts and other fixed interest securities and deposits. The advantages of these investment areas were discussed earlier in this chapter in relation to insured funds.

The individual investor needs the time and the knowledge to make these decisions, or must obtain suitable investment advice.

8 — Death Before Retirement

Introduction 8.1

On the death of a member of a personal pension scheme, the accumulated fund is available to provide benefits for the member's spouse, dependants or (in some circumstances) for others.

In some cases, benefits must be provided wholly or partly in the form of income. These situations can arise where the personal pension arrangement contains protected rights, or where a transfer value has been received from an occupational pension scheme. The detailed provisions regarding these circumstances are covered in sections **8.11** and **8.12** below respectively.

It is also possible for the member to make specific arrangements which require benefits to be paid in income form on their death. Otherwise, it will generally be possible to choose whether to use the fund to provide income, or to pay the benefit as a lump sum.

Income benefit 8.2

The range of individuals for whom income benefits can be provided following the death of a member is restricted to the member's spouse and/or dependants.

'Spouse' means a legally married spouse at the date of death, and does not automatically extend to include common law spouses or same sex partners (though both these groups are likely to fall within the definition of dependants).

The term 'dependant' means someone who was financially dependent on the member at the time of the member's death. The Inland Revenue accepts that an unmarried partner of the member would be regarded as fulfilling this criterion if the couple were financially interdependent. This would cover a situation where the couple relied on their joint incomes to support their standard of living.

There is no difference in the Inland Revenue's treatment of partners whether of the same or opposite sex.

> ### Example – Unmarried partner
>
> Two men live together as a couple, and have done so for some years. Both work, and earn similar levels of salary.
>
> They bought the house in which they live in joint names, using a mortgage from a building society, also in joint names. They share living expenses, such as food and utility bills, though each has a separate bank account.
>
> One is a member of a personal pension scheme, and dies before taking retirement benefits. His partner would be regarded as being within the definition of a dependant, because although he was not financially dependent on the deceased, the couple were financially independent.

Where the member had been legally married but became divorced before death, and was making maintenance payments to their ex-spouse at the time of their death, the ex-spouse would be regarded as being dependent.

Children   8.3

Children are automatically regarded as falling within the definition of dependant if at the time of the member's death they were either:

(*a*)   under the age of 18;
(*b*)   over the age of 18 but still in full-time education or vocational training; or
(*c*)   dependent on the member because of disability.

Income benefits provided for children must generally cease when the child reaches the age of 18, or (if later) ceases full-time education. (In this chapter, the term 'education' should be read as including vocational training.) Note that there is no upper age limit for payment of the income benefit provided full-time education is continuing. Also, where the child is dependent because of disability, the income benefit can continue indefinitely, potentially throughout the child's life.

Where a child takes a gap year between school and further education, this will not be regarded as a cessation of education in this context. The break however must be for not more than one academic year, and the place in full-time education must have been confirmed. It is possible for income benefits for the dependant to be continued in these circumstances through the gap year, but it is also permitted for the benefit to be suspended until the recommencement of education or vocational training. This is a matter for the rules of the personal pension scheme.

The decision as to whether a particular individual qualifies as a dependant of the member is for the trustees or scheme administrator to make in the light of the scheme rules. The Inland Revenue will not normally challenge their judgement.

The term 'survivors' is used to include both a spouse and any dependants of the member.

Survivor annuity 8.4

Where an annuity is provided for a survivor, it will generally be payable from the date of the member's death, and will continue for the lifetime of the survivor. There are however a number of exceptions to this general rule.

As discussed in section **8.3** above, an annuity paid to a dependent child must cease at the later of the attainment of age 18 or cessation of full-time education, unless the child concerned is dependent on the member as a result of disability.

With an annuity which is being provided for the widow or widower of the member (but not if it is provided for any other survivor), it is possible for the commencement of the annuity to be deferred under *section 636(5)* of the *Income and Corporation Taxes Act 1988 (ICTA 1988)* to a time not later than the widow or widower's 60th birthday. This may be appropriate if the surviving spouse has other resources, or has a source of income in their own right which would support them until they reach age 60. However, should the surviving spouse die before reaching the date when the annuity becomes payable, there can be no lump sum death benefit payable, and the fund would be lost. The payment of such a lump sum is specifically ruled out under *s 637A(2)(c), ICTA 1988*.

Types of annuity 8.5

An annuity provided for a survivor can be provided on a level basis, or can include escalation or index linking, or can be investment linked. These types of annuity are covered in more detail in **Chapter 5: Retirement Benefits**. As with annuities provided for a member at retirement, there is no limitation, from a legal or Inland Revenue point of view, on the extent to which the annuity can increase in payment. In practice, maximum levels of escalation available in the market place will reflect current inflation expectations.

It is possible for the survivor's annuity to be guaranteed payable for a minimum period of up to ten years, even if the survivor dies before the end of that period. Where death occurs during the guarantee period, the annuity will continue to be paid until the end of the guarantee period. There are no circumstances where these payments can be commuted for a lump sum, irrespective of the length of the guarantee period.

Where the survivor's pension is subject to a guarantee, the right to the outstanding instalments may be assigned by will, or in the distribution of the estate under the intestacy rules, but otherwise must be non-assignable, non-commutable and non-surrenderable.

Limitation   8.6

The total amount of all annuities paid to survivors must not exceed the total amount that could have been provided for the member had they retired the day before their death. This limitation is contained in *s 636(3)(b), ICTA 1988* and the limitation is calculated on the assumption that no part of the member's benefit would have been given up to provide a cash lump sum.

Income withdrawals   8.7

A survivor who is entitled to an annuity can instead elect to take benefits in the form of income withdrawals. (Under *s 636A(1), ICTA 1988*, note that this choice lies with the survivor, not the trustees or scheme administrator.)

Income withdrawals may generally continue until the earlier of

(*a*)   the survivor's 75th birthday; and
(*b*)   the date on which the deceased member would have reached age 75.

An annuity must be purchased no later than this point, though the survivor may choose to stop taking income withdrawals and purchase an annuity earlier, if they so wish.

However, if the survivor's annuity would not have been payable for life, then income withdrawals must also cease at the time when the annuity would have ceased. This will often apply if the recipient of the income withdrawals is a minor child and in this case income withdrawals must cease by age 18, or if later, the cessation of full-time education, unless the child is dependent because of incapacity.

This situation can also arise where an annuity payable to a surviving spouse would have ceased in the event of remarriage, and then the income withdrawals must also cease on remarriage.

The minimum and maximum levels of income withdrawals are calculated on a similar basis to that which applies where a member takes income withdrawals in retirement. The maximum level of withdrawal is 100% of the annuity calculated on Government Actuary's Department (GAD) rates, based on the age and sex of the survivor. The minimum withdrawal is 35% of the maximum.

Full detail of the operation of income withdrawal limits is given in **Chapter 6: Income Withdrawals**.

Death of survivor whilst taking income withdrawals   8.8

If the survivor dies whilst in receipt of income withdrawals, the remaining fund will be paid as a lump sum. Because the income withdrawals arose on the death of the member before taking retirement benefits, this lump sum is free of tax.

The payment of this lump sum can be made to a range of beneficiaries, which is not restricted to the member's spouse and dependants.

The conditions for payment are the same as those relating to the distribution of a lump sum on the death of the member themself before taking retirement benefits, and these are covered in section **8.10** below.

Death whilst annuity deferred to 60   8.9

Note that where a spouse has elected to defer the payment of an annuity until a time not later than age 60 (see section **8.4** above), this benefit can only be taken in the form of an annuity, and it is not permitted to take income withdrawals as an alternative.

Lump sum on death   8.10

If there is no requirement for benefits payable as a result of the member's death before retirement to be provided as income, they can be paid as a lump sum.

Where a lump sum is payable, it can be:

(*a*)   paid to the member's legal personal representatives;
(*b*)   paid to a beneficiary nominated by the member;
(*c*)   paid under the terms of a trust established by the member; or
(*d*)   distributed at the discretion of the scheme administrator.

Usually the benefit will be paid at the discretion of the scheme administrator and this is both simple and flexible. Payment can be made quickly following receipt by the scheme administrator of proof of the member's death, and the benefit will not form part of the member's estate for tax or legal purposes. In particular, there will generally be no inheritance tax liability (but see section **8.22** below) and there will be no need to await the grant of probate on the estate of the deceased.

Generally, as part of the application process for the personal pension, a member is asked to give details of those to whom they would wish payment to be made in the event of their death. This information, often referred to as a 'letter of wishes', or 'expression of wish' is intended to guide the scheme administrator in the exercise of discretion. However, the member's wishes are not binding on the administrator.

The member may change their letter of wishes at any time, and because the letter is not binding, it creates no rights, and there are no inheritance tax implications of any such change.

Some personal pension arrangements allow the member to choose to make a binding nomination, but if this is the case, the benefits would be regarded as part of the estate for inheritance tax purposes. An inheritance tax liability on the estate could arise, or be increased, as a result. Once made, such a nomination is irrevocable.

In general, payment of benefits is made rapidly following death, but it is permitted for the money to be held under the rules of the scheme for a period of up to two years if the scheme administrator is unable to decide to whom benefit should be payable. If interest accrues on the money during this period, it can also be paid out as part of the lump sum, without any liability to income tax. If payment is not made within two years, the remaining fund must be transferred outside of the scheme to a separate account.

Where the personal pension arrangements are set up on a contract basis, it is possible for the benefits to be made subject to a trust established by the member. In these circumstances, on the member's death before taking retirement benefits, the trustees would receive the death benefits and would apply them as required under the terms of the trust. The terms of the trust must be that, if the member survives, the retirement benefits are the member's. (It is not possible for the trust to relate to the death benefits alone.)

Protected rights   8.11

Where the member is contracted out of the State Second Pension (S2P), or was in the past contracted out of the State Earnings Related Pension Scheme (SERPS) by means of a personal pension, they will have built up protected rights within the arrangement. This is covered in detail in **Chapter 12: Contracting Out**.

Where the member dies before retirement benefits are taken, the protected rights benefits cannot be paid as a lump sum if there is a surviving spouse. In the past, the requirement that benefits must be in income form applied only if there was a qualifying survivor (ie essentially a widow or widower of the member who is either over 45 or who is entitled to child benefit in respect of a child of their marriage). However, the requirement now applies whenever there is a surviving spouse.

Exceptionally, the protected rights benefits can be paid as a lump sum on grounds of triviality if the annuity payable to the surviving spouse would otherwise be £260 *per annum* or less. The payment in these circumstances must be made to the surviving spouse, but would be free of income tax.

If there is no surviving spouse, then the protected rights benefits can be paid in lump sum form (irrespective of their value), and would be paid in accordance with any direction given by the member in writing or otherwise to the member's estate.

Protected rights are generally held in a separate personal pension arrangement. If other contributions are being made by the member and/or the member's employer, these will usually be held in one or more separate arrangements.

However, where protected rights and non-protected rights are held within a single arrangement and the member dies leaving a surviving spouse, the requirement to pay benefits in income form will apply to the whole fund, not just the protected rights portion.

There is an exception to this rule where all or part of the non-protected rights portion arises from the receipt of a transfer value. In this case (subject to the rules of the personal pension) the non-protected rights may be paid as a lump sum.

Effect of transfers   8.12

In some circumstances, where the personal pension has received a transfer from an occupational pension scheme, restrictions will apply to the ability of the scheme to pay death benefits in lump sum form.

These restrictions will apply only where the individual is a regulated individual in relation to the employment from which the transfer value arose.

Regulated Individuals   8.13

Regulated individuals are those to whom the certification requirement in connection with transfers applies, and the definition is covered in detail in section **5.13**. However, an individual who was a controlling director of the company from whose scheme the transfer value was paid, either at the time of transfer or at any time in the preceding ten years falls within the definition.

So too does any other individual who was aged over 45 at the date of the transfer and whose earnings for any year of assessment falling wholly or partly within the period of six years prior to the date of transfer are, or were, more than the earnings cap at its level for the year in which the transfer took place.

The restriction on lump sum death benefits applies only if:

(*a*)   the individual dies before taking retirement benefits;
(*b*)   the personal pension arrangement includes all or part of a transfer value in respect of which the member was a regulated individual; and
(*c*)   there is a surviving spouse, or a dependant for whom benefits are specifically provided under the arrangement.

In such cases, the maximum amount which can be paid as a lump sum is 25% of the value of the fund.

Note that in calculating the maximum lump sum, any protected rights benefits may be taken into account, though no part of the protected rights benefits themselves may be taken in the form of cash. If there is no surviving spouse, nor a dependant for whom benefits are specifically provided, the whole of the fund may be paid as a lump sum in the usual way.

Example – Effect of protected rights

An individual dies, aged 53, before taking retirement benefits from his personal pension arrangement. The fund, which was built up entirely from a transfer, amounts to £220,000, of which £30,000 is protected rights. They are survived by their spouse, who is 50 years old.

If they were a regulated individual in respect of the transfer value, the maximum lump sum payable on death would be 25% of £220,000 = £55,000. (This can be paid in full from the non-protected rights fund.)

If they had not been a regulated individual, then the whole of the non-protected rights fund (£190,000) could have been paid as a lump sum.

The protected rights fund cannot be paid as a lump sum, because the individual is survived by their spouse.

Note that in the example above, the prohibition on paying lump sum benefits from an arrangement housing benefits which are partially in the form of protected rights does not apply. This is because the benefits arose from receipt of a transfer value.

Transfers received before 6 April 2001 8.14

Although the certification requirements applicable to transfer values prior to 6 April 2001 were different, and essentially covered a wider range of individuals, it is only necessary to impose the restrictions contained in section **8.13** above where the individual was both:

(*a*) subject to certification requirements at the time of the transfer; and

(*b*) would have been subject to them under the post-6 April 2001 provisions.

If this is not so, benefits may be paid in lump sum form in the normal way.

Multiple arrangements or beneficiaries 8.15

It is possible for a single recipient of benefits to take benefits in different forms from different arrangements, for example taking some benefits in lump sum form, some in the form of an annuity income, and some in the form of income withdrawals.

Similarly, if there is more than one beneficiary under a single arrangement, each beneficiary can (within the restrictions discussed in this chapter) choose to take benefits in different forms. For example, one beneficiary might choose to receive income by means of annuity purchase whilst another chooses income withdrawals.

Income tax position 8.16

Income benefits, whether provided by means of annuity purchase or through income withdrawals, are subject to income tax under Schedule E, the tax being collected through the PAYE system.

Benefits being paid in lump sum form on the member's death before retirement benefits have been taken are payable free of income tax.

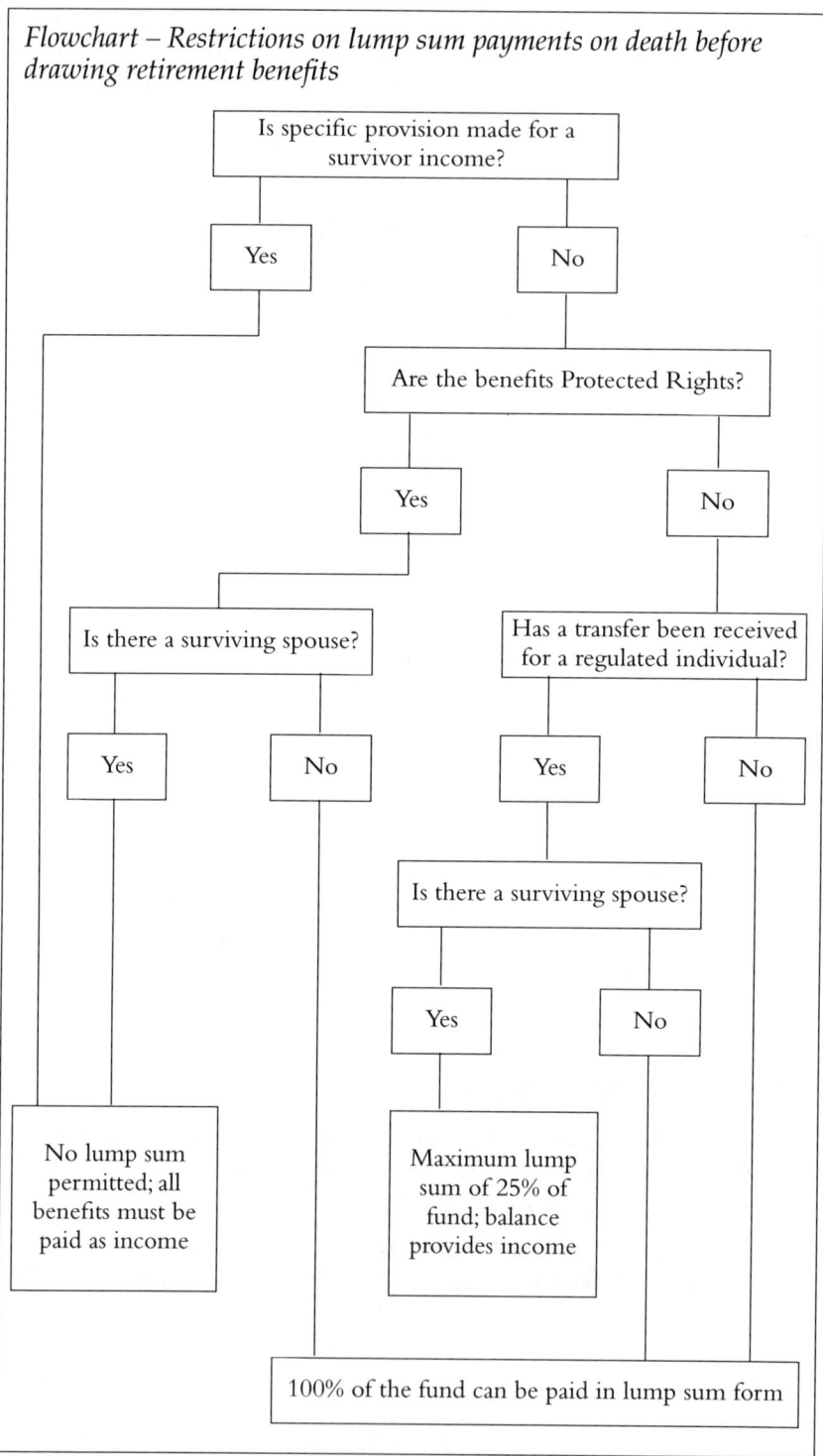

Flowchart – Restrictions on lump sum payments on death before drawing retirement benefits

Term assurance 8.17

It is possible under *s 637, ICTA 1988* to arrange a term assurance contract under personal pension rules. This can be attractive because, subject to limits, the premiums to the term assurance qualify for tax relief in the same way as contributions for retirement benefits.

The term assurance contract must be arranged with an authorised insurance company, and must expire no later than the member's 75th birthday. It can be arranged as a freestanding policy, which will allow it to be assigned (for example to a lender to back a mortgage) or to be written into trust.

Generally, the provision of any term assurance cover is likely to require the member to provide medical evidence to the insurance company concerned.

The level of cover can subsequently be increased, subject to the limits on contributions, and the terms of the contract, including any requirement for further medical evidence.

If the term assurance contract is terminated early, its terms may allow for the cover to be continued under a new policy, not written under personal pension rules. However, the expiry date of the new policy must be no later than that under the original contract.

Limits on contributions for term assurance 8.18

The limitation on contributions for term assurance was changed with effect from 6 April 2001, but the old (pre-6 April 2001) basis continues to apply where the term assurance came into effect before that date.

In addition, where a personal pension arrangement was established before 6 April 2001, and included the option for the member to activate term assurance cover (even if it was not activated at the time) the old rules will also apply. It does not matter when the term assurance cover is activated (even if on or after 6 April 2001), nor whether the activation is dependent on the provision of satisfactory medical evidence.

Limits: arrangements established before 6 April 2001 8.19

The limitation on the amount which can be paid towards the provision of term assurance under the pre-6 April 2001 rules is 5% of the individual's net relevant earnings.

Note that the limit does not change with age, so the level of life assurance cover which can be obtained reduces at older ages, because premium rates become more expensive.

Also, total contributions paid by the member, including those for life assurance benefits, must lie within normal limits. Life assurance contributions therefore reduce the scope for the individual to fund for retirement benefits.

> ### Example – Life cover contribution limit (pre-6 April 2001 basis)
>
> A 38-year-old has a pre-6 April 2001 term assurance contract under personal pension rules. In 2003/04 their net relevant earnings are £30,000.
>
> The maximum they can pay in contributions to the term assurance contract is 5% of £30,000 = £1,500.
>
> The maximum the individual can pay in total to personal pension arrangements, for retirement and death benefits, is 20% of £30,000 = £6,000.
>
> Suppose the individual pays £1,000 to the term assurance contract. The maximum they can then pay for retirement benefits is £6,000 less £1,000 = £5,000.

Note that under the pre-6 April 2001 basis, there is no requirement for the member to be contributing towards retirement benefits in order to establish a term assurance policy. A number of insurance companies offered free-standing term assurance arrangements, which could accommodate this.

Limits: arrangements established on or after 6 April 2001
8.20

The limitation under contracts established on or after 6 April 2001 is that the amount paid for life assurance in any tax year must not exceed 10% of the member's 'relevant pension contributions' in the same tax year.

Relevant pension contributions are those paid towards retirement benefits under personal pension arrangements either by the member or by an employer on the member's behalf.

The formal definition is contained in *s 640(3A), ICTA 1988*, and this states that relevant pension contributions are those '...paid towards securing benefits...under arrangements made under a personal pension scheme on or after 6 April 2001'. This has sometimes been interpreted as meaning that contributions for retirement benefits could only be taken into account if the arrangements to which they are paid were themselves established on or after 6 April 2001. The Revenue has however confirmed that this is not its interpretation, and that the requirement is merely that the contributions for retirement benefits are paid after 6 April 2001.

Once again, total contributions paid by the member, including those for life assurance benefits, must lie within normal limits.

Example – Life cover contribution limit (6 April 2001 and after)

A 49-year-old has net relevant earnings of £33,000 in 2003/04. They pay £2,000 to a personal pension arrangement for retirement benefits. They currently have no term assurance policy under personal pension rules.

If the individual now starts a term assurance policy, the maximum amount they could pay in contributions would be 10% of £2,000 = £200.

Their total contributions of £2,200 lie well within their overall maximum of 25% of £33,000 = £8,250.

Note that in calculating the maximum term assurance premium, as 10% of contributions for retirement benefits, the amount of the contributions which are paid to the term assurance contract itself do not count as contributions for retirement benefits. As a result, if it is intended to maximise life cover benefits, then 1/11th of total contributions can be used for this purpose.

Example – Maximising term assurance premiums

Suppose that the individual in the last example now wants to maximise total personal pension contributions, and to contribute the largest amount possible for life assurance within this.

The maximum total personal pension contribution would be £8,250.

The maximum term assurance premium would be one–eleventh of £8,250 = £750, with £7,500 being paid towards retirement benefits. The term assurance premium is then 10% of the amount paid towards retirement benefits.

Note that where the individual is making contributions at the level of the earnings threshold, perhaps because of low, or zero net relevant earnings, the rules apply in exactly the normal way.

Example – Term assurance within the earnings threshold

An individual has no net relevant earnings, but is eligible to contribute up to the earnings threshold of £3,600.

If they decide to contribute £3,600 in total and want to maximise the term assurance premium within this, they would pay one eleventh of £3,600 = £327 to the term assurance.

They would also make a contribution of £3,273 for retirement benefits.

Although there is no direct link to the age of the individual, as age increases, the maximum limit on personal pension contributions as a percentage of net relevant earnings increases with age (see section **3.7**). Thus the maximum term assurance premium will increase with age if the individual also increases the amount they contribute for pension benefits.

Interaction of limits   8.21

Where an individual has term assurance arrangements under both the old and the new rules, it is possible to pay up to 5% of net relevant earnings to the old arrangement, and 10% of relevant pension contributions to the new.

As always, total contributions for retirement benefits and life assurance must not exceed normal limits.

Example – Interaction of limits

A 44-year-old has net relevant earnings of £38,000 for 2003/04.

During 2003/04, they pay contributions to a number of arrangements as follows:

Personal pension established in 1992:	£2,500
Personal pension term assurance, started in 1994:	£1,000
Personal pension established in 2002:	£2,000
Total	£5,500

Suppose the individual now wants to maximise the amounts they pay for life cover, without increasing contributions for retirement benefits.

The existing term assurance contract is subject to the pre–6 April 2001 rules, so the maximum contribution to it is 5% of £38,000 = £1,900. The individual is already paying £1,000, so they could increase the contribution by a further £900.

> They could also start a new term assurance policy with a contribution of up to 10% of the amount being paid for retirement benefits. This would be 10% of (£2,500 + £2,000) = £450.
>
> If the individual did so, total contributions (£5,500 + £900 + £450) would still be within their overall limit of 20% of £38,000 = £7,600.
>
> Medical evidence is likely to be required in respect of both the increase in cover under the existing policy and the start of cover under the new policy.

Importantly under the new rules, because the limit on contributions for term assurance is based on the contributions being paid for retirement benefits, it is not possible for an individual to arrange a term insurance contract unless they are also contributing for retirement benefits.

Inheritance Tax   8.22

Benefits arising on the death of the member before taking retirement benefits will not generally lead to any Inheritance Tax (IHT) implications.

Where an existing term assurance policy, or a contract based personal pension, is written into trust, the value of the death benefits will usually be regarded as negligible for IHT purposes. However, where this occurs in circumstances where the member is in poor health, care is needed. The Inland Revenue may regard the transfer into the trust as being of significant value in the light of the member's circumstances, and it may therefore create IHT difficulties. No query would usually be raised if the member survived for a period of two years after the transfer.

Note also that where death benefit is paid under a binding nomination made by the member, this will be regarded as part of the estate for IHT purposes.

9 — Incapacity

Introduction 9.1

Retirement benefits under personal pension arrangements are generally only available from the age of 50, but if the member becomes incapacitated, benefits other than protected rights can be taken immediately, irrespective of age, under *section 634(3)(a)* of the *Income and Corporation Taxes Act 1988 (ICTA 1988)*.

Protected rights arise if the individual has been contracted out by means of a personal pension (see **Chapter 12: Contracting Out**) or if the personal pension arrangement has received a transfer value from a contracted out occupational scheme (see section **12.18**). Protected rights cannot be taken earlier than age 60, even in cases of incapacity.

Meaning of incapacity 9.2

The legislation states that benefits can be taken early if the member becomes 'incapable through infirmity of body or mind of carrying on his own occupation or any occupation of a similar nature for which he is trained or fitted'. This is a demanding requirement.

The scheme administrator is required by the Inland Revenue to obtain medical evidence to show that 'the individual has become incapable of carrying on [his] occupation and is unlikely to be able to return to it' (*Inland Revenue Guidance Notes (IR76) para 8.6*).

Form of benefits 9.3

Where benefits are taken early on grounds of incapacity, the usual rules, as discussed in detail in **Chapters 5: Retirement Benefits** and **6: Income Withdrawals** apply to the form in which the benefits can be taken.

A tax free lump sum, generally of 25% of the fund, can be taken at pension date. The remainder of the fund must provide income, either through annuity purchase, or the provision of income withdrawals and the income will be taxed as earned income under PAYE.

Note that there is no provision under personal pension legislation to allow the whole of the fund to be taken in the form of cash, even where the individual is in serious ill-health. This is a significant difference between personal pension and occupational pension provisions. Under the latter, full commutation for cash is allowed if the individual has retired through incapacity and has a life expectancy of less than one year.

There is nothing to prevent benefits being taken on a phased retirement basis (see section **5.5**) if required, in cases of incapacity. It remains true that it is advantageous to leave as much of the fund as possible invested in a tax advantaged environment for as long as possible.

Example – Incapacity

A 42-year-old self-employed roofing contractor is permanently incapacitated following a fall, and can no longer work.

They have contributed to a personal pension arrangement for a number of years, and have built up a fund of £60,000, none of which is protected rights.

The individual can start their retirement benefits immediately. If they do so, they could take up to £15,000 in the form of a tax free cash sum. The remainder of the fund would then be used to purchase an annuity or to provide income withdrawals.

Alternatively, they could phase their retirement. Suppose the individual decided to take immediate benefits from half of the fund. They could take up to £7,500 in cash, and the remaining £22,500 would provide income.

The rest of the fund (£30,000) would remain invested in the normal way. The individual could then choose to take benefits from this at any time up to their 75th birthday.

Practical application   9.4

The facility to draw benefits early in cases of incapacity can be of great value, particularly if the member is close to the age of 50 and has already built up a substantial fund. In these circumstances, the fund may provide an adequate level of income to support the member in their retirement.

In some cases, the member will be able to obtain an impaired life annuity on favourable terms. Annuities of this type, which are discussed in more detail in section **5.34**, may be available where life expectancy is reduced. However, where the member is incapacitated, it does not necessarily mean that life expectancy is markedly reduced. This can mean that the fund is applied at normal annuity rates, reflecting the member's relatively young age, or must sustain income withdrawals for a potentially very long period.

Example – Annuity rates

The examples below are taken from the Government Actuary's Department rate tables, as used for the calculation of income withdrawal limits, and assume a 5% gilt yield. They give an indication of the level annuity, with no survivor's benefits, which could be purchased at various ages, and the figure is also the maximum permitted level of income withdrawal.

The annual income available for a fund of £100,000 would be:

Age	Male	Female
25	£530	£520
35	£560	£540
45	£610	£580
55	£720	£660
65	£910	£810

The situation is made more difficult if the individual is young, and/or has not built up a large fund by the time of their incapacity. In these circumstances, it may be entirely impractical to draw retirement benefits early.

Also, the position is more difficult for females than males, because of their generally longer life expectancy.

Incapacity insurance 9.5

In the past, one way of dealing with the potential difficulties which can arise on incapacity has been to include incapacity insurance within the arrangement. This option is no longer available where arrangements are established on or after 6 April 2001, but it continues to exist under older arrangements.

Up to 25% of the total contributions under such arrangements are permitted to be used for this purpose.

The insurance provides for the benefits from the arrangement to be increased to the level that was expected to be available at the anticipated retirement age selected at outset. This then would ensure that benefits would be realistic, even if incapacity occurs at a young age.

This has never been a complete answer to the problem however. Often contributions start at a relatively low level, and the initial expected benefit level may not therefore be sufficient. Also, the cost is met from the total personal pension contribution, which reduces the amount invested for retirement, and also itself impacts on the level of benefit provided under this form of insurance.

In addition, the cost of the cover was often off-putting for members, and in practice, incapacity insurance has not proved a popular option.

When included, either at outset or at a later date, medical evidence may be required. (An arrangement established before 6 April 2001 may include the option to introduce the insurance later, and this is still permitted, even if the option is not taken up until 6 April 2001 or later.) Medical evidence may also be required at the time of any subsequent increase in cover.

Note that the definition of incapacity used by the insurer may be harsher than that permitted by the Inland Revenue, as discussed in section **9.2** above.

Waiver 9.6

An alternative, and generally more popular approach, is to provide for a waiver of contribution to be included.

The intention here is not to provide for benefits to be taken early if the individual is incapacitated, but instead to provide that the personal pension fund continues to increase in size, even if the individual cannot afford to continue to pay contributions personally. The result is that, in spite of the incapacity, the fund should still be large enough to provide sufficient benefits at retirement.

The basis of operation of waiver was changed with effect from 6 April 2001, but the 'old' basis which applied before that date continues to be relevant, because it still applies to arrangements started before the change was made. We therefore consider both the old and new rules in turn.

Employer contributions 9.7

Note that waiver can cover any employer contributions as well as those paid by the individual member.

Pre-6 April 2001 basis 9.8

The 'old' basis applies where waiver was included in a personal pension arrangement before 6 April 2001. It also applies if an arrangement started before that date included the facility to add waiver later, even if the member only decides to activate it later. The date when the cover is activated is irrelevant, so the old basis would apply if waiver was activated now under an arrangement started before 6 April 2001.

The basis of these arrangements is that the cost of the waiver is built into the personal pension contribution, and so qualifies for tax relief.

The total contribution, including the cost of waiver, must lie within normal limits.

In addition, the cost of waiver, together with the cost of any incapacity insurance (see section **9.5** above) must not exceed 25% of the total contribution to the arrangement(s) concerned.

The cover is written as a true waiver. This means that, in the event of a claim, the individual no longer has to pay contributions, but the personal pension is treated as if contributions were continuing. For example, if the arrangement is unit-linked, additional units would be allocated in exactly the same way as if the contributions were being paid, but no money would be collected from the individual.

This is often described as the product provider paying the contribution on behalf of the member, and this certainly explains the effect. From a technical point of view, the provider is not eligible to make contributions on behalf of the member, so it is important that the provision is documented as a waiver.

Effect on limits and relief 9.9

Two other important effects flow through from the waiver approach. The first is that no tax relief is available on the contributions waived – as nothing is paid, there is nothing to qualify for relief. The waiver must therefore provide for the gross contribution level, not the amount net of basic rate tax relief which the individual would actually have paid.

The second is that the normal eligibility requirements and contribution limits do not apply, again because nothing is actually being paid.

This can be important in practice, because the onset of incapacity will often have changed the member's financial position fundamentally. This may mean that their net relevant earnings might no longer be sufficient to support the level of contributions which had previously been paid. Indeed in many cases, there will no longer be any net relevant earnings at all.

Before 6 April 2001, those with no net relevant earnings could not pay personal pension contributions. If a member ceased to have net relevant earnings as a result of incapacity, they would therefore have to stop paying contributions personally (even if they had the financial resources to continue), and so, if waiver had not been included, they would be forced to forego the tax advantages of pension investment.

Although the situation has eased with the introduction of the earnings threshold, and the ability of non-earners to contribute, difficulties can still arise with limits (see section **9.11** below).

Example – Operation of waiver (pre-April 2001 arrangement)

An individual contributes £300 per month (gross) to a personal pension, which they started in 1988. (They would actually pay £234 net of basic rate relief, with the product provider claiming £66 in tax relief each month.)

The individual has included waiver on the whole amount, and 3% of the contribution is used to pay for this. Their net relevant earnings for 2003/04 are £60,000 and they are 30 years old.

The total contribution (including the cost of the waiver) is £3,600 in 2003/04 and this must lie within the normal contribution limits. In the individual's case, the limit would be 17.5% of £60,000 = £10,500, so this condition is met easily. The cost of waiver is included in the amount of the contribution on which the individual is entitled to relief.

Suppose the individual is incapacitated on 31 May 2004, and their net relevant earnings fall to £20,000 in 2004/05, and £10,000 in 2005/06. They have no net relevant earnings at all thereafter.

The waiver will start to operate (probably after a deferment period – see section **9.17** below), and will provide for the contributions that would have been due from that point onwards. The personal pension will then continue to increase in value as if contributions were being paid. No contributions would be collected from the individual once the waiver starts to operate.

The waiver will provide £300 per month. This cannot be treated as paid net of basic rate tax relief, and there is therefore no reclaim of relief from the Inland Revenue. This follows from the contribution being waived rather than paid.

Contribution limits do not apply for the same reason, so the reduction in their earnings following incapacity does not affect the operation of the waiver.

Basis applicable from 6 April 2001   9.10

As part of the overhaul of the tax treatment of personal pensions from 6 April 2001, the ability to build in waiver or incapacity insurance to personal pension arrangements was ended (though as already discussed, existing arrangements were not affected).

Waiver can still be provided, but must now be arranged outside of the personal pension itself. In the event of a claim, the waiver can pay contributions direct to the product provider, but they will be treated as paid by the member.

As a result of these changes, the cost of the waiver no longer forms part of the personal pension contributions which qualify for tax relief, and it is no longer taken into account in determining maximum contribution levels.

If the member becomes incapacitated, and the waiver operates to pay contributions on the member's behalf, these contributions must fall within normal limits and will qualify for tax relief in the same way as any other contributions. The individual will also need to continue to satisfy the eligibility conditions for contribution payment.

As a result, the waiver needs only to cover the contribution net of basic rate tax relief.

Example – Operation of waiver (arrangement made on or after 6 April 2001)

Let us again assume that the individual from the previous example has a personal pension to which they contribute £300 per month gross (£234 net of basic rate relief), but this time suppose that the arrangement started in 2002. They have a waiver of contribution arrangement alongside (but outside) the personal pension and this is intended to cover the net contribution of £234 per month. They pay the cost of the waiver separately from (and in addition to) the personal pension contributions.

Because the cost of the waiver is outside the personal pension, no relief is available, and it is not taken into account in determining maximum contributions.

When the waiver comes into operation, following the individual's incapacity, the waiver would provide £234 per month, and the product provider can claim basic rate relief on it, assuming the grossed up contribution is within contribution limits.

In 2004/05, although their net relevant earnings have fallen to £20,000, the individual can still make contributions up to the earnings threshold of £3,600, and can do so indefinitely under the current basis of personal pension contribution limits.

Unfortunately, the need to separate waiver from the personal pension has resulted in this cover becoming difficult to arrange in the market. There are practical difficulties for insurers, because generally the cover needed is at a relatively low level, and administration costs are therefore high relative to the premium, particularly where the personal pension contributions are themselves modest.

A possible solution is to include provision for ongoing contributions in more general income protection cover (see section **9.27** below). However, insurers limit the extent of this cover as a proportion of pre-incapacity earned income, and this is likely to mean that financial resources are already stretched if the benefit comes into payment, and it may therefore be difficult to afford the contributions.

In addition, for larger contributions, difficulties can arise with limits as discussed in section **9.11** below.

Effect of limits 9.11

When an individual is incapacitated, their net relevant earnings are likely to fall, and will often reduce to nothing. The ability for non-earners to contribute up to the earnings threshold means that usually, there will be no difficulties with eligibility, and contributions within the earnings threshold can still be paid.

If higher contributions are to be made, they can only be justified under the normal age and earnings related scale (see section **3.7**). If earnings have ceased, this will not be possible in the long term.

The basis year and cessation rules can help however. The basis year rules (which are covered in detail in section **3.30**) allow contributions to be based on net relevant earnings in the current tax year, or any one of the last five tax years.

Example – Use of basis years on incapacity

Suppose that in our previous example, the individual's contributions were £400 per month (gross) rather than £300, and they are therefore in excess of the earnings threshold. Suppose also that the level of the individual's net relevant earnings (NRE) for 2003/04 (£60,000) is the highest level they have ever earned.

The basis year rules allow these to be used for limit purposes as follows:

Year	Actual NRE	Basis year chosen	NRE for limit purposes
2003/04	£60,000	2003/04	£60,000
2004/05	£20,000	2003/04	£60,000
2005/06	£10,000	2003/04	£60,000
2006/07	Nil	2003/04	£60,000
2007/08	Nil	2003/04	£60,000
2008/09	Nil	2003/04	£60,000

After 2008/09, the net relevant earnings figure for 2003/04 is too far back to be used under the basis year rules.

In addition, if all earnings have ceased entirely, the cessation rules (see section **3.34**) may allow the use of historic net relevant earnings for a longer period.

Example – Use of cessation rules on incapacity

Using the same details as the last example, the cessation rules allow 2003/04 to be used as the reference year in 2009/10 and 2010/11, so increasing the scope for contributions in those years.

Year	Actual NRE	Basis year chosen	NRE for limit purposes
2003/04	£60,000	2003/04	£60,000
2004/05	£20,000	2003/04	£60,000
2005/06	£10,000	2003/04	£60,000 (Cessation year)
2006/07	Nil	2003/04	£60,000 (Break year)
2007/08	Nil	2003/04	£60,000
2008/09	Nil	2003/04	£60,000
2009/10	Nil	2003/04	£60,000
2010/11	Nil	2003/04	£60,000
2011/12	Nil	n/a	Nil

The cessation rules only apply for the five tax years following the cessation year (2005/06), so after 2010/11 they cannot be used any longer. The maximum contribution level in 2011/12 would therefore revert to the earnings threshold.

Once the period during which the application of the basis year and/or cessation rules is available expires, contributions will only be possible within the earnings threshold of £3,600 per year.

There are also some potential difficulties in relying on the use of the cessation rules. In particular, they will cease to apply if the individual once again has a source of earnings, which could easily arise if a partial recovery was made, and the individual took up (for example) part-time employment at a relatively low earnings level.

The result could be a substantial reduction in the contribution limit.

Example – Effect of a new source of income

Suppose the same individual took up a part-time employment in 2008/09.

Year	Actual NRE	Basis year chosen	NRE for limit purposes
2003/04	£60,000	2003/04	£60,000
2004/05	£20,000	2003/04	£60,000
2005/06	£10,000	2003/04	£60,000 (Cessation year)
2006/07	Nil	2003/04	£60,000 (Break year)
2007/08	Nil	2003/04	£60,000
2008/09	£2,000	2003/04	£60,000
2009/10	£4,500	2004/05	£20,000
2010/11	£4,800	2005/06	£10,000
2011/12	£5,000	2011/12	£5,000

The cessation rules cease to apply once earnings restart. The basis year rules are still available, so (for example) the net relevant earnings figure for 2004/05 can be used as the basis of contributions in 2009/10.

However, the maximum net relevant earnings figure that can be taken into account in 2009/10 and 2010/11 is substantially reduced because of the existence of the new earnings source.

Note that the cessation rules cease to apply whatever the source of the earnings, which could be employment (pensionable or non-pensionable) or self-employment.

Also, under the proposals currently being considered for the simplification of the tax treatment of pensions, there may be additional problems, because the basis year and cessation rules may not survive the proposed changes. The proposals are covered in detail in **Chapter 15: Simplification of Tax Treatment**.

Ceasing to be eligible 9.12

The situation could be worse still if the individual ceases to be eligible to contribute to a personal pension. In this case, contributions would have to cease, even though they would have been covered by the waiver.

This could arise if the individual became non-resident in the UK, for example, as a result of moving to a warmer climate for health reasons. The eligibility rules allow contributions to continue in any tax year if the individual has been resident at some time in the previous five tax years, but not otherwise.

This problem does not arise under the pre-6 April 2001 basis, because continuing eligibility is not required during the period the waiver is operating.

Level of tax relief 9.13

The tax position on waiver under the old and new rules will often be equivalent in effect. The old rules allowed tax relief on cost, but because no relief was available on the contributions waived, the gross contribution needed to be insured. The new rules give no relief on cost, but allow relief on the contributions funded by the waiver, so only the net contribution needs to be covered.

Example – Effect of change in tax relief I

A basic rate taxpayer contributes £780 per year to a personal pension. The equivalent gross contribution is £1,000 per year.

Suppose waiver would cost 3% of the contributions covered.

Under the old (pre-6 April 2001) basis, the gross cost of waiver would be £30, and the individual would pay £23.40 net of basic rate tax. The waiver would cover the £1,000 gross contribution.

Under the new rules, the individual would cover only the net contribution of £780, and the cost would be £780 × 3% = £23.40. No relief is available, so the net cost to the individual is the same as before.

Under the new rules, waiver would provide £780 per year if the personal pension holder was incapacitated, and the product provider would reclaim basic rate relief from the Inland Revenue to gross the contribution up to £1,000.

(This example assumes that the cost of the waiver remains the same, though the practical difficulties discussed in section **9.10** above may mean that rates are more expensive for cover on the post-6 April 2001 basis.)

However, this assumes that the rates of relief are the same. If the member was a higher rate taxpayer when paying contributions from income, but is only a basic rate taxpayer when the waiver comes into operation, the new rules are disadvantageous. The loss of relief on the cost would outweigh the relief on the contributions covered by the waiver.

A member likely to be in this position should insure the level of their contribution net of basic rate tax, not higher rate.

Example – Effect of change in tax relief II

A higher rate taxpayer contributes £1,560 per year to a personal pension, net of basic rate relief. The equivalent gross contribution is £2,000 per year, and the net cost to the individual after allowing for higher rate relief is £1,200.

Suppose waiver would again cost 3% of the contributions covered.

Under the old (pre-6 April 2001) basis, the gross cost of waiver would be £60, and the net cost after higher rate relief would be £36. The waiver would cover the £2,000 gross contribution.

Under the new rules, the individual would probably cover the contribution net of basic rate relief, ie £1,560. The cost would be £1,560 x 3% = £46.80. No relief is available.

The waiver would provide £1,560 per year if the individual was incapacitated, which would be grossed up to £2,000 by basic rate relief claimed by the product provider. If they are then a basic rate taxpayer, they will not receive any further relief.

The personal pension receives £2,000 per year under each basis, but the net cost to the individual has increased from £36 to £46.80 under the new rules.

Terms of waiver   9.14

The terms applicable to waiver of contribution arrangements vary considerably, and should be considered carefully in evaluating cover. The variations are similar to those which arise on an income protection or PHI policy.

In some cases there are options for the member, which must generally be selected by the member at outset, for example, the deferment period (see section **9.17** below). In other cases, for example, in determining any exclusions from cover, the decision is a matter for the insurer.

In general, the terms are similar for pre and post-6 April 2001 cover, and the factors to consider are the same.

Definition of incapacity   9.15

Generally, the definition of incapacity will fall broadly in line with the Inland Revenue definition of disability, as discussed in section **9.2** above, though there is no requirement on the part of the Inland Revenue that the incapacity should necessarily be permanent in order to allow waiver (as distinct from early payment of benefits) to operate.

However, it is open to the insurer to apply a harsher definition, for example requiring the individual to be unable to follow any occupation before admitting a claim (rather than his 'own occupation or any occupation of a similar nature for which he is trained or fitted').

Alternatively, there could be a condition that waiver would only apply if the individual was not in receipt of any earned income.

Broadly, the harsher the definition of incapacity, the cheaper the cover is likely to be, but the less likely it is to come into operation.

Exclusions   9.16

It is usual to exclude certain causes of incapacity, for example, self-inflicted injury, misuse of alcohol or drugs, and injury arising from participation in a criminal act. If incapacity arose as a result of an excluded occurrence, the waiver would not pay out at all.

HIV and AIDS-related conditions are commonly excluded, though sometimes if these conditions arose through receipt of a contaminated blood transfusion, benefits may still be provided.

Pregnancy is generally also excluded, though there may be cover to some extent for associated complications.

Some arrangements may exclude certain activities relating to the individual's work, or leisure pursuits, for example, involvement in hazardous sports such as hang-gliding. In some cases, the availability of benefits may also be restricted if the individual resides overseas, particularly in areas where medical assistance (and any medical evidence provided to the insurer) may be of doubtful reliability.

Deferment period   9.17

The waiver will usually not come into effect until the end of a defined period following incapacity, usually known as the deferment period or deferred period. This avoids the insurer having to deal with short term claims which may fall wholly within the deferment period, and reduces the period for which waiver pays out in the case of longer term claims.

The longer the deferment period, the lower the cost of the cover will be.

Commonly deferment periods of three, six or twelve months are available, and the period is chosen at outset. Some insurers offer a wider range.

Successive periods of incapacity 9.18

Where an individual returns to work after suffering incapacity, but subsequently once again becomes incapacitated as a result of the same cause, waiver may restart immediately, rather than a further deferment period being applied.

Usually this will only apply if the second occurrence of incapacity occurs within a maximum period set by the insurer. Note that this provision is not included under some arrangements, and the terms of the cover provided under a specific PP arrangement would need to be checked.

Payment of contributions during deferment 9.19

The waiver, once it starts to provide benefits at the end of the deferment period, will not generally backdate those benefits to the time when incapacity first occurred.

During the deferment period, under some arrangements, the member must maintain contributions themself, or the cover would lapse. Under other arrangements, cover will be maintained regardless of whether contributions continue during the deferment period.

In the event of incapacity, it is particularly important that the member understands the basis of the cover provided, otherwise the cover could lapse at the very time it is most needed.

Cessation date 9.20

Generally, the cessation date of the waiver, in other words the point up to which the contributions will be provided for under the waiver, will be linked to the member's expected retirement date. If the member does not become incapacitated by then, but does not draw their benefits, the cover will nevertheless cease at this date, even if contributions are continuing.

Availability of partial waiver 9.21

There is no objection to the provision of partial waiver, which allows the waiver to continue in part if the individual suffers incapacity and the waiver pays out, but they later return to work in a part-time or lower paid capacity (*Inland Revenue Guidance Notes (IR76) para 4.16*).

It is up to the insurer whether to include this provision within the cover, and to specify the terms on which it is available.

Increases in cover 9.22

The amount of the contributions on which waiver cover is required may vary from time to time, generally as contribution levels increase. Cover should be maintained in line with increases, and this is usually permitted.

Medical evidence requirements 9.23

Both at outset and on increases in cover, the insurer may require medical evidence, and may impose special terms if it takes the view that the individual represents a higher than average risk. Some arrangements allow increases without medical evidence within certain limits, or, under arrangements where there are automatic increases applied to contributions, in line with those automatic increases.

Where medical evidence is not required, this simplifies the procedures attaching to contribution increases, both for the member and their advisers.

Increases in contributions waived during incapacity 9.24

If an individual starts to make personal pension contributions, the level of those contributions is likely to increase over the years, as earnings and disposable income increase. This progression will be interrupted if the individual becomes incapacitated.

If waiver of contributions provides only for contributions at their level at the time of incapacity, the build up of the fund will continue, but will not be as fast as would have been the case if contributions had continued and had been increased over the years.

Some insurers therefore allow cover to be provided on the basis that during a claim, the amount of the contribution funded by the waiver increases at an agreed rate. This might be a fixed rate, for example, 3% per year, or at a rate linked to an index such as the Retail Prices Index.

Note that this is a different feature to the ability to increase cover before incapacity arises (see section **9.22** above).

The cost of providing for increases in the contributions waived is inevitably more than providing for level contributions, with the differential being greatest at young ages. It does however provide a more realistic level of cover over the long term.

Example – Increases in contributions waived

A 28-year-old self-employed caterer has just started to make personal pension contributions. They provide for waiver, on a level contribution basis, alongside their personal pension arrangement, based on an expected retirement age of 65.

Suppose they become incapacitated at the age of 30, and their contributions are then at the level of £50 per month. If the individual remains incapacitated, the contribution level provided for under the waiver will remain at £50 per month through to age 60.

Had they included increases in the level of contribution waived at 3% per year, the contributions waived would have gradually increased, and would have reached a level of approximately £120 per month by the time the individual is 60. The fund built up by then would be significantly greater as a result.

Rates and guarantees of rates 9.25

Waiver is an insurance arrangement, so the rates charged by the insurer would always be an important consideration.

Note that some insurers guarantee their rates for the duration of the cover, whilst others reserve the right to vary them in the light of experience. Where there is a right to vary the rates, the cover may be cheaper initially, because the lack of guarantee allows the insurer to quote a keener rate. However, the member takes the risk of a subsequent increase.

Contributions covered 9.26

Although most personal pensions are very flexible in allowing variations in the level of contributions paid, this may impact on the availability of waiver of contribution. Some insurers will only cover contributions which the member has made a commitment to maintain on a regular basis.

Others will cover all contributions, but usually with an averaging formula, to even out major fluctuations in contribution levels. This can be important, particularly for individuals whose income varies widely.

Checklist – Variations in waiver cover

The main areas where the terms of waiver can vary are as follows.

- Definition of incapacity.
- Exclusions.
- Deferment period.
- Successive periods of incapacity.
- Payment of contributions during deferment.
- Cessation date.
- Availability of partial waiver.
- Increases in cover.
- Medical evidence requirements.
- Increases in contributions during incapacity.
- Rates and guarantees of rates.
- Contributions covered.

Income during operation of waiver   9.27

Waiver is a very appealing concept, and is a good way of ensuring that the member is provided for at a reasonable level in retirement. However, the concept requires personal pension benefits to be deferred until the age at which the individual expected to retire before they became incapacitated. The income position between the point of incapacity and retirement must also be provided for, and waiver alone cannot therefore provide sufficient protection against the financial effects of incapacity.

A common way of dealing with this is by means of an income protection (also known as permanent health insurance or PHI) policy.

Note that the income payments provided by such a policy taken out on a personal basis do not count as relevant earnings (see section **2.2**).

Where an employed individual is covered by a group PHI policy taken out by their employer, the basis is generally that the employment continues, with the employer paying salary to the employee, and being reimbursed from the PHI policy. In these circumstances the continuing salary does count as relevant earnings, assuming the employment is not pensionable (see section **2.7**).

Death benefits   9.28

A further point worth considering in cases of incapacity is the basis of death benefits. Incapacity may reduce life expectancy (though this is not always so) and in such cases, great importance may be attached to the position which would apply on death.

If retirement benefits are taken early on grounds of incapacity, and the income benefits are provided by means of annuity purchase, the benefits on death will depend on the type of annuity purchased. In particular they will reflect whether arrangements have been made to include a minimum guaranteed payment period, or income benefits for one or more survivors (see section **5.30**). In any event, there is likely to be a loss of value if death occurs soon after disability.

If income withdrawals are taken, the fund is available on death, and can usually be paid as a lump sum, but if so, there is a 35% tax charge (see section **6.11**).

On the other hand, if death occurs before retirement benefits are taken, the fund is usually available in full as a lump sum, without tax liability (see section **8.10**). If waiver is in operation, this would not affect this position, and the fund available would be building up through the contributions waived, as well as any investment growth achieved.

In appropriate cases, this further emphasises the importance of providing for pre-retirement income from sources other than the personal pension in the event of incapacity.

10 — Divorce

Introduction

When a married couple get divorced, whatever the circumstances, and however difficult they may be, it will be necessary to reach agreement regarding the division of assets, or ultimately to have a basis imposed by the courts. As well as more obvious and more accessible assets, the value of the pension rights which have been built up by either or both spouses must be taken into account, under the *Matrimonial Causes Act 1973 (MCA 1973)*.

In many cases, the value of pension rights will be amongst the most valuable of the assets involved in the settlement, often second only to the marital home. The way in which these rights are dealt with can therefore have a major impact, both immediately, in terms of the way in which other assets are divided, and also in the long term, in relation to the retirement income of both spouses, or possibly, the benefits payable on earlier death.

In this chapter, we consider the way in which rights under personal pension arrangements are taken into account. Essentially the same conditions also apply to benefits under retirement annuity contracts. (These contracts are dealt with more generally in **Chapter 14: Retirement Annuity Contracts**).

Pension rights under occupational schemes must similarly be taken into account on divorce, and we also consider how these are dealt with if transferred to a personal pension under the pension sharing provisions.

In general through this chapter, for ease of illustration, we will assume that only one spouse has pension rights. However, where both spouses have such rights, their value and the balance between them will be taken into account, and the same principles apply in terms of the division of rights on divorce.

At the time of divorce, it is more likely to be the husband who has pension rights rather than the wife. The government's consultation paper on pensions and divorce, (*Pension sharing on divorce: reforming pensions for a fairer future*, published in June 1998), suggested that the husband was around four times more likely to have such rights than the wife. Although this was the result of research regarding occupational pension scheme benefits, an imbalance seems likely to apply to personal pensions too. Again for simplicity, we will therefore assume in this chapter that it is the husband alone who has pension rights, and will often refer to him as the member.

In reality, the sex of the individual with the pension rights makes no difference to the way in which those rights are treated on divorce.

The provisions described in this chapter are those relevant to England and Wales. The position in other countries within the United Kingdom may vary to an extent in detail.

Offsetting   10.2

Historically, pension rights have generally been dealt with by offsetting their value against other assets, though even this basis is relatively recent, since in the past it has been possible for members not to disclose their pension rights when negotiating the divorce settlement.

Under an offsetting agreement, by taking account of the value of the member's pension rights, his entitlement to a share of the other assets involved in the settlement will be reduced.

Example – Offsetting

A couple are getting divorced. The husband has a personal pension arrangement, under which a fund of £100,000 has built up.

The couple's other assets amount to some £300,000, and the settlement involves an equal division of their total assets.

Under an offsetting arrangement, the wife would therefore receive £200,000 of the non-pension assets, and the husband would receive £100,000. The husband would continue to be entitled to all of the eventual benefits from the pension fund of £100,000, making his share of the total assets the same, at £200,000.

The attraction of the offsetting approach in dealing with pension rights is its simplicity. No specific action is necessary in relation to the pension rights themselves, but the agreed division of assets is still reached overall.

However, a major disadvantage in some circumstances is that, particularly where the pension rights are significant, there may be relatively little by way of other assets allocated to the member with the pension rights.

Example – Offsetting difficulties

Suppose in our last example, the value of the husband's pension fund had been £250,000 rather than £100,000, but that the other details are the same. The total assets of the couple, including the value of the pension rights is therefore £550,000.

The wife's share would be half of £550,000 = £275,000.

This would use almost all of the non-pension assets, leaving the husband with the pension fund of £250,000, but only £25,000 of other assets.

If the member has already reached, or is close to the age of 50, when retirement benefits can be drawn, this may not represent too great a practical difficulty. However if he is significantly younger than this, the lack of immediately realisable assets may create significant practical difficulties.

In the example above, the spouse with no pension rights was granted the overwhelming majority of the non-pension assets. This might well include the marital home. The husband, with little by way of immediately accessible resources, must still find somewhere to live, and must set up home afresh. This may be difficult to achieve.

Although the example is fairly simplistic, in that the division of assets (which is very often not 50:50) is likely to take more realistic account of the needs of each spouse, the problem is nevertheless real.

In addition, a significant problem can be that in some cases, where the major asset is the home, the lack of liquid assets might mean that it becomes necessary to dispose of the property, which in reality might not be the preferred solution for either party.

A further issue will sometimes be that the ex-spouse may no longer be entitled to benefits from the pension scheme on the member's death, particularly if she is no longer dependent in any way. This loss may need to be taken into account in agreeing the division of assets generally.

Earmarking 10.3

As more and more people build up pension rights of significant value, there will be increasing numbers of cases where the problem of imbalance in the division of other assets makes the offsetting approach difficult to operate in practice. For this reason an alternative basis was introduced under *section 66* of the *Pensions Act 1995 (PA 1995)*, and came into effect from 1 August 1996. This is known as 'earmarking'.

The principle is that, by means of a court order, the personal pension scheme provider can be required to earmark all or part of a member's benefits to his ex-spouse, and must therefore pay the benefits to the ex-spouse when they fall due.

Although earmarking is most familiar in relation to occupational pension schemes, it also applies to personal pension schemes and retirement annuity contracts under *ss 25D(3),(4), MCA 1973*, these sections having being inserted by the *PA 1995*.

Note that the introduction of earmarking did not mean the end of the offsetting approach. Both approaches remained (and still remain) possible.

Practical difficulties 10.4

The earmarking provisions in effect establish a form of deferred maintenance, so that, at the time the member retires, provision is made for the ex-spouse from what would otherwise have been the member's pension. Whilst this seems a reasonable basis at first sight, there are a number of practical difficulties.

For the most part, these relate to the fact that the benefits are still treated as those of the member of the personal pension scheme (or holder of the retirement annuity contract). Therefore, retirement benefits will generally become payable sometime between the member's 50th and 75th birthdays, irrespective of the age of his ex-spouse.

The member alone chooses (within these time parameters) when benefits are actually drawn. Even assuming an amicable arrangement and reasonable levels of co-operation between the ex-spouses, the time at which the member wishes to take retirement benefits may not be the same as the time at which the ex-spouse wants, or needs to have the benefits which have been earmarked for her. In addition, it is not difficult to imagine situations where the divorce is anything but amicable, and where the member therefore decides to delay the taking of retirement benefits for as long as possible, in order to create the maximum inconvenience for his ex-spouse.

In some cases, where there is a substantial age difference between the parties, it may be impossible within the legislation to provide benefits for the ex-spouse at the time she might reasonably want them.

Example – Effect of age differences

Using a divorced couple as an example, part of the ex-husband's retirement benefits under his personal pension have been earmarked for the ex-wife. However, he is 30 years younger than her.

The earliest age at which he can access benefits is 50, by which time the ex-wife will be 80 years old (assuming she survives).

If the ex-husband decides to draw his benefits at 65, along with his State pension, the ex-wife would then be 95.

If the ex-husband waited until he was 75 before drawing benefits, the ex-wife would need to survive until she was 105 in order to receive the earmarked benefits.

Similarly, if the ex-spouse is considerably younger than the member, the earmarked benefits may emerge whilst she is still working, and may have run out on the member's death before the ex-spouse reaches retirement.

The member also controls the investment of the fund prior to drawing retirement benefits, and it may be that the approach he takes is not in line with the attitude to risk, or the needs of the ex-spouse.

The order can however require the member to take part of his benefits in the form of cash, to the extent allowed within the personal pensions legislation, and can require a proportion of the cash sum to be paid to the ex-spouse.

The earmarking order will reflect the basis of division of benefits determined by the court, and this will be decided in the light of all the circumstances of the divorce. As with the division of assets overall, the amount of the member's benefit earmarked for the ex-spouse is not necessarily a half share, and in fact usually would not be so.

Earmarking is perhaps not a welcome development for schemes. Inevitably, the existence of an earmarking order, which may remain in existence for a long period, will increase and complicate the administration and record-keeping of the scheme, particularly when benefits are paid, and must be divided between two recipients. The scheme will need to have maintained records of both parties too. All these factors may in turn create additional costs.

Transfers   10.5

The member may also choose to transfer benefits from one provider to another, or in some cases from a personal pension scheme or retirement annuity contract to an occupational pension scheme. Although such a transfer may not meet with the wishes of the ex-spouse, it is again the member who controls this decision.

However, the legislation does require that the earmarking order be treated by the receiving scheme as if the order had been made in relation to it rather than the transferring scheme. In other words, the terms of the ear-marking order will still apply.

Taxation 10.6

Benefits which are paid to an ex-spouse under an earmarking order remain taxable on the member. There is no tax liability on the ex-spouse.

This can often be disadvantageous, since, if there is a difference in the tax rates applicable to the ex-spouses, it is most likely that it is the member with pension rights who is subject to the higher rate.

In addition, only the member's personal allowance is available, and the ex-spouse's cannot be used, even if she has no other taxable income.

Death of the member before retirement 10.7

If the member dies before taking retirement benefits from his personal pension, and if as a result a lump sum becomes payable, the court order may require that a proportion of this be paid to the ex-spouse. This may then provide some protection for the ex-spouse, and this may be very nec-essary, because in these circumstances there will be no eventual retirement benefits to be paid to her under the earmarking order.

However the terms of the order are for the court to decide, and may not necessarily include such provision.

In addition, as discussed in section **14.27**, under some retirement annuity contracts, the benefits payable in the event of death before retirement may be poor. Under many such contracts, the payment on death is restricted to merely a return of contributions with no growth, or with a modest rate of interest. In these circumstances, any death benefit is likely to be less than adequate for the needs of the ex-spouse.

Furthermore, some retirement annuity contracts provide no return at all on death before retirement, and so any earmarking order would not be capable of producing any actual benefit in these circumstances.

Death of the member after retirement 10.8

Even after retirement benefits start to be paid to the member, problems can still arise on the member's death. The ex-spouse is receiving a propor-tion of the member's pension and when the member dies, the pension benefit will probably cease, leaving the ex-spouse with no benefit.

Because the member once again controls the choice of income benefit, he may well choose not to include any guaranteed minimum payment period. To do so would decrease the level of benefit he would receive during his lifetime, and in the event of his early death, would simply serve to provide more benefits for the ex-spouse.

In many cases, the ex-spouse may not fall within the definition of a survivor, as would be necessary to enable her to be provided with ongoing income benefits after the member's death. If maintenance payments are being made, she would qualify on the grounds of being financially dependent, but otherwise, qualification is not automatic. She would have to be able to show that dependence arose in some other way.

Expiry of earmarking order   10.9

The earmarking order automatically expires if the ex-spouse remarries. This can inevitably cause difficulties and is a further disadvantage of the earmarking approach from the point of view of the ex-spouse.

The order will also cease to have effect if the ex-spouse herself dies, leaving no remaining entitlement to her estate.

Conflicts   10.10

The earmarking order clearly does not provide for a 'clean break' divorce, since the benefits received by the ex-spouse depend on the circumstances and choices made by the member. Generally a clean break approach is favoured by courts and tends also to be what both parties to the divorce prefer.

In addition, as discussed above, there are many circumstances such as the member's death or the ex-spouse's remarriage which will affect the nature, timing and value of the benefits which the ex-spouse will receive. This provides a significant level of uncertainty as far as the ex-spouse is concerned, and this will also generally be seen as a disadvantage.

Within the terms of a divorce settlement, aspects which are regarded as disadvantageous to one party will often be seen as favourable to the other. It follows from this that there may be a conflict between the ex-spouses as to whether the earmarking approach should be adopted. During the negotiation stage, it may well be that the spouse with pension rights favours such an approach, whilst the spouse without pension rights finds it inappropriate and unacceptable.

If agreement cannot be reached, then it is up to the courts to impose a basis of dealing with the pension rights, along with all the other relevant assets.

To date, very few earmarking orders have been made.

Pension sharing 10.11

Pension sharing was introduced under the *Welfare Reform and Pensions Act 1999,* and the *Finance Act 1999.* This was intended as a response to the various problems which had been identified in relation to the earmarking basis, and also as an attempt to facilitate a clean break settlement.

The concept is that the value of the pension rights should be shared at the time of divorce rather than at the time of the member's retirement. This means that thereafter, the member will control the residue of his pension rights, but the ex-spouse will be in complete control of her rights, even though they originally arose from the member.

Pension sharing is available only for divorce proceedings which started on or after 1 December 2000.

As was the case when earmarking was introduced, pension sharing provides an alternative approach, but does not replace the other possible approaches. All three – offsetting, earmarking and pension sharing – therefore remain available.

Pension sharing order 10.12

Pension sharing is put into effect in relation to any particular divorce by means of a court order, and once again the terms of the sharing of rights are determined by the court in the light of the circumstances. The order is a prerequisite of the *decree nisi* being made absolute. Generally the rights will not be shared equally, because the respective shares of member and ex-spouse will also take account of the division of other assets.

The court order will specify the proportion of the member's fund under his personal pension or retirement annuity contract which is to be transferred to his ex-spouse. The pension share will be actioned by means of a transfer of the value of those rights to a new or an existing personal pension scheme for the ex-spouse.

Note that where the rights being transferred arose under a retirement annuity contract, the transfer will still be made to a personal pension scheme because it is no longer possible to establish new retirement annuity contracts.

Also, pre–Royal Assent arrangements (ie arrangements established before 27 July 1989 – see section **5.11**) are not permitted to accept transfers of pension credit rights.

The rights transferred are referred to as a 'pension debit' in relation to the member, and a 'pension credit' in relation to the ex-spouse.

Note that it is not necessary for the ex-spouse to meet the normal eligibility conditions for personal pensions in order to allow such a transfer to be made, though the ex-spouse will need to choose the personal pension scheme to be used. (It is necessary for the ex-spouse to apply for membership of the scheme in order for the transfer to be effected.)

Retirement benefits 10.13

Once the transfer is made, the ex-spouse who has received the pension credit will be able to control her pension arrangements in the normal way. For example, it will be the ex-spouse who controls the investment of the fund prior to retirement, and whether any further transfer is made at any future time.

Benefits will be payable according to her own age rather than that of the member from whom the rights were transferred. As discussed above, this may be particularly important where there is a significant age difference between the former spouses.

Retirement benefits will be available to the ex-spouse in accordance with normal rules, and so generally must commence between the ages of 50 and 75. They can be started earlier if the ex-spouse becomes incapacitated. (Pension credit benefits cannot be paid early on the basis of a special occupation, even if the member was in such an occupation. This is because they were not provided from contributions made from earnings which derived from the ex-spouse pursuing a special occupation. The provisions relating to special occupations generally are covered in **Chapter 13: Special Occupations**.)

The full range of usual options is available to the ex-spouse at retirement, including the ability to take part of the total fund in the form of tax free cash. Income benefits can be provided either by the purchase of an annuity or (up to the ex-spouse's 75th birthday) by means of income withdrawals.

Arrangements can be made to provide for a minimum guaranteed payment period and/or a survivor's pension. The definition of a survivor for this purpose (see section **5.30**) would be determined in relation to the ex-spouse, and not in any way in relation to the member from whom the pension rights were transferred.

Example – Survivor benefits

Following a divorce, a pension sharing order was made in relation to part of the husband's personal pension fund, and a transfer was made to a new personal pension set up for his ex-spouse.

Some years later, his ex-spouse remarried. When she retires, she can purchase an annuity which includes provision for a survivor's benefit payable to her new husband if she predeceases him.

Tax free cash 10.14

The value of the fund derived from a pension credit which has been transferred from a member's personal pension arrangement to his ex-spouse's may generally be included in the fund when calculating the 25% maximum tax free cash sum at retirement.

Safeguarded rights (see section **10.20** below) arising from the transfer of protected rights under a pension sharing order cannot however be taken in the form of cash.

Benefits transferred from occupational schemes 10.15

Where a pension credit under a personal pension arises as a result of benefits which have been transferred from an occupational pension scheme under the terms of a pension sharing order, they are generally treated in the same way as any other personal pension benefits. As part of this, they will generally be taken into account in calculating the 25% tax free cash limit at retirement.

However, in some cases, the pension credit rights themselves may be non-commutable. This could occur in particular if they arise from a transfer from a scheme where no commutation would have been available (for example from a free-standing AVC scheme).

Otherwise, unless safeguarded rights (see section **10.20** below) are included, the usual 25% limit on tax free cash applies in the normal way. There is no situation where a certification limit applies (as it sometimes does where a member transfers his own rights from an occupational scheme to a personal pension – see section **5.13**).

Death before retirement 10.16

The value of pension credit rights may be paid in full as a lump sum on death before taking retirement benefits.

Effect on contribution limits 10.17

The receipt of a transfer value representing a pension credit has no effect on the contribution limits which would otherwise be applicable to the ex-spouse.

If she is eligible to make contributions, then she may do so in the normal way, subject to normal limits. Conversely, if she is not otherwise eligible, although the pension credit rights can still be transferred into a personal pension, she will still not be able to make any contributions in her own right.

Effect on ceding member 10.18

As far as the member is concerned, his pension fund will be reduced by the amount of the pension debit. He is not affected in any other way.

In particular, there is no effect on the contribution limits which would normally apply, nor on the requirements relating to the timing and form of his remaining benefits.

The ex-spouse may remain within the definition of survivor in respect of death benefits (see section **5.30**) if she is in receipt of maintenance. However, unless making provision for a survivor's pension for her is part of the overall divorce settlement, in practice, the member is probably unlikely to make such provision voluntarily.

Pension sharing after benefits start 10.19

A pension sharing order may be made where benefits are already being taken in income form, whether by means of an annuity or by income withdrawals. If the member was taking income under an annuity, the ex-spouse must also take the benefits arising from the pension credit in the same form.

Where the member is taking income withdrawals (see **Chapter 6: Income withdrawals**) the ex-spouse may continue to draw benefits in this form, or may choose to purchase an annuity with the fund transferred to her personal pension arrangement. Note that the scheme administrator under the transferring scheme must provide a certificate to the receiving scheme showing that no amount can be paid to the ex-spouse in lump sum form (since the entitlement to cash only arises at pension date, which by definition has now passed).

Safeguarded rights 10.20

The benefits which are subject to the pension sharing order may include protected rights. These might have been built up by the member as a result of contracting out by means of the personal pension, or through receipt of a transfer value from an occupational pension scheme, which itself included contracted out rights.

In such circumstances, the protected rights which are transferred become 'safeguarded rights'. They must be ring-fenced from the other benefits arising under the ex-spouse's personal pension, including any protected rights attaching to the ex-spouse in her own right.

Although the provisions relating to safeguarded rights are broadly similar to those which apply to protected rights, there are differences. In particular, benefits must generally come into payment between the ages of 60 and 65 (not 75), but can be paid earlier in cases of ill health. Also, unlike protected rights, it is not a requirement that survivors' benefits be provided.

However, the prohibition on taking benefits in the form of cash does apply, as does the requirement to provide escalation (see section **5.3**).

Simplification 10.21

Currently, there is no overall maximum benefit level that can be provided under personal pension or retirement annuity contract legislation. Clearly the reduction in the member's fund as a result of the pension debit will reduce his ultimate benefits, but, as already discussed, there is nothing to stop him building up his rights by payment of further contributions within normal limits.

One aspect of the simplification proposals, which are dealt with in **Chapter 15: Simplification of Tax Treatment**, is the intention that there should be an overall limit on total provision under pensions legislation. The initial proposal is that this limit should be reduced in the case of the member by the amount of the pension debit, but that the pension credit paid to the ex-spouse should not be regarded as part of her lifetime limit.

This proposal is still the subject of consultation at the time of writing, but it may be an important aspect of advice on the treatment of pension rights on divorce generally, particularly in the case of those making, or intending to make, substantial contributions.

11 — Interaction with Occupational Schemes

Introduction   11.1

There is only limited interaction between personal pension schemes and occupational schemes, but where it does arise, the implications are important. In this chapter we discuss a number of areas, including situations where there are choices to be made between personal and occupational schemes, and some aspects of transferring benefits between them.

A further area of interaction is in terms of the benefit limits which apply under the occupational scheme.

Retained benefits   11.2

Where an individual is a member of an approved occupational pension scheme, limits apply to the benefits which are payable. In some cases, these will be affected by the existence of benefits arising under personal pension arrangements (and retirement annuity contracts).

Where these benefits arose in relation to a period of employment or self-employment which preceded the employment to which the occupational scheme relates, they will generally be treated as retained benefits. (Preserved benefits arising from occupational schemes relating to previous employments are also treated in the same way.)

There are two situations where the personal pension benefits would not be treated as retained benefits, and can be ignored. These are:

(a)   where the individual was a member of an occupational scheme which was not itself contracted out, and the personal pension was funded entirely by the minimum contributions payable by the National Insurance Contributions Office (NICO) of the Inland Revenue in respect of periods when the member contracted out (see **Chapter 12: Contracting Out**); and

(b)   Where benefits arose from contributions payable during periods when the individual was eligible only under the concurrency rules (see section **2.20**).

Under occupational schemes, for members subject to the current approval regime, introduced by the *Finance Act 1989 (FA 1989)*, the maximum pension benefit at retirement which the scheme can provide is generally:

●   1/60th of final remuneration for each year of service; or, if greater

- the lesser of 2/3rds of final remuneration less retained benefits, and 1/30th of final remuneration for each year of service.

If the benefits provided are no greater than 1/60ths, then retained benefits can be ignored, but if greater, then any retained benefits must be taken into account.

Example – Effect of retained benefits

An occupational scheme member has completed 15 years service at their retirement age of 65. Their current earnings are £60,000, and their employer wants to increase benefits to the maximum allowed.

The individual also has benefit rights under a personal pension scheme, to which they contributed when self-employed. The benefit is a pension of £12,500 per year.

The maximum benefit that could be provided for them under the occupational scheme is:

(a) 15/60 × £60,000 = £15,000; or if greater
(b) The lesser of 2/3 × £60,000 less £12,500 = £27,500 and 15/30 × £60,000 = £30,000

The lesser of the two figures under (b) above is £27,500. This exceeds the figure from (a) above, so the maximum which can be provided under the occupational scheme is a pension of £27,500 per year.

Although the structure of benefit limits under earlier approval regimes (which can still apply to members who joined an occupational scheme some years ago, and have not changed jobs), the essential basis of the treatment of retained benefits is the same.

Tax free cash   11.3

Under the *FA 1989* approval regime for occupational pension schemes, the maximum permitted tax free cash sum at retirement is the greater of:

(a) 3/80ths of final earnings for each year of service; and
(b) 2.25 times the pension benefit provided under the occupational scheme

No specific provision needs to be made for retained benefits in calculating cash benefits, though the pension benefit calculated in (b) above may have been restricted by retained benefits, as in the example above.

Valuation of retained benefits 11.4

In order to take account of retained benefits, they will need to be valued. The administrator of the occupational scheme is responsible for the testing of limits, which may be required on entry to the scheme, on the occasion of an improvement in benefits, or at the point benefits are taken. There are various situations which can arise, and the rules are complex, but the details below are intended to provide a brief guide.

If benefits are in payment from an annuity, they are valued at their current level. Any cash taken earlier is also taken into account, but no additional value is placed on the fact that the amount was paid earlier than the time the occupational scheme benefits are being taken.

Where benefits are being taken by income withdrawals, the valuation is based on the maximum level of withdrawals currently available, irrespective of the amount actually being drawn.

If benefits are not yet in payment, the valuation is based on the existing personal pension fund. If the exercise is being conducted before the occupational scheme benefits are taken, the personal pension fund must be projected forward to the expected retirement date under the occupational scheme, and then converted to an income using an assumed annuity rate.

Controlling directors 11.5

In the case of controlling directors, it is also necessary to take into account any benefits under personal pension schemes and/or retirement annuity contracts where they were funded from contributions arising out of earnings from the same employment prior to their joining the occupational scheme.

For controlling directors subject to the *FA 1989* regime, these are treated as if they arose from the occupational scheme itself.

Example – Controlling directors

A controlling director is a member of their company's occupational pension scheme. They are about to retire, and have completed 16 years service. Their final earnings are £84,000.

The occupational scheme started only ten years ago, and before that, the individual funded a personal pension, under which a pension of £12,000 per year is payable.

Additionally, they have a preserved benefit of £5,000 per year from the occupational scheme of a former employer.

The £5,000 per year preserved benefit is a retained benefit. The maximum benefit which the occupational scheme could provide, ignoring the personal pension benefit, is therefore the greater of:

(a)   16/60 × £84,000 = £22,400; or if greater
(b)   the lesser of 2/3 × £84,000 less £5,000 = £51,000 and 16/30 × £84,000 = £44,800.

The maximum would therefore be £44,800 per year. However, the personal pension benefit relates to the same employment, and so reduces the maximum directly. The occupational scheme can therefore provide a maximum of only £44,800 − £12,000 = £32,800 per year.

Note that this is a harsher treatment than would be the case if the personal pension benefits were treated as a retained benefit. If this were so, the maximum occupational scheme benefit would be:

- 16/60 × £84,000 = £22,400; or if greater
- The lesser of 2/3 × £84,000 less (£5,000 + £12,000) = £39,000 and 16/30 × £84,000 = £44,800.

This would give a maximum permitted benefit of £39,000 per year.

For controlling directors subject to earlier approval regimes, these benefits are treated as retained benefits, as described in section **11.2** above.

Transfers   11.6

Benefits can be transferred from personal pension arrangements to occupational schemes, and from occupational schemes to personal pension arrangements. In general, individuals will take up the opportunity to transfer if they feel that as a result, they may improve potential benefits, but there are other factors to consider.

Transfers to occupational schemes   11.7

Although there is no legal obstacle to a transfer being paid from a personal pension to an occupational scheme, there is also no obligation on the receiving scheme to accept it. This is a matter for the trustees to determine.

If they are prepared to accept the transfer value, what benefits are provided in return for it is also decided by the trustees. The individual must decide whether to accept the terms offered.

Note that where the personal pension includes protected rights (see section **12.14**), these can only be transferred if the occupational scheme is contracted out. If it is not, only the non-protected rights can be transferred.

In some cases, the receiving scheme will offer benefits on a money purchase basis. This may offer little advantage, because it simply alters the range of investment links available, and there is no guarantee of improved performance. If a surrender penalty is applied on transferring, this may reduce the potential advantage of transferring, if it exceeds the value of future charges due under the personal pension.

Sometimes benefits are offered in the form of added years under a defined benefit scheme. For example, if the scheme provides benefits on the basis of 1/60th of final salary for each year of service, the transfer value might mean that the individual is treated as having five additional years of service, and is therefore entitled to an additional 5/60ths of final salary as a pension at retirement.

The provision of benefits on a defined benefit basis through added years may be attractive to some individuals. However, value for money might be difficult to determine, though generally added years favour those who stay in the scheme for a long period, particularly if they enjoy higher than average salary increases. Conversely, they tend not to work well for those who leave the employment well before retirement, or whose salary progression is disappointing.

Whatever form the additional benefits under the occupational scheme take, they will still be treated as retained benefits, as described in section **11.2** above.

Advantages and disadvantages 11.8

The main consideration will usually be the likelihood of the transfer producing better benefits at retirement than would have been available under the personal pension.

There is a further possible advantage which may be relevant to particular cases. If an occupational scheme accepts a transfer from a personal pension, it must provide preserved benefits for the individual if they leave the scheme, even if they have not completed the normal legal requirement of a minimum of two years' pensionable service.

However, there are also a number of disadvantages. In particular, the transferred benefits are now part of the occupational scheme benefits, and can only be accessed at the same time as main scheme benefits. Phased retirement is not permitted under occupational schemes, at least at the moment, and income withdrawals, if allowed under the scheme rules, are on a more restrictive basis than would be the case under a personal pension.

In addition, the tax free cash benefit at retirement will be subject to occupational pension scheme limits, and may be less than would be available under a personal pension. Similarly, death before retirement benefits may also be restricted.

As always with transfers, each case needs individual consideration, to determine the balance of advantage.

Transfers from occupational schemes 11.9

If a transfer is made from an occupational scheme to a personal pension, considerable care is needed and again, individual consideration is necessary. The possibility of a transfer generally arises after the individual has left the occupational scheme, and usually the employment. It is unlikely to be attractive to leave such a scheme in order to transfer when continuing membership is an option (see section **11.10** below).

It may be difficult to determine whether the transfer is good value if it derives from a defined benefit scheme, because the value of a guaranteed future benefit is often difficult to assess. The receiving personal pension scheme or an adviser will calculate the 'critical yield' (ie the investment return required in order to match the benefits given up under the occupational scheme). The individual must then consider whether they are confident of achieving or exceeding this yield under their personal pension arrangement.

If the individual chooses a transfer from a defined benefit scheme, they must appreciate that they are giving up a guaranteed benefit in return for a money purchase arrangement, where benefits will depend on investment performance and annuity rates at the point of retirement. They will only receive a greater retirement benefit if the critical yield is exceeded.

Amongst the other issues to be considered are:

(*a*) the position on death, in which event the personal pension fund would be available to provide benefits in the usual way, but some occupational schemes would provide greater benefits for survivors, though under many, death benefits after leaving service are poor;

(*b*) the position on incapacity, where some occupational schemes provide enhanced benefits, but personal pension arrangements generally do not;

(*c*) the ability under personal pensions for the individual to control aspects such as the investment choices and the timing and form of retirement benefits;

(*d*) under personal pension arrangements, the individual can determine whether benefits are available for a particular dependant, but some, for example common law and same sex partners may be excluded under the rules of the particular occupational scheme concerned;

(*e*)   the availability of phased retirement under the personal pension;

(*f*)   the flexible basis of income withdrawals available under personal pensions, compared to the occupational scheme, where – even if available – the basis is less flexible because of Inland Revenue requirements;

(*g*)   the limitation of tax free cash under personal pensions to 25% of the fund excluding protected rights (which may be more or less favourable than the basis under the occupational scheme);

(*h*)   the possible impact of the certification requirements (see section **5.14**) on both death and retirement benefits;

(*j*)   differences in the detail of benefit conditions, for example the fact that all benefits can be taken in the form of cash in cases of serious ill-health under occupational schemes, but not personal pension schemes;

(*k*)   the possibility of preserved rights under the occupational scheme being improved if the scheme finds itself in surplus, or endangered if it is in deficit in the future;

(*l*)   the alternative of transferring either to a new employer's occupational scheme (if there is one), or to a *section 32* buy-out policy, which gives individual control, but maintains many of the occupational pension provisions, also needs to be weighed.

Opting out   11.10

Individuals who are eligible to join an occupational scheme have the right to decline to join, or to leave the scheme if they have already joined. If they do so, the employment is regarded as non-pensionable and they are eligible to contribute to a personal pension.

However, it is unlikely that this will be an attractive option in many cases. The fact that the employer must contribute to an occupational scheme means that an employee who chooses not to join, or not to remain a member, gives up that employer contribution.

Although it is possible for the employer to make a similar contribution to a personal pension scheme, in practice, this is seldom done, and the employer is certainly under no obligation to do so. It would also be possible, though very unusual, to use the available contribution to finance other benefits or even a salary increase.

Choices for the employer   11.11

An employer seeking to provide a pension scheme for employees may also choose between an occupational scheme and a group personal pension.

The occupational scheme has been the traditional route, and remains the only route if the employer intends providing the scheme on a defined benefit basis. However, if the scheme is to be on a defined contribution basis, a group personal pension is a valid alternative.

The disadvantage is that the group personal pension is in reality only a collection of normal personal pension arrangements, and these are controlled by the employees, not the employer, even if funded wholly or partly by the employer. As a result, employees may not relate the scheme to the employer in the same way as they would an occupational scheme, and so may have a lower appreciation of its value as an employee benefit.

In addition, the employee could choose to access benefits at any time within the normal age limits of 50 to 75, without any reference to the employer. This may undermine the employer's intention if this is to ensure that the employees are well provided for in retirement. Taking benefits early will inevitably mean that the level of benefits available in retirement is reduced.

However, the employer's obligations are less too. For example, the legal obligations to disclose details of the scheme to employees fall largely on the product provider of the group personal pension, whereas they fall on the trustees or the employer in the case of an occupational scheme.

Also, personal pensions are completely portable, so they follow the employee when they leave service. The employer has no further dealings with the personal pension arrangements or the benefits for a member who is no longer employed, and need keep no records for this purpose.

There remain some obligations, particularly as regards paying over employee contributions to the product provider, where the contributions have been deducted through payroll. These must be paid over by the 19th of the month following the month in which the deduction is made.

There is no obligation on the employer to contribute however, whereas there must be an employer contribution to an occupational scheme.

Benefit limits, and the form of benefits are very different under occupational schemes, though group personal pension arrangements follow the normal personal pension basis. In reality, most of these schemes are well below maximum levels anyway, so the impact of limits is modest, though the different calculation of maximum tax free cash benefits at retirement may be relevant.

Note that the employer is obliged to designate a stakeholder pension scheme unless an exemption applies (see section **1.25**).

Concurrency 11.12

The concurrency rules allow an individual who is a member of an occupational pension scheme to contribute to a personal pension scheme at the same time and in relation to the same source of earnings. They are discussed in detail in section **2.20**.

There are various conditions that must be met, and in particular, controlling directors and those whose earnings exceed £30,000 are excluded. (These requirements are also expanded in section **2.20**.) However, where applicable, there are considerable attractions.

Comparison with AVCs 11.13

Making personal pension contributions under the concurrency rules will often be more attractive for those eligible than the traditional alternatives of additional voluntary contributions, either to an arrangement within the occupational scheme (in-house AVCs) or to a separate, free-standing arrangement (FSAVCs).

There are various reasons for this. Where an individual makes in-house AVCs, although they may be able to choose between a number of investment links or even between a number of different providers, the range is determined by and is selected by the trustees of the scheme. It may be therefore that there is no selection which ideally meets the individual's own requirements or objectives.

Timing of benefits 11.14

In addition, the in-house AVC arrangement is subject to the rules of the occupational scheme itself. Inland Revenue requirements regarding, for example, the timing of taking benefits from AVC arrangements have relaxed considerably in recent years, and benefits can now be taken at any time between the ages of 50 and 75, irrespective of whether the member remains in service, and irrespective of the timing of their main scheme benefits.

However, many schemes have not included this flexibility within their rules, because of the complications which could arise for scheme administration. In many cases therefore the individual would be limited to drawing their in-house AVC benefits at the same time as the main scheme benefits.

With a personal pension established under the concurrency rules, the availability of retirement benefits is fully in line with normal personal pension provisions, which will allow benefits to be taken any time between the ages of 50 and 75.

It is also possible to phase retirement benefits under a personal pension, by taking benefits from different parts of the total fund at different times (see section **5.5** for further details). Phased retirement is not possible under occupational scheme rules, including those applicable to in-house and freestanding AVCs.

Charges   11.15

Although the costs involved in in-house AVC arrangements are generally low, particularly where these costs are subsidised by the main scheme itself, personal pension charges are also generally low, particularly now, given the influence of the limit on charges under stakeholder pension arrangements (see section **1.29**).

Free-standing AVC arrangements provide the individual with the ability to choose both the provider and the investment links, but the charges under these arrangements are often considerably more than under a personal pension, though they have started to reduce because of competitive pressures.

Confidentiality   11.16

A personal pension will also give the individual complete confidentiality from their employer. Privacy is often cited as an advantage of free-standing AVC arrangements, and to an extent this is true in that the employer will not be aware of the level of contributions being made, nor of the build up of the investment fund. However, it is required that the free-standing AVC provider notify the trustees of the occupational scheme of the existence of the FSAVC arrangement, so that benefit limits can be checked when necessary.

There is no such requirement where an individual establishes a personal pension under the concurrency rules.

Limits and cash   11.17

A further important point is that benefits provided under both in-house AVC arrangements and FSAVC arrangements must be taken into account in assessing Inland Revenue limits under occupational pension schemes. Contributions to these arrangements must also lie within the 15% of earnings limitation which applies to total member contributions under occupational pension scheme legislation.

Concurrent personal pension arrangements, on the other hand, are entirely ignored for the purpose of occupational pension scheme limits, both on benefits and on contributions. The Inland Revenue's view is undoubtedly that, in practical terms, the limitation on eligibility for these arrangements to those who are neither controlling directors nor particularly high earners, means that it is highly unlikely that limits will be infringed. This is certainly reasonable, and the advantage is therefore more to do with the simplicity of explanation and operation rather than any significant chance that occupational pension limits will be exceeded.

This simplicity can be particularly relevant when dealing with the availability of tax free cash at retirement.

Under personal pension rules, 25% of the fund (excluding any protected rights) can be taken in the form of tax free cash at retirement (full details are covered in section **5.8**). With AVCs, generally no cash at all is available from the AVC arrangement itself (though there are some exceptions, in particular for arrangements started before 7 April 1987, and for some added years arrangements).

However, it is possible within Inland Revenue rules that the existence of pension benefits deriving from an AVC arrangement can increase the amount of cash which the occupational scheme itself can provide. The rules involved are complex, and will certainly be difficult for most occupational pension scheme members to understand. The simplicity of personal pensions therefore has much to commend it.

Checklist – Main advantages of personal pensions under concurrency rules

- Ability to choose the product provider.
- Control of investment choices.
- Control over the timing of benefits (within Inland Revenue requirements).
- Ability to phase retirement.
- Availability of low cost arrangements.
- Complete confidentiality from the employer and occupational scheme trustees.
- No interaction with occupational scheme contribution limits.
- No interaction with occupational scheme benefit limits.
- Availability of part of the fund as tax free cash at retirement.
- Simplicity.

Group life assurance schemes 11.18

Employers often arrange group life assurance cover for employees under occupational pension scheme rules. There are considerable attractions in doing so, because the cover is generally available on very competitive premium rates, and often with little or no medical evidence, provided a reasonable size group is covered.

Membership of such a scheme does not of itself make the employment pensionable, and so the employee remains eligible to contribute to a personal pension (see section **2.9**). As a result, an employer might choose to arrange a group life assurance scheme under occupational pension rules, and a group personal pension for retirement benefits. This would be a cost-effective and flexible approach.

12 — Contracting Out

Introduction 12.1

It is possible for individual employees, who are not already contracted out by means of an occupational pension scheme, to contract out of the State Second Pension Scheme (S2P) by means of a personal pension.

This partly reflects the Government's intention to support the idea of a partnership between State and private pensions, but also partly reflects the need to reduce the financial pressure on State pension provision.

Because membership of S2P is open only to employees, contracting out is also only open to employees. It has at various times been suggested that the self-employed be eligible for S2P, but, so far at least, this has not occurred.

There will also be certain groups of employees who are not accruing benefits under S2P. For these employees therefore, contracting out is not a relevant concept. The employees involved are those whose earnings are below the Lower Earnings Limit (£77 per week in 2003/04) and also those married women who took the opportunity to pay reduced rate National Insurance Contributions when this option was available prior to 12 May 1997, and have not subsequently reverted to full contributions.

Concept of contracting out 12.2

Employees who contract out give up S2P benefits and in return, part of the National Insurance Contributions paid by the employee themself, and by their employer, are rebated to a personal pension. These amounts are invested to provide benefits for the employee at retirement, and generally the motivation is that the employee anticipates that this will produce greater benefits than those they have given up under S2P. There may be other reasons, and these are considered later in this chapter (see section **12.20** below).

The decision to contract out, once made, is not a permanent one. Employees can change their decision each year if they wish, and they will only give up S2P benefits in respect of periods when they have chosen to contract out. Thus at retirement, most will receive a combination of benefits, partly from S2P itself, and partly from the arrangement or arrangements which they have used to contract out.

Although the underlying principle is that S2P benefits are given up in exchange for the rebate, it is important to be aware that, in some cases, not all of the individual's benefits will be foregone. In these circumstances (which are discussed in more detail in section **12.10** below) the individual will continue to have some S2P benefits in respect of periods when they have been contracted out.

It is not possible however to contract out of the State basic pension arrangements, and these continue to provide the foundation of retirement planning for many people.

SERPS 12.3

Prior to the introduction of S2P in April 2002, the State Earnings Related Pension Scheme (SERPS) was in place. S2P is a modification of SERPS, designed primarily to focus benefits to a greater extent on the lower paid.

Between 1988 and 2002, it was possible to contract out of SERPS by means of a personal pension in broadly the same way as it is now possible to contract out of S2P. There have been some differences made to the detailed operation of contracting out historically, and these are considered in section **12.17** below.

Pay As You Go 12.4

One of the reasons behind the availability of contracting out is that it reduces the financial pressure on the State pension arrangements. This pressure is largely a result of the method of funding adopted, which is usually referred to as 'Pay As You Go'.

This approach means that, rather than building up an invested fund to back the benefits for individual employees, the pension benefits paid to current pensioners are provided directly from contributions paid by those currently at work. This approach would not be acceptable in relation to private pension arrangements, because of the uncertainty of ongoing contributions, for example from an employer. However most people would consider that such a commitment entered into by the State is rather more reliable.

This approach removes a number of potential problems, including the fact that it would be a difficult proposition to manage the investment of a fund covering the long term pension entitlement of millions of people, without this in itself having a distorting effect on the investment markets as a whole.

In addition, benefits which derive from a scheme backed by individual funding would be uncertain if they depended on the investment performance achieved, and on annuity rates at retirement. Given the fact that State pensions are intended to meet basic needs, this could be difficult to justify to disappointed pensioners if investment conditions were adverse.

A further point is that it would be many years from launch before a funded scheme could produce benefits at a level high enough to make a real impact on the living standards of pensioners generally. A Pay As You Go scheme on the other hand can allow changes in benefit levels to be actioned quickly following a change in contribution levels.

However, there are also difficulties associated with the Pay As You Go approach. In particular, the level of National Insurance Contributions required to fund benefits for current pensioners depends only partly on the amount of pension provided for each one. The other major factor is the relationship between the number of pensioners in receipt of benefits and the number of people at work in respect of whom National Insurance Contributions are paid. Life expectancy has increased considerably over recent years, with increases in living standards and improvements in medical treatment, and this has led to an increase in the number of pensioners, whilst the number of people in work has remained broadly the same. This trend is expected to continue into the future.

The support ratio (the ratio between the number of employed National Insurance contributors to pensioners) has worsened considerably and is likely to continue to do so for some time into the future. The figures in the table below illustrate the projected future trends and clearly illustrate why the financial pressure on the arrangements is likely to grow.

Table – Actual and projected numbers of contributors and pensioners (millions) and the support ratio

Year	2000/ 2001	2010/ 2011	2020/ 2021	2030/ 2031	2040/ 2041	2050/ 2051	2060/ 2061
Contributors	20.2	21.6	22.2	21.5	21.4	21.3	21.0
Pensioners	11.0	12.3	12.6	15.2	16.4	15.8	15.6
Support ratio	1.8	1.7	1.8	1.4	1.3	1.4	1.3

Source: *Government Actuary's Department Quinquennial Review*, February 2000.

The importance of this issue to the economy as a whole is highlighted by the proportion of the total National Insurance fund expenditure which is made up of pension benefits. In 2000/01, out of a total of £48.6 billion, pension expenditure was £38.7 billion, ie just under 80% of the total (Source: Government Actuary's Department).

Because contracting out reduces the liability of the State for future pensioners, it reduces the future burden on the arrangements, and therefore reduces the upward pressure on National Insurance Contributions. However, from a governmental point of view, contracting out means an immediate reduction in net National Insurance receipts (after allowing for the contracting out rebate), in return for a long term reduction in liability.

If contracting out terms were too favourable, and the result was that huge numbers of people took up the option to contract out, this could create considerable short term funding problems. It is therefore important that the level of rebate available is reasonable, but not overgenerous.

Structure of S2P   12.5

Whether or not to contract out is an important choice for employees and this means that they, and their advisers, need a good understanding of the benefit structure provided. The fact that some contracted out employees will also continue to have benefits under S2P further underlines this point.

Because S2P is a modification of its forerunner, SERPS, we first consider the basis of SERPS.

SERPS benefits   12.6

SERPS was introduced in 1978, with the intention of providing an earnings related tier of benefits to ride on top of State basic pension provision.

The benefit structure changed a number of times over the period during which SERPS was in operation, but the basis in place immediately before the introduction of S2P was that individuals could, over a full working career, build up an entitlement of 20% of the band of earnings to which SERPS applied. This band of earnings (which is also the band of earnings on which S2P benefits are based) are those between the Lower Earnings Limit and the Upper Earnings Limit (between £77 and £595 per week in 2003/04).

To protect the accrual of benefits against the effects of inflation, the earnings figures taken into account for this purpose are revalued each year in line with changes in national average earnings generally. This is one of the few areas within the State benefits system where an inflation proofing provision is linked to earnings rather than prices. Final benefits are then based on the average of these revalued earnings figures throughout the individual's working career. The result should then provide a fair reflection of the real value of the individual's earnings.

Maximum SERPS benefits can be accrued over a full working career, which is 49 years for a man, and (currently) 44 years for a woman. This reflects the period between age 16 and State pension age. Where an individual does not belong to the scheme for the whole of their working career, benefits are reduced proportionately. This might arise because the individual is self-employed for a period, or because they have been contracted out.

Note however that for those who were eligible to join SERPS in 1978, the build up of benefits was accelerated. Full benefits could be achieved by anyone with 20 years or more remaining before State pension age, provided that they were members of SERPS throughout that remaining period. Once again, a proportionate reduction applies if this is not the case. The effect is that the annual accrual rate of SERPS was considerably higher for those who joined at inception than for those joining later.

In addition, SERPS accrual was initially based on a target benefit of 25% rather than 20%, which increased accrual rates still further. This basis was retained for those reaching State Pension Age no later than 5 April 2000.

Example – SERPS accrual

Suppose a male employee reached age 45 just after SERPS started on 6 April 1978, and remained in the scheme until reaching State Pension Age. He would have 20 years as a member of SERPS.

His expected benefit was 25% of average revalued band earnings, so the accrual rate was 1.25% per year of membership.

An individual joining the scheme at age 16 in 2001/02, and assuming SERPS had continued unchanged, would have had an expected benefit of 20% of average revalued band earnings, and this would accrue over a 49 year working career. This gives an accrual rate of just under 0.41% per year.

The reduction to 20% was made with effect from 6 April 1988, though benefits accrued in earlier years were preserved on the old basis. Also, those reaching State Pension Age before 5 April 2009 are subject to a sliding scale, limiting the effect of the reduction in benefits. This minimised the effect on those closest to retirement, who would have least time to make up the lost benefits by other means.

Level of SERPS benefits   12.7

The level of benefits provided by SERPS was considerably higher than is sometimes appreciated. The examples below show the benefit entitlement (in today's terms) at different earnings levels, assuming the maximum 20%

benefit is accrued under the scheme. It also shows the total benefits available, including the State basic pension, assuming the individual is a single person, both as a monetary amount and as a percentage of total income.

Examples – Total State benefits under SERPS basis

Total earnings	Band earnings	Maximum SERPS benefit	State basic pension	Total State pension	% of income
£5,000	£996	£199	£4,027	£4,226	84.5%
£10,000	£5,996	£1,199	£4,027	£5,226	52.3%
£20,000	£15,996	£3,199	£4,027	£7,226	36.1%
£30,000	£25,996	£5,199	£4,027	£9,226	30.8%
£40,000	£26,936	£5,279	£4,027	£9,306	23.3%
£50,000	£26,936	£5,279	£4,027	£9,306	18.6%
£100,000	£26,936	£5,279	£4,027	£9,306	9.3%

The overall level of income replacement provided by the combination of the basic pension and SERPS was highest at low income levels, but at these levels, the proportion of income spent on necessities is also high. Because of this, pension benefits need to be at a proportionately high level to support even basic living standards. This explains the thinking behind the Government's decision to replace SERPS with a modified scheme (S2P), and to design that scheme in a manner which provided often substantial increases in benefit for those on low incomes.

Benefits already earned under SERPS are preserved, and benefits accrue under S2P on the new basis from April 2002.

The State Second Pension Scheme (S2P)   12.8

Increasing benefits under the State pension arrangements can be very costly because of the large number of pensioners currently and prospectively qualifying for benefits. If benefits were to be increased for the lower paid, there needed to be other adjustments through the scheme, in order to keep costs within manageable proportions. Although the structure of S2P fulfils its prime purpose of focusing benefits towards the lower paid, the financial constraints have meant that it also introduces a considerably greater level of complexity.

Instead of benefits accruing at the same rate across all earnings between the Lower and Upper Earnings Limits, under S2P, these earnings are divided into three bands. The maximum entitlement which can be built up over a full working career in respect of earnings within these bands is as follows:

Earnings band	Maximum entitlement
Up to Lower Earnings Limit (£4,004 pa)	0%
Lower Earnings Limit to Lower Earnings Threshold (£11,200 pa)	40%
Lower Earnings Threshold to Upper Earnings Threshold (£25,600 pa)	10%
Upper Earnings Threshold to Upper Earnings Limit (£30,940 pa)	20%
Over the Upper Earnings Limit	0%

As with SERPS, benefits accrue uniformly over the individual's full working career, at a rate reflecting the maximum target benefit above.

The increase in target benefit (relative to the SERPS basis) on the first band of earnings from 20% to 40% boosts benefits for the lower paid, but this – on its own – would do very little for those whose earnings are just above the Lower Earnings Limit. These are often very vulnerable people, perhaps working part-time whilst caring for a disabled person.

To address this issue, special provisions apply to those who earn more than the Lower Earnings Limit but less than the Lower Earnings Threshold. Whilst National Insurance Contributions are based on actual earnings, benefits are calculated assuming earnings are equal to the Lower Earnings Threshold. As the examples below show, the overall effect is a very substantial increase in benefits for those on low levels of earnings.

Example – S2P benefits at low earnings levels

A male individual is employed on a part-time basis, and earns £5,000 per year. His S2P benefits are calculated as if he earned an amount equal to the Lower Earnings Threshold (ie £11,200 per year).

In today's terms, and assuming a full working career in S2P, his expected benefit would be 40% of (£11,200-£4,004) = £2,878 per year.

In addition, the State basic pension would be £4,027, giving total benefits of £6,905 per year, which is more than 100% of earnings.

The effect diminishes as earnings increase, as shown in the table below. The total benefits from the State as shown in monetary terms, and as a percentage of earnings. The percentage figures under the old SERPS basis are also shown, for comparison purposes.

Examples – Total State benefits under S2P basis

Total earnings	Maximum S2P benefit	State basic pension	Total State pension	% of income	% under SERPS basis
£5,000	£2,878	£4,027	£6,905	138.1%	84.5%
£10,000	£2,878	£4,027	£6,905	69.1%	52.3%
£20,000	£3,758	£4,027	£7,785	38.9%	36.1%
£30,000	£5,199	£4,027	£9,226	30.8%	30.8%
£40,000	£5,279	£4,027	£9,306	23.3%	23.3%
£50,000	£5,279	£4,027	£9,306	18.6%	18.6%
£100,000	£5,279	£4,027	£9,306	9.3%	9.3%

The higher maximum benefit on the first of the three bands of earnings means that those earning up to £11,200 are accruing benefits considerably faster than would have been the case under SERPS. This advantage is then gradually clawed back over the next band of earnings, and the bands are calculated so that once the top of the second band is reached, the rate of benefit accrual is the same as would have applied under SERPS.

On the third band, the benefits are the same as they would have been under SERPS. The net effect of this is that those earning less than £25,600 will receive better benefits under S2P than would have been the case under SERPS, and those earning above this level receive the same benefits.

Example

A female employee earns £28,000 per year. Under SERPS, her maximum benefit at retirement, in today's terms, would have been:

20% of (£28,000–£4,004) = £4,799 per year (excluding State basic pension).

Under S2P, the calculation would be:

40% of (£11,200–£4,004) =   £2,879
10% of (£25,600–£11,200) =   £1,440
20% of £28,000–£25,600) =   £ 480
                              £4,799

This inevitably means that if the current structure of S2P were to be maintained, the cost of benefits would be greater than would have been the case under SERPS. The Government's stated long term intention is that the cost of S2P should be approximately the same as SERPS, and therefore a second phase of changes is planned. When this takes place, the benefit basis will be amended so that all members accrue benefits as if they were earning an amount equal to the Lower Earnings Threshold. This will have the effect of turning S2P into a second tier flat rate scheme, providing the same benefits for all members who complete the same period of membership, irrespective of their earnings history.

Originally, it was intended that the second tier of changes would come into effect five years after the introduction of S2P, subject to stakeholder pensions being successful in significantly increasing the extent of private pension provision. This has not so far occurred, and the Government indicated in December 2002 that the decision would for the moment be kept under review.

In the meantime, S2P benefits will continue to accrue on the basis described in this section, and when (and if) the change to a flat rate basis is made, benefits earned prior to the date of change will be preserved.

Contracting out with personal pensions 12.9

In order to allow an individual to contract out by means of a personal pension scheme, the scheme documentation must include specific provisions relating to the way in which the National Insurance rebate will be dealt with, and must have been granted a contracting out certificate by the Inland Revenue.

A personal pension which includes the necessary provisions is known as an Appropriate Personal Pension Scheme (APPS).

Note that being a member of an APPS does not necessarily mean that the individual is contracted out. Many providers offer only one scheme, and this will include some employed members who have decided to contract out, and some who have decided not to. It will also include self-employed individuals, to whom contracting out does not apply. The provisions relating to contracting out are simply not activated for those who are not contracted out.

S2P benefits foregone 12.10

Generally when an employee contracts out by means of an APPS, they will forego all S2P benefits which would have accrued in respect of the contracted out period.

However, for those who earn more than the Lower Earnings Limit, but less than the Lower Earnings Threshold, the S2P benefits foregone will be calculated based on actual earnings. The benefits under S2P would have been calculated as if earnings equalled the Lower Earnings Threshold, and the additional benefits provided as a result of this are retained under S2P.

Although we are only concerned here with contracting out by means of personal pension arrangements and not occupational schemes, it is important to be aware that the basis of calculating benefits foregone is different under occupational schemes. Essentially the benefits foregone under contracted out occupational schemes are those which would have accrued had SERPS continued in its pre-2002 form, rather than having been replaced by S2P. This means that all those earning less than £25,600 will still have additional benefits held under S2P, even though they are contracted out, whilst only those earning less than £11,200 will be in this position where contracting out is achieved through a personal pension.

The rebates available for those contracted out under occupational schemes are adjusted to reflect this difference.

National Insurance rebate   12.11

Where a member contracts out by means of an APPS, the National Insurance rebate is paid direct to their personal pension scheme by the National Insurance Contributions Office (NICO) of the Inland Revenue. This will occur a few months after the end of the tax year to which the rebate relates.

The calculation of the rebate is undertaken by NICO and there is no alteration to the level of contributions paid by employer or employee through payroll. For this reason the calculation must await the provision of year end information by the employer.

The advantage of this approach is that the individual's employer does not need to be involved, or even be informed of the individual's decision to contract out. The individual simply makes application via their product provider.

If it were necessary for the employer to amend payroll systems, to accommodate different National Insurance Contribution levels, this could involve the employer in extra expense. It could therefore be that in some cases, the employer might try to dissuade the employee from contracting out in the first place.

The amount of the rebate is based on earnings between the Lower and Upper Earnings Limits, and differs with age, but also differs between the three bands of earnings in relation to which benefits accrue at different rates (see section **12.8** above).

Examples of rebate levels relative to Band 3 earnings (between the Upper Earnings Threshold and the Upper Earnings Limit) are given below.

Examples – Contracted out rebates under APPS arrangements 2003/04 (Band 3)

Age attained at 6 April 2003	Rebate as % of earnings
15	4.2%
25	4.6%
35	5.0%
45	6.2%
55	10.5%

The percentage is lower at young ages and higher at older ages. This reflects the fact that a rebate paid in respect of a younger employee can be invested for considerably longer than one paid for an older employee, and should therefore benefit from a higher level of investment growth.

From an equitable point of view, the percentage rebate should continue to increase as age increases, but in fact the level of rebate is capped at 10.5%, which is reached at age 52. At ages below that at which this cap is reached, the level of rebate is calculated by the Government Actuary to represent fair value for money relative to the benefits foregone, and based on assumptions determined by him. It follows that where the level of rebate is restricted by the cap, it will represent less than fair value on those assumptions.

We consider the advantages and disadvantages of contracting out in sections **12.20** and **12.21** below, but clearly the imposition of the cap will be a negative factor in many cases.

The rebate on Band 1 earnings (between the Lower Earnings Limit and the Lower Earnings Threshold) is double that on Band 3 earnings, because the rate of accrual of S2P benefits is double. Similarly, it is halved on Band 2 earnings, because the accrual of S2P benefits is halved.

Reviews of the rebate 12.12

The level of the contracted out rebate is reviewed periodically, usually at five year intervals. The next review is due to take effect from 6 April 2007. Any changes must be announced at least twelve months in advance.

Tax relief 12.13

The amount of the rebate available to those contracted out by means of a personal pension is increased by the addition of basic rate tax relief (on a grossed up basis) on the employee portion of the rebate. This portion is always 1.6% of earnings between the Lower and Upper Earnings Limits.

Note that the employee portion is not in any way related to age, and also that it does not vary between the earnings bands. The value of the tax relief element is therefore always just over 0.45% of earnings between the Lower and Upper Earnings Limits.

The grossing up for basic rate relief occurs automatically, and the tax relief is also paid direct to the personal pension by NICO. There is no clawback of this relief if the employee concerned is a non-taxpayer, or is only subject to tax at the 10% starting rate. However neither is there any ability to claim higher rate relief if the employee is a higher rate taxpayer.

The thinking behind this relief is to provide broad equality with the situation which arises under occupational pension schemes where the individual's National Insurance liability is reduced through payroll. This saving might be used to subsidise a member contribution to the scheme, which would qualify for tax relief.

The total amount paid by way of National Insurance rebate and the accompanying tax relief is referred to as 'minimum contributions'.

Protected rights   12.14

Minimum contributions must be accumulated to provide protected rights, which are subject to specific provisions which differ from those applicable to other personal pension benefits. This means that the personal pension provider must maintain separate records of these contributions and the growth achieved on them. Generally protected rights are housed in a separate arrangement, and if this is not done, the special requirements and restrictions will apply to all benefits, not just those arising directly from the minimum contributions.

It is not possible to segment protected rights benefits, nor to split the minimum contributions in respect of any particular year between a number of providers. (It is however possible to choose a different provider each year if the individual so wishes.)

Requirements   12.15

Protected rights benefits cannot be accessed until age 60 at the earliest, but benefits can be deferred until the normal upper age limit of 75.

It is not possible to pay protected rights benefits earlier than 60, even in cases of incapacity, and neither do the special early retirement ages normally applicable to those in special occupations (see **Chapter 13: Special Occupations**) apply to protected rights.

No part of the protected rights benefits can be paid in the form of cash, and generally the protected rights fund must be ignored in calculating the 25% cash limit on other benefits. There is an exception to this rule in the case of pre-Royal Assent arrangements, which is discussed in section **5.11**.

The absence of a cash benefit reflects the fact that tax free cash is not available from S2P itself, and this is therefore not an unreasonable restriction. Nevertheless, it would be an encouragement for individuals to contract out if cash were available, and one of the possible changes mooted by the Government in their consultation paper *Simplicity, Security and Choice: Working and saving for retirement*, issued by the Department for Work and Pensions in December 2002, was to lift this restriction. It was also suggested that the prohibition on drawing benefits earlier than 60 might be removed.

Protected rights benefits for the moment must provide only income, and can do so either through annuity purchase or income withdrawals. Where an annuity is purchased, the rates applied by the insurance company must be on a unisex basis rather than the more usual basis, which differentiates between males and females.

Provision must be made to include a 50% spouse's benefit on the death of the member, if married, and in addition the annuity must escalate at the lesser of 5% *per annum* or the increase in the Retail Prices Index.

More detailed discussion of the requirements is included in section **5.36**.

Income withdrawals are available as an alternative to annuity purchase, and special GAD rates apply, to reflect the basis of protected rights annuities, and in particular, the inclusion of escalation and spouse's benefits.

Income withdrawals cannot be continued beyond age 75, by which age, at the latest, the individual must have bought an annuity.

Note that although protected rights income must include escalation if provided by an annuity, there is no requirement for income withdrawals to increase year by year in the same way. The requirement is simply that the amount withdrawn in any year lies between the 35% and 100% limits.

Death before retirement   12.16

If the individual dies before taking retirement benefits, the protected rights fund will often have to be used to provide income benefits. This will generally be the case where the individual dies leaving a surviving spouse, and the detailed provisions are covered in section **8.11**.

In the absence of a surviving spouse, the protected rights can be paid as a lump sum on the death of the member, and will be free of income tax, though the benefits are usually paid to the estate, and may be liable to inheritance tax if received by a non-exempt beneficiary.

Checklist – Protected rights

The main requirements relating to protected rights are as follows.

- Retirement benefits can be accessed only between the ages of 60 and 75.
- There is no provision for earlier access, even in cases of incapacity or special occupations.
- No part of the benefit can be taken in the form of cash at retirement.
- The protected rights fund must usually be ignored when calculating the cash available at retirement from the rest of the personal pension fund.
- It can however be included under pre-Royal Assent personal pensions.
- If income benefits are provided by means of an annuity, escalation at the lesser of 5% *per annum* or the RPI increase must be included.
- Provision must also be made for a 50% spouse's benefit on the member's death.
- Income withdrawals are available as an alternative to an annuity, but an annuity must be purchased no later than the member's 75th birthday.
- Phasing retirement benefits is not permitted in respect of protected rights benefits.
- On death before taking retirement benefits, the fund must be used to provide income if the member is survived by a spouse.
- Otherwise, the fund can be paid out as a lump sum.

Historical variations   12.17

Although SERPS started in 1978, it was originally only possible to contract out by means of a defined benefit occupational pension scheme. Contracting out on a money purchase basis, including contracting out under personal pensions, was introduced in 1988. However, even since then, a number of changes have been made to the basis of contracting out.

For example, at one time it was necessary to include within the annuity purchased by the protected rights fund, a provision for a spouse's pension on the member's death, even if the member was unmarried at the point of retirement. This provision has now been abolished, and no longer applies even in respect of contracted out periods prior to the change.

The requirement for escalation of a protected rights annuity changed with effect from 6 April 1997, prior to which the requirement was for escalation at the lesser of 3% *per annum* or the increase in the Retail Prices Index. This lesser requirement still applies in relation to benefits relating to service before 6 April 1997, and so if an individual now purchases an annuity covering protected rights which accrued partly before that date and partly after, the escalation provisions will differ.

A further important aspect of contracting out which has undergone a number of changes is the relationship between total benefits and the amount of benefit foregone on contracting out. As already discussed, the current situation under S2P is that an individual who contracts out will generally give up all benefit, with the exception that those earning less than the Lower Earnings Threshold of £11,200 per year will still have residual S2P benefits (see section **12.10** above).

Between 1988 and 1997, the situation was considerably more complex. Contracting out required giving up not the whole of the employee's SERPS benefits, but only a benefit equivalent to the guaranteed minimum pension (GMP). This concept arose from the basis upon which defined benefit occupational schemes contracted out at the time. This was based on the philosophy that contracted out individuals under such schemes should be guaranteed not to be worse off as a result of being contracted out. The GMP benefit was designed to provide for this.

Essentially, GMP approximates SERPS benefits, but with the proviso that any difference between the benefit that would have been provided under SERPS and the GMP benefit which a defined benefit scheme has to provide would be retained under SERPS. For example, SERPS benefits in payment are fully inflation proofed in line with the RPI, whilst the extent to which GMP benefits must escalate is limited to a maximum of 3% *per annum*. If RPI inflation exceeds 3%, the excess continues to be provided under SERPS.

Between 1988 and 1997, if an individual was contracted out by means of a personal pension, their SERPS entitlement was not completely lost, but instead was reduced by what would have been the GMP had they been a member of a defined benefit scheme. There will therefore in many cases be a residual benefit retained under SERPS. (Note however that there was no guarantee that the member would not be worse off as a result of contracting out under a personal pension.)

The level of contracting out rebate at the time was calculated taking into account the residual SERPS benefits, so although it perhaps seems a strange concept, the overall result is a reasonable one.

From 6 April 1997, the GMP test for defined benefit schemes was abolished, and so the basis of dealing with contracting out under personal pensions also needed to change. Over the period from 1997 to the introduction of S2P in 2002 therefore, contracting out meant that the individual gave up all of their SERPS entitlement. This fulfilled the basic concept of contracting out for the first time, and created a relatively simple situation, though one which was short lived.

Transfers of contracted out rights 12.18

Where transfers are received into a personal pension scheme from a contracted out occupational pension scheme, complications can arise. If the scheme was contracted out on a money purchase basis, then protected rights will have arisen in much the same way as under personal pensions (though the detailed mechanism differs). On transfer, the value of the occupational pension scheme protected rights becomes protected rights under the personal pension and is treated in accordance with the rules discussed above.

Where the transferring scheme was contracted out on a defined benefit basis, and GMP benefits arose in respect of service before 6 April 1997, the value of those benefits will be segregated, and will be treated as protected rights. Again the provisions described above apply to these rights.

After the abolition of the GMP test in April 1997, it became impossible to identify any particular part of the transferred rights as representing the contracted out rights. As a result, all post-April 1997 rights are treated as protected rights when transferred to the personal pension.

If this is a significant part of the transfer (which is increasingly the case as the post-April 1997 service is potentially greater), this can be a serious disadvantage. It means that benefits could not be taken until at least age 60 and no part of them can be taken in cash, whereas it would generally have been possible to take some benefits in cash under the occupational scheme. As a result, a transfer to a personal pension may not be advisable.

Example – Transfer of post-April 1997 rights

An individual has been a member of a contracted out final salary scheme since May 1997. They left the employment to which it related in May 2003, with a preserved pension of £8,000 per year, payable at retirement. Alternatively, they could take a reduced pension of £7,500 per year, together with a tax free cash sum of £30,000. (These figures would be revalued between the date of leaving and retirement.)

If the individual transferred these rights to a personal pension scheme, they would all be regarded as protected rights, because they all relate to contracted out service under a defined benefit scheme, after 6 April 1997.

As a result, no cash benefit would be available at retirement from the personal pension scheme, and benefits could not be drawn before age 60.

The contracting out decision   12.19

It can be difficult for employees to determine whether or not they should contract out. The assumptions made by the Government Actuary in calculating the level of rebate are quite stringent, particularly those relating to the effect of charges under the personal pension. These reflect stakeholder pension requirements, and this may understate the actual level of charges made under many personal pension schemes.

There will therefore be few situations where contracting out can be regarded as providing anything like certainty of improved benefits.

Advantages of contracting out   12.20

Some individuals will prefer that their rights to benefit are identified with them personally, and are capable of being valued, in a way which is not possible if those rights remain under S2P.

Contracting out means that those rights are held under a personal pension in the individual's own name and are not simply part of the State pension scheme. This will mean that the value of those rights cannot be eroded in any way by future changes to the State scheme. For example, should there be a decision in future to increase State pension age (in much the same way as State pension age for women is already increasing from 60 to 65), this could reduce the value of benefits which remain under S2P, though this would depend on the detail of the basis of change adopted.

There is no current indication that the Government plans to do this, and indeed it has only recently committed to maintaining the State pension age. However it is undeniable that a change could occur in future, given the financial pressures as discussed in section **12.4** above.

There is also the potential to improve on the level of benefits which S2P would provide, through the achievement of strong investment performance, at a level greater than the Government Actuary has assumed in calculating the level of rebate. Contracting out will therefore inevitably appeal more to an individual who is optimistic about future investment prospects than someone who is pessimistic.

Clearly younger employees, with a long period over which to invest the rebate, will find contracting out most attractive, if they feel investment conditions will be favourable.

In addition, there are attractions in term of the timing and form of benefits. State pension age for men is 65, and although it remains 60 for some women, for the majority it is now later, and in many cases is also 65. Although protected rights are not available as early as other personal pension benefits, the ability to access protected rights from 60 is still attractive to many people.

An additional consideration, where the individual is unmarried, is that there is now no requirement to make provision for a hypothetical spouse in respect of protected rights, and this should enhance the level of income available to the individual.

A further advantage is the ability to take benefits in the form of income withdrawals, with the fund remaining invested, and this may again appeal to those with an optimistic outlook on the future of investment markets.

The ability to take account of the protected rights fund in calculating tax free cash from a pre-Royal Assent personal pension will also add a further modest advantage for those with such contracts (see section **5.11**).

A further relevant point is that the benefits provided under S2P on the death of a member before retirement are limited, and at most will be 50% of the member's own benefits. Only a legally married spouse can benefit, so an unmarried partner of a deceased employee would receive nothing from S2P by way of inherited rights. Where an individual is contracted out, and rebates have been paid to the personal pension to form a protected rights fund, this fund is available in full to provide benefits on death, which could mean an income for a legally married spouse, but in other circumstances could be paid as a lump sum.

Disadvantages of contracting out 12.21

On the negative side, possibly the main disadvantage of contracting out is the loss of a guaranteed income benefit. S2P is a defined benefit scheme and provides certainty of benefits calculated according to a known formula. Taking the National Insurance rebate in lieu of these guaranteed benefits not only opens up the opportunity of receiving enhanced benefits, but also exposes the individual to the possibility of reduced benefits as a result of poor investment returns or a downturn in annuity rates.

The situation is made rather more difficult because the timing of the receipt of the rebate is uncertain. This is because it depends on the timing of the completion of the rebate calculation by the Inland Revenue, following receipt of the relevant information from the employer. This can make it difficult to decide on the way in which the rebate should be invested, and more difficult still to be sure that the timing of the investment will be favourable.

As already mentioned the calculation of the rebate is based on the expectation of low levels of charge under the personal pension, and many arrangements will in practice have higher levels of charge, meaning that the investment return required to match or exceed the S2P benefits given up is that much higher.

Once the maximum rebate of 10.5% of earnings between Lower and Upper Earnings Limits is reached, it inevitably becomes more difficult to argue for contracting out on the basis of the likelihood of improved ultimate benefits. Although the attraction of a visible and quantifiable pension fund may still appeal to some individuals, the likelihood of ultimately reduced benefits increases as age increases.

Making the decision 12.22

In the end the decision will almost always be finely balanced, and most commentators now feel that there is very limited advantage in contracting out. Certainly those who decide to do so be sure that they fully appreciate the risk involved.

It is also important to keep the decision under review on an ongoing basis. An individual who contracts out this year can change their mind and go back into S2P next year if they so choose. There is also nothing to stop them changing their mind again in some subsequent year and deciding to contract out again.

The decision will always be a personal one, though it is probably fair to say that those with modest retirement resources may be well advised to stick with the security of S2P rather than taking the risk of contracting out and relying on investment markets and future annuity rates to provide for a significant aspect of their income benefits.

13 — Special Occupations

Retirement 13.1

As discussed in **Chapter 5: Retirement Benefits**, although there is a great deal of flexibility in terms of the timing of retirement benefits under personal pension arrangements, there is generally a requirement that benefits commence strictly between the ages of 50 and 75. There is an exception to this rule in cases of incapacity, when benefits can be taken at any time, and this is discussed in detail in **Chapter 9: Incapacity**.

Early retirement ages 13.2

It has however been recognised for many years that there are certain special occupations where retirement at an age earlier than 50 is normal, and indeed is generally necessitated by the nature of the activity involved. Typically, though not without exception, the individuals concerned are professional sportspeople such as football players or cricketers. The requirement of the legislation is given in *section 643(3)* of the *Income and Corporation Taxes Act 1988 (ICTA 1988)*, and is that the Board of the Inland Revenue 'are satisfied that his occupation is one in which persons customarily retire before [50].'

The Inland Revenue publishes a list of special occupations which they recognise as meeting this requirement, and the details are shown in the table below.

Note that where a special early age applies, it is still open to the individual to delay drawing retirement benefits to a later date, which can be anywhere between the early retirement age and their 75th birthday.

Table – Professions with agreed early retirement ages for personal pensions

Age 30	Skiers (Downhill)
Age 35	Athletes
	Badminton Players
	Boxers
	Cyclists
	Dancers
	Footballers
	Ice Hockey Players
	Jockeys – National Hunt
	Models
	Rugby League Players

Age 35 – *continued*
    Rugby Union Players
    Squash Players
    Table Tennis Players
    Tennis Players (including Real Tennis)
    Wrestlers

Age 40   Cricketers
    Divers (Saturation, Deep Sea and Free Swimming)
    Golfers
    Motor Cycle Riders (Motocross or Road Racing)
    Motor Racing Drivers
    Snooker/Billiards Players
    Speedway Riders
    Trapeze Artistes

Age 45   Jockeys – Flat Racing
    Members of the Reserve Forces

Retirement annuity contracts 13.3

There are many differences between personal pensions and retirement annuity contracts, and these are dealt with in **Chapter 14: Retirement Annuity Contracts**. Note however that, since the earliest age at which retirement benefits can generally be accessed from a retirement annuity contract is 60, there is a further group of recognised occupations where a retirement age of 50 or 55 is permitted. These occupations are in addition those given in the personal pension list above, which can apply equally to personal pensions and retirement annuity contracts.

Table – Additional professions with agreed early retirement ages for retirement annuity contracts

Age 50   Croupiers
    Money Broker Dealers
    Newscasters
    Offshore riggers
    Royal Navy Reservists
    Rugby League referees
    Territorial Army members

Age 55   Air pilots
    Brass instrumentalists
    Distant Water Trawlermen
    Firemen (part-time)
    Inshore Fishermen
    Midwives or Health Visitors who are female
    Money Broker Dealer Directors

Age 55 – *continued*
> National Health Service Psychiatrists
> Nurses
> Physiotherapists
> Singers

Sources of earnings   13.4

Individuals with earnings deriving from these special occupations will very often have sources of earnings from other activities which are not directly part of the pursuit of the occupation concerned. For example, a sports professional will have earnings which are the direct result of their sports activity, such as tournament earnings and appearance money, but in addition may have income from sponsorship or coaching.

Contributions can only be made to a personal pension with a special early retirement age in respect of earnings directly relating to the occupation concerned, and only to the extent allowed by the normal limitations based on net relevant earnings from that occupation (or the earnings threshold if this gives a higher figure).

The individual is free to establish a separate personal pension arrangement (or arrangements) in respect of other sources of net relevant earnings, but these must conform with normal rules (ie benefits can commence only between the ages of 50 and 75, except in cases of incapacity).

It is also required that the individual advise the scheme administrator immediately if they are no longer following the recognised special occupation, and in these circumstances, contributions to any arrangements with a special retirement age must cease.

Example – Two sources of income

A 28-year-old professional tennis player earns £30,000 from tournaments in 2003/04, but also earns a further £20,000 from coaching.

They could contribute up to 17.5% of £30,000 = £5,250 to a personal pension with a pension age of 35.

They could make further contributions of up to 17.5% of £20,000 = £3,500 to a personal pension with a pension age between 50 and 75.

If they only have sufficient resources to pay a contribution of £5,250 or less, it would make sense to use a personal pension with an early pension age. They would then have the flexibility to draw benefits at any time between 35 and 75.

Total contributions must remain within normal limits based on total net relevant earnings, even if split between two (or more) personal pension arrangements, one with a special retirement age, one with a normal age.

It is possible to contribute up to the earnings threshold of £3,600 to an arrangement with a special retirement age, even if earnings from the special occupation are low. (This is confirmed in the *Inland Revenue Guidance Notes (IR76) para 8.8.*) However, if a further arrangement is established to pension earnings from another source which is not part of the special occupation, normal limits apply to total contributions. In particular, a further earnings threshold does not become available.

Example – Application of earnings threshold

A 26-year-old earns a small amount from tournament prize money as a professional golfer. In 2003/04, their income from this source is £6,600. In addition, they give golf lessons at a local club, and earn £20,000 from this.

They can establish a personal pension arrangement with a pension age of 40, based on their tournament earnings. The maximum contribution is the greater of:

(a)   17.5% of £6,600 = £1,115; and
(b)   the earnings threshold of £3,600.

The individual can therefore contribute up to £3,600 for 2003/04 to the arrangement with the pension age of 40.

If they do this, and then wish to make further provision in respect of their earnings from golf lessons, the overall maximum contribution is based on total net relevant earnings (£6,600 + £20,000 = £26,600) and is therefore the greater of:

- 17.5% of £21,600 = £4,655; and
- the earnings threshold of £3,600.

As the individual has already contributed £3,600 to the other personal pension arrangement, the maximum additional amount they can contribute is £4,655 − £3,600 = £1,055.

Retirement options

13.5

As already mentioned, considerable flexibility is available under personal pensions with early retirement ages. It is possible for retirement benefits to start at the special retirement age, or at any time after that age, subject to the normal upper limit of age 75.

Benefits can also be phased over this period if required, as described in section **5.5**.

The normal options apply regarding the form of benefits, so that up to 25% of the fund under the personal pension arrangement can generally be taken in the form of a tax free lump sum, with the balance being used to provide an income. This income can be provided through purchase of an annuity, or through income withdrawals, subject to the normal rules and limits as discussed in **Chapters 5: Retirement Benefits** and **6: Income Withdrawals**.

Protected rights 13.6

Note that if the individual contracts out of the State Second Pension (S2P), the normal rules as discussed in **Chapter 12: Contracting Out** apply.

This means that the protected rights benefits which result from contracting out will not be accessible until age 60, and no part of the protected rights themselves can be taken in the form of cash.

The maximum tax free cash sum of 25% available from the rest of the personal pension must be calculated excluding the protected rights, except in the case of pre-Royal Assent arrangements (ie arrangements started before 27 July 1989 – see section **5.11**).

Practical application 13.7

It seems reasonable that an individual who follows an occupation from which they are likely to retire early should be able to recognise this in terms of the structure of their pension arrangement. This is why special occupations have been recognised in the past by the Inland Revenue.

However, this does not mean that it is always an option which is practicable.

For example, although there are numerous well known and well publicised sports professionals who earn very large sums indeed, many others earn much more modest amounts. This will make it difficult to build up a large enough pension fund to give a realistic opportunity of early retirement. There will have been relatively few years during which to pay contributions, and only a short time for the fund to be increased through investment returns.

Annuity rates at young ages are substantially more expensive than at older ages, reflecting the longer life expectancy of the individual. This would also affect the limits on the level of income withdrawals which would be available, based on Government Actuary's Department rates.

In any event, in most cases, the individuals involved will not stop work when their involvement in their special occupation ceases, but instead will move on to other occupations. This could for example include coaching, sports commentating, or an entirely different and perhaps more conventional career. This would then provide the individual with the opportunity to build up further pension benefits related to the earnings from these activities, and available at a retirement age within the normal range.

Where the individual has a new source of earnings, they may not need to take benefits from the arrangement related to their special occupation at the agreed early age. There could also be a tax disincentive if the new career is producing high earnings, so that any pension income would be subject to higher rate tax.

In practice therefore, the availability of an early retirement age does not necessarily mean that benefits will (or should) be taken early.

Additions to the list   13.8

It is possible for applications to be made to the Inland Revenue to allow further occupations to be added to the list.

The *Inland Revenue Guidance Notes (IR76)* indicate that the applications should include:

(*a*)   details of the occupation concerned;
(*b*)   the proposed early pension age; and
(*c*)   evidence from the relevant professional or representative body demonstrating why the proposed early age is considered to be appropriate for that occupation.

Although the list of occupations has expanded over the years, in the light of the comments below regarding the effect of the pensions simplification proposals, it may be that the Inland Revenue will be reluctant to accept any further applications.

Effect of pensions simplification   13.9

The proposals for pension simplification put forward by the Inland Revenue in December 2002 are dealt with in detail in **Chapter 15: Simplification of Tax Treatment**. One of the less well-publicised provisions within these proposals is the suggestion that the availability of early retirement ages for special occupations should be withdrawn entirely.

Bear in mind that it is also proposed to raise the normal minimum age at which benefits can be accessed from 50 to 55. The change would therefore be quite significant in terms of the reduction in flexibility it involves for those in special occupations.

In general, one of the central concepts within the simplification proposals is that the new rules (assuming they are introduced) should apply to existing as well as new arrangements. However, the Inland Revenue have indicated that the issue of dealing with existing personal pension arrangements with early retirement ages is undecided, and that views are genuinely being sought as part of the consultation process.

It is stressed that these proposals are still at the consultation stage at the time of writing, and readers who might be affected, or who advise those who might be affected, will wish to remain up to date with developments as they occur over the coming months.

Doctors and dentists 13.10

Doctors and dentists who operate in NHS general practice are subject to special rules in respect of contributions to personal pensions. The term 'General Practitioners' (GPs) is generally used to cover both doctors and dentists in this context, and in this chapter, we follow this convention.

The individuals concerned are taxed under Schedule D, and are treated for most purposes as being self-employed. However, they undertake work for the NHS, and are eligible for membership for the National Health Service Pension Scheme (NHSPS), which is an occupational scheme. Schemes of this type are generally available exclusively to Schedule E employees, and it is the peculiarity of their position in being eligible for the NHSPS which has resulted in their special treatment for personal pension purposes.

National Health Service Pension Scheme 13.11

To put a consideration of the personal pension position into context, we first look briefly at the structure of the National Health Service Pension Scheme (NHSPS), as it applies to GPs. This is fundamentally different to the basis which applies to employed NHS staff, such as hospital doctors.

In particular, for employed staff, the NHSPS provides benefits linked to final pay, but for GPs, the basis reflects average pensionable pay, adjusted for inflation. The make-up of a GP's earnings can vary considerably throughout their career, and the proportion of NHS income can fluctuate widely. In many cases, the amount of NHS income can reduce towards the latter stages of the GP's career, as they undertake more private work. In these circumstances, benefits based on final pay would not provide a fair reflection of the NHS work undertaken through the individual's career as a whole.

Table – NHSPS Main benefit provisions for GPs

Retirement Age	Generally the GP can retire between 60 and 65, though optional early retirement with reduced benefits is available from 50. Late retirement is also usually possible.
Pension	1.4% of uprated pensionable pay throughout the period of membership. (This equates to 1.4% per year of average uprated pay.) Pensionable pay from past years is uprated in line with recommendations by the relevant Pay Review Body, so that benefits ultimately reflect average inflation adjusted pay.
Tax free cash at retirement	Generally three times the annual pension benefit. Note that this is in addition to the pension benefit, and it is not necessary (nor possible) for the GP to commute any part of the pension.
Death in retirement	If death occurs within five years of retirement, a lump sum is paid equivalent to the balance of a five year pension guarantee. However, this is subject to a maximum of twice the average of uprated annual pensionable pay less the tax free cash sum paid at retirement. A pension of 50% of the GP's own pension continues to a surviving legal spouse and there are additional pensions for dependent children. (Widower's benefits generally only reflect service from April 1988.)
Death in service	A lump sum is payable of twice the average of uprated annual pensionable pay. A pension of 50% of the pension the GP would have received on incapacity early retirement is paid to a surviving legal spouse and there are additional pensions for dependent children. (As on death in retirement, widower's benefits generally only reflect service from April 1988.)
Inflation proofing	All pensions in payment are fully inflation proofed in line with the Retail Prices Index.
Member contributions	6% of pensionable pay.

The details in the table are intended only as a summary. There are many detailed provisions related to the scheme, and further details are available from the NHS Pensions Agency, through their website www.nhspa. gov.uk.

Pensionable Pay 13.12

One of the issues when considering the benefits available from the NHSPS in the case of a GP is the way in which pensionable pay should be determined. Generally under occupational schemes, this is a relatively straightforward matter because, when dealing with Schedule E employees, earnings are taxed through PAYE at the time they are received, and the level of pay can be determined immediately.

In contrast to this, the GP is taxed under Schedule D and will prepare accounts in the same way as any other self-employed person, based on the gross income received and the expenses etc which can be deducted from that income to determine taxable profit. The profit figure cannot therefore be determined until after the end of the accounting period concerned.

If profit were the basis of pensionable pay under the NHSPS, this would mean an unacceptable delay in calculating the basis of benefits under the scheme.

In addition, GPs generally receive income from sources other than the NHS. This might be from a substantial involvement in private practice, which in some cases will produce income which exceeds that received from the NHS. In other cases, the other income might arise from relatively small items, such as signing certificates and so forth on behalf of patients. Whilst the NHSPS is intended to provide pension and other benefits in relation to earnings received from the NHS, it is not intended to cover earnings from other sources. Whilst the source of such other income could be determined easily enough, the apportionment of expenses of various sorts would be very onerous, and possibly contentious, if it was attempted on a precise basis.

As a result, a hypothetical calculation is undertaken to allow for practice expenses. Not all parts of the NHS fees received are regarded as pensionable, but most are, and an expenses deduction is made by the Health Authority (HA) or Dental Practice Board (DPB) in order to arrive at pensionable pay. The rate of deduction (which differs between medical and dental practitioners) is agreed annually after consideration by the relevant pay review body and in consultation with professional associations.

As well as being the basis for benefits under the NHSPS, it is important to determine pensionable earnings because of the impact which they have on personal pension contribution limits. This is discussed in section **13.17** below.

Happily it is not necessary for the GP or for their advisers to duplicate the calculation made by the Health Authority or Dental Practice Board. Instead pensionable pay can be calculated simply from the contributions paid by the GP to the NHSPS. These are paid at the rate of 6% of pensionable pay and therefore by taking the amount of the contribution and multiplying by 100/6, the pensionable pay figure can be established.

> *Example – Calculation of pensionable pay*
>
> A GP pays NHSPS contributions of £4,200 in 2003/04.
>
> Their NHSPS pensionable pay is therefore:
>
> £4,200 × 100/6 = £70,000.

Limits on pensionable pay 13.13

There are two limits which may apply to pensionable pay under the NHSPS. One is the normal earnings cap which applies to members who join the NHSPS on or after 1 June 1989. The limit is £99,000 for 2003/04.

A separate limit applies to dental practitioners, for historic reasons. The latest available figure is £101,300, which applies in respect of the year to 31 March 2003. In the past, this limit has usually been lower than the earnings cap, but currently is higher. However, for dentists who joined the NHSPS on or after 1 June 1989, the earnings cap of £99,000 overrides the higher separate limit applicable to dentists.

These limits will be reflected in the contributions paid by GPs and it therefore should not be necessary to make separate allowance for this in calculating NHS pensionable pay.

Extra Statutory Concession A9 13.14

GPs are able to claim tax relief on their contributions to the NHSPS under Inland Revenue Extra-Statutory Concession A9 (ESC A9). The provisions within *s 594, ICTA 1988* regarding contributions by members to occupational pension schemes only provide relief in the case of an employee, and hence the need for the position of GPs to be covered by this concession.

The extra-statutory concession also covers the effect of claiming this concessionary relief on other pension arrangements the GPs might make. Originally the concession was drafted to deal with retirement annuity contracts (see **Chapter 14: Retirement Annuity Contracts**), but the practice has been extended and modified where necessary to apply under personal pension rules as well.

Options available to GPs 13.15

As a result of the special provisions for GPs, a number of options arise in relation to pension provision. They can:

(a)   opt out of the NHSPS;

(b)   join the NHSPS and claim tax relief on their contributions under ESC A9; or

(c)   join the NHSPS, but waive their right to claim tax relief under ESC A9.

We deal with each of these options in turn.

Opt out of NHSPS 13.16

It is generally agreed that opting out of occupational pension schemes is seldom advantageous. This applies just as much in the case of a GP as it does to any other member or potential member of an occupational pension scheme. Opting out would mean giving up benefits which would otherwise be provided partly through employer contributions. Most GPs are therefore members of the NHSPS, and as a result the scheme provides benefits payable on death and on retirement (see section **13.11** above).

If a GP were to opt out, they would not be paying contributions to the NHSPS, and the terms of the extra-statutory concession would not apply. The GP would therefore be treated for personal pension purposes in the same way as any other self-employed person. They would calculate their net relevant earnings in the usual way, and all the usual contribution rules and limits would apply in relation to them.

Join NHSPS and claim relief on contributions under ESC A9 13.17

Where a GP is a member of the NHSPS, and takes advantage of ESC A9 in order to claim concessionary relief on their NHSPS contributions, their pensionable pay must be deducted from net relevant earnings when calculating personal pension contribution limits. The result is referred to as non-NHS earnings.

Example – Non-NHS earnings

A 48-year-old female GP's income is derived partly from the NHS, and partly from private practice. For 2003/04, their total Schedule D earned income is £74,000 (this is their net relevant earnings figure) and they pay contributions to the NHSPS of £2,100.

If they claim concessionary relief, they can only pay personal pension contributions based on their non–NHS earnings, ie their net relevant earnings less their NHS pensionable pay. Pensionable pay is £2,100 x 100/6 = £35,000, and non–NHS earnings are therefore £74,000 less £35,000 = £39,000.

Their maximum personal pension contribution would therefore be 25% of £39,000 = £9,750.

Note that non–NHS earnings are essentially those earnings not pensioned under the NHSPS. There is not necessarily any direct relationship with the profit actually generated from fees received from sources other than the NHS.

NHS pensionable pay is calculated based on an assumed allowance for expenses, as discussed in section **13.12** above. It is possible for a GP whose only source of income is from the NHS to have income regarded as non–NHS earnings for personal pension purposes if actual expenses are less than those allowed for in the calculation of pensionable pay.

The earnings cap   13.18

The application of the earnings cap in relation to GPs is important. In the case of GPs claiming concessionary relief on NHSPS contributions, the earnings which can be pensioned through a personal pension are limited to a maximum of the earnings cap less NHSPS pensionable pay.

This means that non–NHS earnings for personal pension purposes will be net relevant earnings (limited by the earnings cap) less NHSPS pensionable pay.

Example – Application of earnings cap

A 52–year–old male GP has total Schedule D earned income from his practice of £120,000 for 2003/04. He pays contributions to the NHSPS of £5,040, and claims concessionary tax relief on them.

Net relevant earnings are limited to the earnings cap of £99,000.

NHS pensionable pay is £5,040 × 100/6 = £84,000.

Non–NHS earnings on which personal pension contributions can be based are therefore £99,000–£84,000 = £15,000.

His maximum personal pension contribution for 2003/04 is therefore 30% of £15,000 = £4,500.

Join NHSPS, but do not claim relief under ESC A9   13.19

It is possible for the GP to join the NHSPS and contribute to it in the normal way, but to decline to claim tax relief on contributions under ESC A9.

Waiving the ability to claim concessionary relief does not affect in any way either the amount of the contributions which the GP pays to the NHSPS, or the benefits which the scheme provides. However there is a significant effect as far as personal pension provision is concerned.

In this situation, the GP is able to pension their net relevant earnings in the normal way, and they are not reduced to take account of pensionable pay under the NHSPS. The effect is that income derived from the NHS can be pensioned twice over.

The disadvantage of selecting this option is that the cost of NHSPS membership is increased in net terms by the lack of tax relief obtained on the GP's contribution, but nevertheless the value for money remains good. For a GP who perhaps wishes to maximise their personal pension provision towards the end of their working career, this can be very attractive.

Example – Waiving concessionary relief

A 62-year-old male GP has net relevant earnings for 2003/04 of £80,000, and he contributes £3,900 to the NHSPS.

His NHS pensionable pay is £3,900 × 100/6 = £65,000.

If he claims concessionary relief, his non–NHS earnings would be £80,000 less £65,000 = £15,000, and his maximum contribution would be 40% of £15,000 = £6,000.

If he waives concessionary relief, he could pay a personal pension contribution of up to 40% of £80,000 = £32,000.

If he pays the maximum contribution, he will have paid:

£3,900 to the NHSPS (net cost £3,900 as no relief claimed).

£32,000 to the personal pension (net cost £19,200 after allowing for 40% relief).

The total amount contributed is £35,900 at a net cost of £23,100 (equivalent to relief at 35.6%). In addition, his NHSPS benefits continue to be paid for partly by employer contributions.

The loss of on the NHSPS contributions will be of little consequence if the personal pension contribution is substantial.

Earnings cap 13.20

Where the GP does not claim concessionary relief, the earnings cap would apply to net relevant earnings in determining contributions in the normal way, and no reduction in respect of NHSPS pensionable pay would be required.

The earnings threshold for GPs 13.21

Generally, the allowable contribution to a personal pension is the greater of the earnings threshold (£3,600) or the percentage derived from the age and earnings related scale (see section **3.7**). This basis applies normally to GPs where they have either opted out of the NHSPS, or have chosen to waive concessionary tax relief on their NHSPS contributions. In either case their total Schedule D earned income (subject to the earnings cap) is regarded as net relevant earnings and in practice it is unlikely that the earnings threshold would exceed the age and earnings related limit.

Where concessionary relief is claimed under ESC A9, personal pension contributions are limited to the age and earnings related scale based on net relevant earnings reduced in accordance with section **13.17** above. This means that it is not possible for a GP whose main source of income is the NHS but who has a small amount of net relevant earnings to claim concessionary relief on NHSPS contributions, but still pay £3,600 to a personal pension, unless this level of contribution is supported by the age and earnings related scale of limits.

Example – Non-availability of earnings threshold

A male GP with net relevant earnings of £75,000 for 2003/04 contributes £3,750 to the NHSPS. He is 42 years old, and claims concessionary relief on his NHSPS contribution.

His NHSPS pensionable pay is £7,500 × 100/6 = £62,500, so his non–NHS earnings are £75,000 – £62,500 = £12,500.

His maximum personal pension contribution would be 20% of £12,500 = £2,500.

He would not be permitted to contribute £3,600, because only the age and earnings related limit is available, not the earnings threshold.

Basis years for GPs   13.22

The basis year rules apply to GPs in the same ways as to other individuals eligible for personal pensions, and where the GP has either opted out of the NHSPS or has waived concessionary relief on NHSPS contributions, there are no particular complications.

Where concessionary relief is claimed in the current year, some care is needed. The net relevant earnings figure used to calculate maximum personal pension contributions can be that for the current tax year, or for any of the previous five tax years, in the normal way. However, in calculating non-NHS earnings to determine maximum personal pension contributions, the net relevant earnings figure must always be reduced by NHS pensionable pay for the current year.

Note that it is whether concessionary relief is claimed on NHSPS contributions in the current year rather than the year from which the net relevant earnings figure is derived that affects the position.

Example – Basis years I

The table below shows the net relevant earnings and NHSPS contributions in recent years for a female GP.

She intends to claim concessionary relief on her NHSPS contributions in 2003/04.

Tax year	Net relevant earnings	NHSPS contributions	Relief claimed
1998/99	£50,000	£2,400	Yes
1999/2000	£45,000	£2,500	Yes
2000/01	£48,000	£2,400	No
2001/02	£63,000	£2,700	No
2002/03	£52,000	£2,900	Yes
2003/04	£55,000	£3,000	Yes

She can nominate 2001/02 as her basis year for 2003/04, and this means that her net relevant earnings will be £63,000.

Her NHSPS pensionable pay is £3,000 × 100/6 = £50,000. (Note that the level of NHSPS contributions in 2001/02 is not relevant, and neither is the fact that she did not claim concessionary relief in 2001/02.)

Her non-NHS earnings for 2003/04 are therefore £63,000 – £50,000 = £13,000.

If the GP waives concessionary relief in the current year, then net relevant earnings from the basis year, with no deduction in respect of NHS pensionable pay, can be used to calculate contribution limits.

Example – Basis years II

Taking the same earnings history as in the previous example, let us now suppose that Marion claimed concessionary relief in all past years, but does not do so in 2003/04. The details are now as follows:

Tax year	Net relevant earnings	NHSPS contributions	Relief claimed
1998/99	£50,000	£2,400	Yes
1999/2000	£45,000	£2,500	Yes
2000/01	£48,000	£2,400	Yes
2001/02	£63,000	£2,700	Yes
2002/03	£52,000	£2,900	Yes
2003/04	£55,000	£3,000	No

She again nominates 2001/02 as her basis year for 2003/04, and her net relevant earnings are therefore £63,000.

There is no reduction in respect of NHSPS pensionable pay, even though she claimed concessionary relief in the basis year (2001/02).

Concurrency rules for GPs   13.23

The concurrency rules under *s 632B, ICTA 1988* (see section **2.20**) do not apply to GPs.

This is because the application of these rules is restricted to those who, throughout the year, hold 'an office or employment' which is pensionable. As GPs are self-employed rather than employed, the concurrency rules cannot apply.

AVCs and FSAVCs for GPs   13.24

Where a GP is a member of the NHSPS, they will be eligible to pay in-house Additional Voluntary Contributions (AVCs) under the NHSPS arrangements in the normal way. If tax relief is claimed by a GP on their ordinary contributions under ESC A9, then relief can also be claimed on their AVCs.

Conversely, if relief on ordinary contributions is waived, although the GP remains eligible to pay in-house AVCs, no relief will be available on them.

The position with free-standing AVCs is different. Where the GP claims relief on ordinary contributions under ESC A9, they can pay free-standing AVCs, and relief can be claimed in the normal way.

However if concessionary relief is not claimed, free-standing AVCs are not permitted to be paid at all.

Example – AVCs and FSAVCs

A 57-year-old GP has total Schedule D earned income for 2003/04 of £82,000, and he pays contributions of £4,320 to the NHSPS. He claims concessionary relief on the NHSPS contributions.

His NHS pensionable pay is £4,320 × 100/6 = £72,000 and his non-NHS earnings are therefore £10,000.

He could pay a personal pension contribution of 35% of £10,000 = £3,500.

In addition, he could pay in-house or freestanding AVCs of 9% of £72,000 = £6,480, with full tax relief.

If he waived his concessionary relief, he could pay a personal pension contribution of up to 35% of £82,000 = £28,700.

However, he would not obtain tax relief on his NHSPS contribution and could not pay anything to a freestanding AVC arrangement. He could pay up to £6,480 by way of in-house AVCs, but these would not qualify for tax relief.

Making the choice 13.25

The pension options for GPs are complicated, and clearly need to be considered in the light of the circumstances of any particular individual. The table below summarises the main points.

Table – Summary of options for GPs

Option	NHSPS benefits	AVC position	Earnings for personal pension purposes
Opt out of NHSPS	None	Not eligible	Net relevant earnings
Join NHSPS and claim concessionary relief	Full benefits	Can pay in-house or freestanding AVCs with full tax relief	Net relevant earnings less NHSPS pensionable pay
Join NHSPS, but waive concessionary relief	Full benefits (but no tax relief on contributions)	Can pay in-house AVCs with no tax relief, but not eligible to pay freestanding AVCs	Net relevant earnings

However it is fair to say that opting out of the NHSPS entirely is unlikely to be advisable, simply because of the level of benefits which would be foregone. The only advantage is the saving of contributions which would otherwise be payable, but the scheme is funded in part by the employer, so the value for money is very good.

We are therefore generally concerned with GPs who are members of the NHSPS.

In general, for GPs whose income consists mainly of NHS earnings, the contributions to the NHSPS will be quite substantial, and the value of tax relief on them will also be substantial as a result. In these circumstances, many GPs will choose to claim concessionary relief and will consider making additional personal pension contributions only in respect of their non-NHS earnings.

Because the benefits from the NHSPS will be at a relatively high level, the need for additional personal pension provision will often be limited. However this will not always be the case, given that the earnings pattern of GPs can be very varied, and NHSPS benefits are based on average earnings (adjusted for inflation) through their career.

Where there is a need for significant personal pension contributions, waiving concessionary relief can have a major impact on the scope for contributions. It may therefore be appropriate in some circumstances to maximise the potential for personal pension contributions by waiving relief.

The decision regarding concessionary relief is one that can be made year by year, so it is possible to maximise personal pension contributions in one tax year, but then revert back to claiming concessionary relief in later years. This may be appropriate if more modest personal pension contributions are to be made in those later years.

14 — Retirement Annuity Contracts

Introduction 14.1

Before the introduction of personal pensions on 1 July 1988, retirement annuity contracts (RACs) were available, and essentially fulfilled a similar purpose. Although no new RACs can be established on or after 1 July 1988, those that were already in force on that date are permitted to continue, and will provide benefits in due course.

Contributions can continue to these existing RACs, and there is no requirement for them to be regular, or to be maintained in any particular way. Thus for example even if an individual started an RAC sometime before 1 July 1988, with a single contribution, and has made no further contribution to it since, they could now (subject to being eligible) make a contribution. This assumes that the RAC contract is worded in such a way as to permit such further payments.

Importantly, although the tax advantages of retirement annuity contracts are the same as those which apply to personal pensions, contribution limits and benefits are subject to detailed provisions which are distinctly different from those applying to personal pensions.

Checklist – Main tax advantages of RACs

- Contributions within limits qualify for tax relief at the individual's highest rate(s) of income tax.
- Growth within the fund is free of tax on income and capital gains, except that dividend tax credits cannot be reclaimed.
- Part of the fund is available at retirement in the form of a tax free cash sum.

In this chapter, we consider RACs, taking into account particularly the differences between personal pensions and RACs, and we also consider the interaction between the two types of arrangement.

Providers 14.2

Under *section 620* of the *Income and Corporation Taxes Act 1988 (ICTA 1988)*, it is a condition of the approval by the Inland Revenue of a retirement annuity contract that it is made 'by the individual with a person carrying on lawfully in the United Kingdom the business of granting annuities on human life'.

This means that RACs could only be offered by life insurance companies and friendly societies, so the range of providers is considerably more limited than applies under personal pension schemes (see section **1.20**).

Note also that, under RAC provisions, there is no equivalent of the self-invested personal pension as discussed in section **7.39**. In general therefore, the range of investment choices available is much narrower than for personal pensions, because it is limited to the funds on offer from life assurance companies and friendly societies. The range may include non-profit, with profit and unit linked funds, but the full range described in **Chapter 7: Investment Considerations** is unlikely to be available. Although some contracts do offer a choice of funds managed by different fund management organisations, again the choice will be far less wide than is often the case under modern personal pension arrangements. This simply reflects the fact that the market at the time did not place as much emphasis on having so many funds to choose from.

Eligibility 14.3

In order to be eligible to contribute to a retirement annuity contract, the individual concerned must have a source of relevant earnings. The meaning of 'relevant earnings' for RAC purposes (given in *s 623, ICTA 1988*) is similar to that which applies under personal pensions, and essentially means income chargeable to tax which arises from:

(*a*)   an office or employment which is not pensionable; or

(*b*)   the carrying on or exercise of a trade, profession or vocation on a self-employed basis (either as an individual or in a partnership).

Earnings arising as a controlling director of an investment company are excluded, as they are for personal pensions.

Nevertheless, although similar in principle, the definition differs in some detailed points.

The exclusion from the relevant earnings definition of income arising from the exercise of share options applies only to personal pensions (see section **3.27**), and not RACs. Where such income is chargeable under Schedule E, and where the employment is non-pensionable, such amounts would therefore be included in the calculation of relevant earnings.

The definition of pensionable employment is however wider than that which applies to personal pensions. In particular, when a member of an occupational scheme leaves pensionable service, they may sometimes be given a refund of contributions, and will then have no preserved benefits.

The period of service whilst a member of the scheme will continue to be regarded as pensionable employment from an RAC point of view, whereas under personal pension legislation, it is regarded as non-pensionable.

Although the period involved is necessarily short (the legislation requires a preserved pension where the member completes two years qualifying service) this provision nevertheless can disadvantage those who move rapidly from job to job.

Section 632(3), ICTA 1988 provides that where the benefits under the occupational scheme are limited to a lump sum on death or disability, this will not render the employment pensionable for RAC purposes. However, there is no exclusion in the legislation in relation to the situation where a scheme provides income benefits, for example for a spouse, on the death of the employee.

By concession however, the Inland Revenue allows periods of membership of such schemes to be regarded as non-pensionable provided no claim arises in the tax year concerned. The nature of this concession means that the individual cannot be certain during any particular tax year that they will not be the subject of a claim at some later point, and therefore contributions cannot be made in respect of the current tax year. They can however be made and carried back to the previous tax year as described in section **14.17** below.

Various conditions apply to the operation of this extra-statutory concession, and in particular the scheme must have been in force at the time the concession was introduced (14 October 1980) and must be fully or partly paid for by the employer.

Opt-outs, non-joiners and deferred retirements   14.4

If an individual is a member of an occupational pension scheme but chooses to opt out of the scheme, pensionable service is regarded as ending on the date when they opt out. Similarly, an individual who, although eligible, chooses not to join such a scheme, is never regarded as having entered pensionable employment.

However, where a member reaches normal retirement date under the occupational pension scheme, but defers benefits because they remain in the same employment, the employment is regarded as still being pensionable, and the earnings are not within the definition of relevant earnings.

Similarly, if in this situation the individual chooses to take their tax free lump sum, but defer income benefits (as is permitted under older occupational scheme approval provisions), the employment again remains pensionable. It is not relevant whether any further contributions are paid.

Unapproved schemes 14.5

A funded unapproved retirement benefit scheme (FURBS) is also regarded as making the employment of its members pensionable, so the earnings are again excluded from the definition of relevant earnings for RAC purposes. This would not be the case under personal pension provisions, where only membership of an approved scheme makes the employment pensionable.

Note that membership of a group PHI scheme where employment is regarded as continuing in the event of a claim does not alone result in the employment being regarded as pensionable.

Golden handshakes 14.6

Under personal pension legislation, golden handshake payments are entirely excluded from the definition of relevant earnings under *s 644(4)(b), ICTA 1988*. However, if such payments arise from a non-pensionable employment, they can be included within the definition for RAC purposes, but only to the extent that they are taxable.

Generally the first £30,000 of any such payment is free of tax, and any further amounts are taxable.

Example – Golden Handshakes

An individual is made redundant by their employer in December 2003, and is given a golden handshake payment of £50,000. Their earnings from the employment, which has always been non-pensionable, are £60,000 in 2003/04, excluding the golden handshake.

Of the £50,000 golden handshake payment, £30,000 is tax free, and £20,000 is taxable as earned income.

The individual's net relevant earnings for personal pension purposes are £60,000.

For RAC purposes, net relevant earnings are £60,000 + £20,000 = £80,000.

Those with no relevant earnings 14.7

Because the requirement for eligibility is to have a source of relevant earnings, note that it is not possible for non-earners to pay contributions to a retirement annuity contract.

Similarly, if an individual has a single source of earnings, which is a pensionable employment, they will have no relevant earnings and cannot therefore contribute to an RAC. There is no equivalent to the concurrency rules which apply for personal pension purposes.

Payment of contributions   14.8

Only an eligible individual is permitted to pay contributions to a retirement annuity contract.

Employer contributions   14.9

Note that it is not possible for employer contributions to be made to an RAC. Prior to the introduction of personal pensions, some employers did arrange for contributions to be remitted to a product provider by the employer, but this process is simply one where the employer is regarded as passing on part of the employee's remuneration. The payments are not regarded as employer contributions.

In some cases, the amount will be deducted from the employee's net remuneration, which is reduced as a result. The employee will be able to claim relief on the contribution in the normal way (see section **14.13** below).

Sometimes the employer might wish to provide a contribution as a benefit for the employee, and in addition to normal remuneration. Such a payment will be regarded as additional remuneration, and will result in a tax liability for the employee. It will also be regarded as part of the employee's relevant earnings.

Example – Employer contributions

A higher rate taxpayer has an RAC, and their employer wants to make a contribution of £1,000, direct to the insurance company concerned.

The individual will be regarded as having received additional gross salary of £1,000, and will have to pay tax of £400 on it from the remainder of their income.

In these circumstances, although the tax liability will eventually be balanced by the tax relief which the employee can claim, there will also be a National Insurance liability, assuming that the employee's remuneration (including the RAC contribution) exceeds the National Insurance threshold. The National Insurance liability is greatest if remuneration lies between the threshold and the Upper Earnings Limit, because both employer and employee National Insurance Contributions will be affected. If above the Upper Earnings Limit, the employer liability will be increased.

From April 2003, the introduction of the additional 1% National Insurance charge on both employer and employee would also apply to such payments.

Contracting out   14.10

No provision is made under retirement annuity legislation to allow an individual to use an RAC in order to contract out of the State Second Pension (S2P), or its predecessor, SERPS. If an employee wishes to contract out, and is not a member of a contracted out occupational scheme, they can do so only through a personal pension.

Contribution limits   14.11

The maximum level of contributions which qualify for tax relief is a percentage of net relevant earnings determined in accordance with the scale below. The scale for personal pension contributions is also shown for comparison purposes.

Age at 6 April	Maximum contribution as % of Net Relevant Earnings (RACs)	Maximum contribution as % of Net Relevant Earnings (Personal pensions)
up to 35	17.5%	17.5%
36 to 45	17.5%	20%
46 to 50	17.5%	25%
51 to 55	20%	30%
56 to 60	22.5%	35%
61 to 74	27.5%	40%

The RAC scale applies in all cases. There is no minimum monetary amount which can be paid regardless of the level of net relevant earnings, as would be the case with the earnings threshold under personal pension legislation. This can make a major difference at low earnings levels.

Example – RAC limits for low earners

A 37-year-old has net relevant earnings of £10,000 in 2003/04. If they have an RAC available, the maximum contribution they could pay to it with tax relief is 17.5% of £10,000 = £1,750.

The maximum contribution to a personal pension would be the greater of 20% of £10,000 = £2,000 and the earnings threshold of £3,600. The PP maximum is therefore £3,600.

This is more than double the possible RAC contribution.

Net relevant earnings is relevant earnings (as defined for RAC purposes – see section **14.3** above) after deduction of business expenses, losses and capital allowances relating to activities which would themselves produce relevant earnings.

Importantly however, net relevant earnings for RAC purposes are not subject to the earnings cap, but are unlimited.

Although the maximum contribution percentages to RACs are lower than those for personal pensions at all ages from 36 onwards, for those earning more than the earnings cap, it will often be the case that the RAC limit is higher in monetary terms.

Example – RAC limits for high earners

A 48-year-old has net relevant earnings of £160,000 in 2003/04. They have an RAC, started in 1986.

The percentage contribution limit to the RAC is 17.5% of net relevant earnings, which is considerably lower than the personal pension limit of 25%. However, this difference is outweighed by the fact that net relevant earnings for RAC purposes is not subject to the earnings cap.

The maximum contribution to an RAC with tax relief is 17.5% of £160,000 = £28,000.

The maximum contribution to a personal pension is 25% of £99,000 = £24,750.

When calculating maximum contributions to RACs, the net relevant earnings figure taken into account must always be that for the tax year to which the contribution relates. There is no provision to base the calculation on any other year, as would occur under the personal pension basis year rules. Similarly, the cessation rules under personal pensions legislation do not apply to RACs. It follows therefore that once net relevant earnings cease, RAC contributions must cease, except to the extent that they can be continued under the carry back rules (see section **14.17** below).

Excess contributions 14.12

In contrast to the position under personal pensions legislation, it is possible to pay contributions in excess of the limits discussed above to an RAC. This is possible because the legislation merely imposes a limitation on the contributions which qualify for relief rather than the contributions which can be paid.

The Inland Revenue discourages such payments, and would take a dim view of any attempt to market actively the ability to do so. Generally it would be unattractive to do so. The contributions would be made from after-tax income, would not qualify for tax relief, and at retirement, the emerging benefits must largely be taken in the form of taxable income. The exercise therefore serves to convert after-tax cash into pre-tax income.

A possible motivation for paying excess contributions would be to increase the capital invested in the tax advantaged environment of a pension fund, but growth would have to be both good and sustained in the long term in order for this to outweigh the disadvantage of the tax on benefits. It is difficult to see circumstances where this could be recommended, particularly given the uncertainty of investment returns, measured against the certainty of the income tax disadvantage.

Claiming tax relief 14.13

Contributions to RACs are paid gross, and the individual must claim all tax relief from the Inland Revenue, generally using their tax return. Tax relief is available at the individual's highest rate(s) of income tax, and is given as a deduction against relevant earnings for tax purposes, under *s 619(1), ICTA 1988*.

This is a more cumbersome system than that which applies to personal pension contributions, and requires a claim to be made to the Inspector of Taxes even by basic and lower rate taxpayers. Note that whereas with personal pensions, lower rate and non-taxpayers benefit from basic rate relief through payment of net contributions, they will not do so under a retirement annuity contract.

Example – Non-taxpayer paying RAC contributions

An individual has net relevant earnings of £4,000 in 2003/04, and has no other income. The £4,000 is covered by their personal allowance, so they are a non-taxpayer.

If they make an RAC contribution of £500, this is paid gross, and their taxable income reduces from £4,000 to £3,500. This is still covered by their personal allowance, and they have no tax liability, but they have not benefited from any tax relief.

If the individual wants to contribute £500 to a personal pension, they pay only £390 themselves, and the product provider reclaims basic rate relief of £110 (ie £500 x 22%) from the Inland Revenue. This is not reclaimed from the individual, even though they are a non-taxpayer. They have therefore benefited from tax relief of £110.

Carry forward of unused reliefs   14.14

Under *s 625, ICTA 1988*, a contributor to an RAC may carry forward unused reliefs over a six year period. The intention here is to allow contributions which have been missed entirely in the past, or have been made at levels below the maximum permitted level, to be picked up in later years.

Tax relief is granted against the liability for the tax year in which the contribution is paid, not the year from which the unused relief is carried forward.

There are a number of conditions which must be met, namely:

(*a*)   the contribution in respect of the current tax year must be paid in full before any unused relief from an earlier year can be carried forward;

(*b*)   the earliest year from which unused relief can be carried forward is that which is six years before the current tax year (for example, in 2003/04, the earliest year which could be considered is 1997/98);

(*c*)   the unused relief carried forward must be used in order, starting with the earliest year available;

(*d*)   the amount of unused relief from any past year is calculated based on the individual's age on 6 April in the past year, and their net relevant earnings in that past year; and

(*e*)   any contributions already claimed in respect of that year, either by payment at the time, or as a result of a subsequent claim under the carry forward provisions, reduces the remaining unused relief available.

This can be a very attractive facility, and one which will appeal particularly to those who have not maximised their contributions in the past, but now have more money available for contributions, perhaps as a result of increased earnings.

Example – Carry forward of unused reliefs

An individual has a retirement annuity contract, to which they have not paid maximum contributions in the past. They are now 56, and want to pick up as much as possible of the unused reliefs in 2003/04, when their net relevant earnings have reached a high point.

The individual's contribution and earnings history is as follows:

Tax year	NRE	Age at 6 April	% limit	Maximum contribution	Contributions already made	Unused relief
1997/98	£20,000	50	17.5%	£3,500	£2,000	£1,500
1998/99	£25,000	51	20%	£5,000	£3,000	£2,000
1999/2000	£25,000	52	20%	£5,000	£5,000	nil
2000/01	£30,000	53	20%	£6,000	£5,000	£1,000
2001/02	£35,000	54	20%	£7,000	£5,000	£2,000
2002/03	£40,000	55	20%	£8,000	£5,000	£3,000
2003/04	£80,000	56	22.5%	£18,000	nil	

The individual must first pay the contribution for the current tax year, ie £18,000. They can then start picking up unused relief. The maximum unused relief available is £9,500 in total.

They can therefore contribute up to £27,500 in total, with tax relief against their tax liability for 2003/04.

Note that the fact that there is no unused relief from 1999/2000 makes no difference, other than providing a zero figure in the calculation. It does not in any way affect the ability to utilise unused relief from other years within the six year period.

A similar facility was available under personal pensions legislation up to and including the tax year 2000/01. It is no longer available in respect of contributions claimed for relief in 2001/02 or subsequent tax years.

The fact that tax relief is given against the liability for the current tax year will usually favour the individual. In the example above, had contributions been paid in full in the past, tax relief would have been available at the rates of tax applicable in each tax year, and in some years this would have meant that tax relief would have been available only at basic rate.

Because earnings are high in 2003/04, even if the individual in the example above paid the maximum possible contribution of £27,500, all of this would attract tax relief at higher rate.

In some circumstances, this basis could be disadvantageous, where the individual would have been paying higher rate tax in the past, but picks up unused relief at a time when only liable for basic rate. In practice, simply because the provision is most likely to be used in years when earnings and therefore tax rates are high, it is more likely to favour than disadvantage the taxpayer.

Partial use of carry forward   **14.15**

In some cases, the individual will wish to use some of the available unused relief, but may not have the resources to use it all, or may simply not wish to. In such cases, the rest of the unused relief will remain available in future years, subject to the maximum six year carry forward period.

Example – Partial carry forward

Suppose that the individual from the previous example pays £22,000 into her RAC, claiming tax relief in 2003/04, rather than the maximum of £27,500.

The situation is then as follows:

Tax year	NRE	Age at 6 April	% limit	Unused relief before 2003/04 contribution	Relief used by 2003/04 contribution	Remaining unused relief
1997/98	£20,000	50	17.5%	£1,500	£1,500	nil
1998/99	£25,000	51	20%	£2,000	£2,000	nil
1999/2000	£25,000	52	20%	nil	nil	nil
2000/01	£30,000	53	20%	£1,000	£500	£500
2001/02	£35,000	54	20%	£2,000	nil	£2,000
2002/03	£40,000	55	20%	£3,000	nil	£3,000
2003/04	£80,000	56	22.5%	£18,000	£18,000	nil

The total unused relief still available from past years, and which could be used in 2004/05, is £5,500.

To utilise this, the individual must first pay the maximum contribution in respect of 2004/05 net relevant earnings. Suppose these net relevant earnings were £80,000, the same as in 2003/04.

The maximum they could then pay, with tax relief in 2004/05, would be £18,000 in respect of 2004/05 net relevant earnings, plus £5,500 in unused relief carried forward. The maximum total contribution would therefore be £23,500.

If the contribution paid in 2003/04 had not been sufficient to fully use the unused relief from 1997/98, the remainder could not be carried forward any further. This is because of the maximum carry forward period of six years. Each year therefore, the availability of unused relief from the furthest year back falls out of account.

Limitation to relevant earnings 14.16

Because tax relief on retirement annuity contributions is given by a reduction against relevant earnings, it follows that the maximum contribution cannot exceed relevant earnings.

Example – Limitation to relevant earnings

Suppose in 2004/05, the individual from our previous two examples had net relevant earnings of only £6,000, and that this was also their relevant earnings figure. Their maximum contribution based on these earnings would be 22.5% of £6,000 = £1,350.

Total unused relief from earlier years is £5,500. However, the most the individual can utilise is £4,650, to bring their total contribution up to £6,000.

Although care is needed not to exceed this limitation, in practice it will often be the practical limitations regarding tax relief which will be more important. In the example above, suppose that the individual's net relevant earnings of £6,000 was their only income. The amount of their income which would actually bear tax would be considerably less than this, because of the personal allowance. The personal allowance for 2003/04 is £4,615, so the amount of income bearing tax would only be £1,385.

If they contributed more than this, they would achieve no effective relief, and this is unlikely to be an attractive proposition.

Moreover, if their total income was £6,000, the part of their income which bears tax would fall wholly within the starting rate band, where the tax rate is 10%. If it is likely that the income emerging from the retirement annuity contract at retirement will be subject to basic rate or higher rate tax, it may be unattractive to pay contributions with 10% relief in order to generate a benefit largely in the form of income which will be taxed at a higher level.

Checklist – Carry forward of unused relief

The main points to remember regarding the facility to carry forward unused relief under RACs are as follows.

- The individual must be eligible for an RAC in the current year.
- The full contribution for the current year must be paid before any unused relief can be carried forward.
- Unused relief can be carried forward from the preceding six tax years.
- Earlier years must be used before later years.
- Unused relief is calculated based on the individual's age and net relevant earnings in each of the years from which relief is carried forward.
- Any contribution paid in an earlier year reduces the unused relief available to be carried forward to the current year.
- The total contribution cannot exceed relevant earnings for the current tax year.
- Tax relief is granted against the liability for the current tax year, not against that for the tax year from which the unused relief is carried forward.
- The current year is the year in which the contribution is paid unless a carry back election (see section **14.17** below) is made, in which case it is the year to which the contribution is carried back.

Carry back   14.17

The concept of carry back was discussed in relation to personal pension contributions in section **4.13**. The concept under retirement annuity legislation is similar, though the facility is in many ways more flexible. It remains the case that if a contribution is carried back to a previous year, the limits applicable are calculated as if the contribution was paid in that earlier year, and relief is granted against the tax liability for that earlier year.

Carry back accelerates tax relief for higher rate taxpayers under personal pension rules (see section **4.13**) but can be even more important for retirement annuity contributions. This is because all tax relief, including basic rate relief, must be claimed from the Inspector of Taxes rather than being given automatically and immediately through payment of net contributions.

There are a number of differences between the operation of the carry back facility on RACs compared to that for personal pensions, which are:

(a)   it is not necessary for the carry back election to be made at the time of, or before, payment of the contribution – it can instead be made afterwards;

(b)   the election to carry back the contribution must however be made by 31 January in the tax year following the year of payment (this contrasts with the rule for the carry back of personal pension contributions, where the election must be made one year earlier-by 31 January in the tax year of payment); and

(c)   if there were no net relevant earnings in the tax year preceding that of payment, the contribution can be carried back two years.

The later deadline for making the carry back election can be very useful. It can be argued that the personal pension deadline of 31 January in the year of payment is not unreasonable because by that date, the tax position for the previous year will be fully known. However the position in relation to the year in which the contribution is paid may not be finalised until much later. The RAC deadline reflects this. Given that the choice the individual has to make is between carrying the back to the previous tax year and claiming relief in the current year, the RAC position is the ideal.

It also follows from the later deadline that contributions paid at any time during the tax year can be carried back. Under personal pensions, the contribution must be paid by 31 January, so contributions paid between 1 February and 5 April cannot be carried back.

Two year carry back   14.18

The provision allowing a contribution to be carried back two years if there were no net relevant earnings in the immediately preceding year is another useful facility. This facility used to be available under personal pensions legislation, but has now been abolished in respect of contributions paid on or after 6 April 2001.

The circumstances in which two year carry back can be used seem relatively unusual, but in fact are not as rare as it might seem at first sight.

As well as situations where an individual's earnings may fluctuate, and may be zero in some years, this facility can also be used where the source of relevant earnings has entirely ceased. An example of this would be where an individual who was in non-pensionable employment enters an occupational pension scheme, and so ceases to have a source of relevant earnings. The two year carry back facility will allow contributions to a personal pension to continue for a considerable period, even though occupational pension benefits are accruing.

In these circumstances, the personal pension may be a useful alternative to in-house or free-standing additional voluntary contribution arrangements for quite some time.

Example – Two year carry back

A 54-year-old has been in non-pensionable employment for a number of years, and has been contributing to an RAC, which they established in 1984. Their current contribution level is £100 per month.

In December 2003, the individual changes jobs, and moves into pensionable employment. Their earnings from the non-pensionable employment were £40,000 in 2003/04, in respect of the period before they moved to their new job, and £20,000 from the new job.

Their net relevant earnings for 2003/04 are the earnings from the first (non-pensionable) job, and so are £40,000 (assuming no deductible expenses). The earnings from the second job are not relevant earnings, and so do not affect limits.

The maximum contribution on which the individual can claim relief against 2003/04 is therefore 20% of £40,000 = £8,000.

If they continue to pay £100 per month throughout 2003/04, the total of £1,200 is well within limits.

The individual could then contribute throughout 2004/05, and carry back the contributions to 2003/04 for tax relief. They could do the same under the two year carry back rules throughout 2005/06. (This assumes they remain in pensionable employment throughout 2004/05 and so have no net relevant earnings in 2003/04.)

If they continue to contribute at the rate of £100 per month throughout this period, the total claimed for relief against 2003/04 would then be £3,600, which is still well within limits.

Remember that the total contributions claimed for relief must lie within limits for the tax year concerned. In the example above, it is assumed that the individual enters pensionable employment relatively late in the tax year, and therefore has a considerable level of net relevant earnings (ie earnings arising prior to entering pensionable employment) in the tax year concerned.

Had they joined the scheme on 1 May, then only one month's earnings would have constituted net relevant earnings, and the scope of RAC contributions would therefore be much more limited. In such a case, it may not be possible to utilise carry back through the whole of the following two years without infringing limits.

Example – Limitation on two year carry back

Suppose the individual from our last example left their non–pensionable employment on 31 May 2003, and their earnings from that employment in 2003/04 were only £10,000.

The maximum contribution in relation to their 2003/04 net relevant earnings is therefore 20% of £10,000 = £2,000.

If they claim relief on the £1,200 they pay during 2003/04 against that year, they will only be able to contribute a further £800 before they exhaust the contribution limit in relation to their 2003/04 net relevant earnings.

In some cases, in these circumstances, it is possible to improve the position by carrying the contributions which were paid in the last tax year when there were relevant earnings back to the previous year. This frees the whole of the allowable contribution limit in relation to net relevant earnings in the last year. This can then be utilised by means of contributions paid over the following two tax years, and carried back.

Example – Carry back in successive years

Returning once again to the individual in the above examples, let us again assume that they left their pensionable employment on 31 May 2003. They could improve their position in relation to RAC limits by carrying all the contributions they pay in 2003/04 back to 2002/03 (assuming this would not infringe limits for 2002/03).

They then have not used any of their allowed contribution limit of £2,000 for 2003/04, and could pay £100 per month for a further twenty months during 2004/05 and 2005/06.

Whether the individual wishes to continue to make contributions whilst accruing benefits under an occupational pension scheme is a question which must be considered carefully. In some cases the individual will decide that the benefits provided by the occupational scheme are adequate for their needs, and that there is therefore no point in continuing to make RAC contributions. There may also be concerns regarding spendable income, particularly if the individual must contribute to the occupational pension scheme itself.

Even if they wish to make further provision themself, they could choose to make additional voluntary contributions to the occupational scheme, or to establish a free-standing AVC arrangement.

The RAC offers some advantages, particularly the fact that part of the benefits are available in the form of tax free cash at retirement. This is no longer generally the case with in-house or freestanding AVC arrangements (though there are some exceptions under in-house AVC arrangements).

There is no interaction between the RAC and occupational pension scheme contribution limits, which simplifies the position considerably (though the RAC benefits would be retained benefits for limit purposes). Also, the RAC is entirely personal, and therefore under the individual's control as far as timing and form of benefits are concerned (subject to Inland Revenue requirements).

Against this, additional voluntary contribution arrangements may offer more choice of provider and of fund links, particularly given that it is now necessarily quite some years since RAC arrangements were designed. In-house AVC arrangements may be very inexpensive, and in some cases will offer the opportunity of purchasing benefits on an added years basis, where the relationship between benefits and final earnings is underwritten by the employer.

It is of course possible to make contributions to the RAC arrangements (within the constraints explained above) as well as AVCs, given sufficient financial resources.

Checklist – Carry back for RAC contributions

The main points to remember regarding the facility to carry back RAC contributions are as follows.

- The contribution can be paid at any time in the tax year.
- The election to carry back must be made by 31 January in the tax year following that of payment.
- The election can relate to the whole, or to part, of the total contribution paid to the RAC.
- The contribution is generally carried back to the tax year immediately preceding that of payment.
- If there were no net relevant earnings in the previous tax year, the contribution can be carried back two years.
- There are no circumstances where a contribution can be carried back more than two years.
- Contribution limits are based on the position in the tax year to which the contribution is carried back.
- The contribution limit for the year to which the contribution is carried back can include unused reliefs carried forward from the six previous tax years.

- Any contribution already paid in the year to which the contribution is carried back reduces the scope for carry back.
- Tax relief is given against the tax liability for the tax year to which the contribution is carried back.
- It is not necessary to be eligible in the tax year of payment, only in the tax year to which the contribution is carried back.
- It is not necessary for a contribution to be paid in respect of the current year before a contribution is carried back.

Interaction of carry back and carry forward   14.19

It is possible to use the carry back and carry forward facilities in conjunction with each other. An individual can pay a contribution in the current tax year, and carry it back to the preceding tax year, and then it is treated for limit purposes as if paid in the previous tax year.

The limits for the preceding tax year include any unused relief brought forward from earlier years, and this can considerably increase the scope for carry back.

The effect is also to make available a further past year from which unused relief can be carried forward.

Example – Combining carry back and carry forward

An individual has an RAC started before 1988. They have not paid maximum contributions in the past, and now wish to do so.

If the individual paid a contribution in 2003/04, and did not elect to carry it back, they could pick up unused relief from 1997/98 onwards.

If they carried the contribution back to 2002/03, they could then pick up unused relief from 1996/97 onwards, so allowing the individual to take into account one extra year. They would then claim tax relief against their tax liability for 2002/03.

There are other issues to take into account, in particular the relative rates at which the individual could obtain tax relief in the current or the carry back year.

In the examples in section **14.18** above, where carry back was used to allow RAC contributions to continue after entering pensionable employment, the point was made that care needs to be taken regarding the limits applicable to contributions in the year when non-pensionable employment ceased. The possibility of bringing forward unused relief from earlier years may reduce this problem.

However, care is still needed to ensure that the total amount of contributions does not exceed relevant earnings for the year.

Example – Effect of picking up unused relief

In the final example in section **14.18** above, the individual ended pensionable employment on 31 May 2003, having had net relevant earnings of £10,000 in 2003/04. They then entered pensionable employment.

As illustrated in the example, the individual could carry back RAC contributions paid in 2004/05 and 2005/06 to 2003/04, but could be handicapped by the contribution limit applicable to 2003/04. In respect of 2003/04 net relevant earnings, the limit would be 20% of £10,000 = £2,000, given that their age is 54.

However, if they had unused relief from earlier years, this would enable higher contributions to be paid and carried back.

The maximum they can claim against 2003/04 will nevertheless be limited to their relevant earnings for 2003/04 ie to £10,000, irrespective of how much unused relief is available.

Choosing between carry back and carry forward   14.20

In some circumstances, an individual will be able to choose between using the carry back or carry forward facilities. This will generally only apply in respect of contributions for the tax year immediately preceding the one in which the contributions are actually paid. It would be possible to carry back a contribution to this year for relief purposes, or alternatively to pick up the unused relief in the current year.

In most cases, the choice will hinge on the relative tax rates, and therefore the rates of tax relief, which could be obtained in the two years. However, the timing of tax relief can also be an important issue, particularly as RAC contributions are paid in full, with tax relief, even at basic rate, claimed from the Inspector of Taxes. (The timing of tax relief on contributions under the self-assessment tax system is discussed in detail in section **4.4**.)

Example – Choosing between carry back and carry forward

A 49-year-old has an RAC started when they were in non-pensionable employment in the 1980s. They have not paid contributions to it for the last ten years, because they were in pensionable employment for most of this time.

However, the individual became self-employed in 2002/03, and had net relevant earnings of £12,000. Their net relevant earnings for 2003/04 will be £50,000.

If they now wish to restart contributions to their RAC, they can pay contributions in respect of both 2002/03 and 2003/04. The contribution for 2003/04 can be claimed against the tax liability for 2003/04.

The individual has a choice in relation to the contribution relating to their 2002/03 net relevant earnings, if they pay it during 2003/04. They can carry the contribution back to 2002/03, in which case they will get tax relief at the rate(s) applicable to 2002/03.

Alternatively, the individual can claim tax relief against 2003/04, using the carry forward facility. This will mean that they get tax relief at 2003/04 rate(s), though it will be longer before the relief is available.

Delaying payment 14.21

Where an individual is currently subject only to basic rate tax, but anticipates moving into higher rate tax in a later year, it can be appropriate to delay making contributions until the higher rate liability materialises. Contributions could then be paid in the later year, with the unused relief being picked up at that point. Where the higher rate liability is certain, or near certain, this strategy can be highly advantageous, but there are drawbacks.

If the financial resources are currently available to pay the contribution, but it is not paid, then an alternative investment must be found to house the money in the period before it becomes appropriate to pay it. This may not be as tax-advantaged as a pension fund would be (though if it is possible to use an ISA, this would also be tax advantaged). In any event, provided the period for which the contribution is delayed is not too extended, it is unlikely that the effect of investing temporarily in a taxed environment would outweigh the advantages of (say) obtaining higher rate relief on the contribution as opposed to basic rate.

However, a major consideration in the current environment is the likely introduction of the simplification rules, which are discussed in some detail in **Chapter 15: Simplification of Tax Treatment**. Although these rules are still at the consultation stage, it appears that neither carry back nor carry forward (at least in their current form) will be available. It will however be possible to pay contributions at levels which in most cases will be much greater than is permitted under current rules, and this will allow individuals to achieve a similar effect to that which could be achieved under the RAC carry forward rules. This may increase the temptation to delay pension contributions if an individual believes that they will become a higher rate taxpayer in the future. Because the potential period of delay may be much longer than the existing rules allow, the effect of tax on investment returns in the interim becomes more important.

Interaction with personal pensions 14.22

There will be situations where individuals wish to contribute to both retirement annuity contracts and personal pensions within the same tax year. Because the limits on contributions are very different, there are necessarily specific rules which relate to the interaction of those limits.

These rules are triggered in any tax year against which the individual claims relief on contributions to both types of arrangement. It does not matter whether the contributions are for retirement benefits, for term assurance, or both.

In the past, this has sometimes led to situations where the interaction rules have been triggered inadvertently by an individual who is funding retirement benefits through RACs, but has also started a term assurance arrangement under personal pension rules. Because it is no longer possible to start a personal pension term assurance without also making contributions for retirement benefits, this is now much less of a problem area than has been in the past.

The interaction rules are also triggered if an individual has a retirement annuity contract to which they pay contributions, but their employer pays contributions on the individual's behalf to a personal pension. This applies whether or not the member themself also pays contributions to the personal pension.

Note however that if an individual with a retirement annuity contract chooses to contract out by means of a personal pension arrangement (see **Chapter 12: Contracting Out**), but no contributions other than the minimum contributions resulting from contracting out are paid to the personal pension, then the interaction rules do not apply.

Contribution limits 14.23

Where contributions are paid to both types of contracts, contribution limits apply, namely:

(*a*)   contributions to the RAC must be within RAC limits; and
(*b*)   total contributions to the personal pension and the RAC combined must be within personal pension limits.

The effect of the interaction depends on the relative limits under the two types of arrangement. For high earners, where the RAC contribution limit may be considerably greater than the personal pension limit (because of the absence of the earnings cap), the fact that total contributions are limited to the personal pension maximum will reduce the maximum.

Example – Interaction between personal pension and RAC limits I

A 52-year-old has net relevant earnings of £200,000. They have paid £1,000 into an existing RAC during 2003/04. They have no unused reliefs from earlier years.

The maximum contribution to their RAC in 2003/04 would be 20% of £200,000 = £40,000. They could therefore pay an additional £39,000 during 2003/04 if they wish.

However, suppose the individual also pays a contribution of £1,000 to a personal pension. They then become subject to personal pension limits, and so their total contributions to both arrangements in 2003/04 cannot exceed 30% of the earnings cap (£99,000) ie £29,700.

This therefore reduces their overall maximum by over £10,000 in 2003/04.

Note that although it is often said that the effect of starting a personal pension when an individual has a retirement annuity contract is to make the RAC subject to the earnings cap, this is not quite accurate. The cap is relevant because overall contributions are subject to the personal pension limit, which is influenced by the cap. However if it was necessary to directly apply the earnings cap to the RAC, this would mean that the RAC contributions in the above example would be limited to 20% of £99,000 = £19,800. This is not the case.

In the example above, it would be perfectly possible to pay £28,700 to the RAC, so that the total of the combined contributions, including the £1,000 paid to the personal pension, is at the maximum overall level of £29,700. Because the RAC contribution is within normal RAC limits, this division of contributions meets the two conditions as stated above.

At lower income levels, the personal pension limit will usually be higher in respect of the current year than the RAC limit, so the introduction of a personal pension will increase the overall scope for contributions, and will not reduce the amount that can be paid to the RAC.

Example – Interaction between personal pension and RAC limits II

A 57-year-old has net relevant earnings of £50,000. They have paid £2,000 into an existing RAC during 2003/04. The individual has no unused reliefs from earlier years.

The maximum contribution to their RAC in 2003/04 would be 22.5% of £50,000 = £11,250. They could therefore pay a further £9,250 to their RAC.

If the individual contributed to a personal pension, the limit on total contributions would be 35% of £50,000 = £17,500. This increases their total scope for contributions by £6,250.

Having paid £2,000 to their RAC already, they can contribute a further £15,500 in total. Of this, up to a further £9,250 can be paid to the RAC, but the balance must be paid to a personal pension.

The individual could choose to pay all of the £15,500 to a personal pension if they wanted to.

Effect of carry back   14.24

The interaction rules are triggered when relief is claimed in the same tax year on contributions to both personal pensions and RACs. The time when contributions are paid is not relevant.

If in the first example in section **14.23** above, the individual had been able to carry back their personal pension contribution and had therefore claimed relief on it against 2002/03, rather than against 2003/04, then the interaction rules would not be triggered for the year 2003/04. Only the RAC contribution would then be claimed against 2003/04.

Interaction including unused reliefs   14.25

Where there are unused reliefs to be picked up, the position inevitably gets a little more complex, but not unduly so.

The two basic conditions mentioned in section **14.23** above still apply, so the contribution to the RAC must be within RAC limits whilst the total contribution must be within personal pension limits.

In principle, the amount of unused relief in respect of past years is calculated in relation to the RAC limit for the past years, but taking account of all contributions paid in those years to both personal pensions and retirement annuity contracts.

> *Example – Calculation of unused relief where interaction rules apply*
>
> An individual has paid both personal pension and RAC contributions over the years, but has not maximised contributions in some years. They now want to pick up unused reliefs in 2003/04.
>
> In 1997/98, their net relevant earnings were £100,000 for RAC purposes, but were limited to the earnings cap at that time of £84,000 for personal pension purposes. In that year, the individual paid, and claimed relief on contributions of £1,000 to an RAC and £3,000 to a personal pension.
>
> On 6 April 1997, the individual was aged 43. The limit for RAC purposes in respect of 1997/98 was therefore 17.5% of £84,000 = £14,700.
>
> The total contributions paid to both RACs and personal pensions were £4,000. Their unused relief for 1997/98 is therefore £10,700.
>
> Assuming none of this has been taken up since through the use of carry forward, this amount can now be picked up, with tax relief against the tax liability for 2003/04.

Comparison of RAC and personal pension limits   14.26

Before 6 April 2001, the way in which limits operated on personal pensions and RACs was similar, and in particular, the carry forward provisions applied to both types of arrangement. The contribution limits in relation to each differed because of the differences in the maximum percentage limit, and also the imposition of the earnings cap for personal pension, but not retirement annuity contract purposes.

At that time, therefore, the comment made in section **14.11** above regarding the relative size of the limits under the two types of contract also applied to cases where unused relief was available. For most individuals the personal pension limits were more generous, but for high earners, the RAC limits, based on uncapped net relevant earnings, might be greater.

From 6 April 2001, the provisions relating to personal pensions were dramatically changed, with the introduction of (amongst other things) the basis year rules, and the abolition of the carry forward rules. This can therefore lead to a wise disparity between the contribution limits.

Where there is unused relief available to an individual who has an RAC, it will often be the case that the RAC limit is considerably more than the personal pension limit, irrespective of earnings. However, the comparison may be complicated by the availability of the basis year rules for personal pension contributions.

Example – Comparison of limits I

An individual has an RAC and their contribution and earnings history is given below.

Tax year	NRE	Age at 6 April	% limit	Maximum contribution	Amounts already paid	Unused relief
1997/98	£20,000	48	17.5%	£3,500	£1,000	£2,500
1998/99	£25,000	49	17.5%	£4,375	£1,500	£2,875
1999/2000	£20,000	50	17.5%	£3,500	£1,500	£2,000
2000/01	£30,000	51	20%	£6,000	£2,000	£4,000
2001/02	£50,000	52	20%	£10,000	£8,000	£2,000
2002/03	£40,000	53	20%	£8,000	£3,000	£5,000
2003/04	£25,000	54	20%	£5,000	nil	

Excluding the current year, the total of unused relief available to the individual is £18,375. The contribution limit in respect of the current year's net relevant earnings is £5,000, so the total scope for RAC contributions is £23,375.

The personal pension percentage limit at the age of 54 is 30% compared to the retirement annuity limit of 20%. Based on net relevant earnings for the 2003/04 tax year, the maximum personal pension contribution would therefore be 30% × £25,000 = £7,500.

However, under the basis year rules, the individual can use the net relevant earnings figure from 2001/02 for the purpose of calculating contribution limits, so their maximum personal pension contribution would be 30% of £50,000 = £15,000.

In this particular example, the RAC limit is the higher.

Where net relevant earnings in the current tax year are considerably less than those in a past year which could be used as the basis year (see section **3.30**), the personal pension basis might be better.

Example – Comparison of limits II

In the last example, suppose that the individual's net relevant earnings in 2001/02 had been £90,000 rather than £50,000. The unused relief for that year under RAC rules would then have been £10,000.

The maximum RAC contribution in relation to the current year's net relevant earnings would remain £5,000, but the total amount of unused relief from previous years would have increased to £26,375, giving a total of £31,375. They would not have been able to utilise the whole of this because their total RAC contribution (including that for the current year) cannot exceed their relevant earnings in the current year of £25,000. The maximum RAC contribution they could pay would therefore be £25,000.

The maximum personal pension contribution would be 30% of £90,000 = £27,000.

Note that whereas RAC contributions must not exceed relevant earnings for the current tax year, no such restriction applies under personal pension limits.

Death benefits   14.27

If an individual dies before taking retirement benefits from a retirement annuity contract, death benefits may be payable. However this is not always the case.

Retirement annuity contracts were often designed on the basis that they provided insurance against living too long (ie reaching retirement). This is a distinctly different concept to that underlying personal pension arrangements, which are perceived as being a method of saving for retirement. Where the first approach is taken, the return on death before retirement is in some cases nothing, in some cases a return of contributions without interest or growth, and in some cases a return of contributions with interest at a pre-set, and usually modest, rate. This is often the case under with profits RACs, and the insurer would expect to be in a position to improve the retirement benefits as a result of restricting the pre-retirement death benefits.

There were however many RACs, particularly those on a unit-linked or deposit basis, where the whole of the fund is returned on death. In some cases, insurance companies and friendly societies who issued policies on a basis where the whole fund was not returned may be prepared to alter the terms of the arrangement by negotiation, to provide for a full fund return on death.

As with personal pension arrangements, it is possible to create a trust to house RAC benefits, on the basis that death benefits are disposed of by the trustees, whilst retirement benefits revert to the member.

Term assurance 14.28

Section 621(1)(b), ICTA 1988 permits the provision of insured death benefits under RAC rules, in much the same way as applies under personal pension legislation (see section **8.17**).

The limit which applies to the contributions which can be used for this purpose is 5% of net relevant earnings, which is the same basis that applies to personal pension arrangements established before 6 April 2001.

Any contributions paid for term assurance under a retirement annuity contract will reduce (or eliminate) the scope for making contributions to a term assurance policy under personal pension rules.

Unused relief provisions also apply to term assurance arrangements, though their operation is complex. In particular, it is not possible to use them if no contributions for retirement benefits are being paid. In order to utilise the unused reliefs, the individual must first pay the maximum permitted total contribution for the current tax year, not just the maximum permitted for term assurance. Once this is done, unused relief can be brought forward from the earliest available year.

However, the unused relief from the next year can only be utilised if the balance of the maximum contribution limit as a whole is utilised for the earliest year.

In practice, and also in the light of the fact that term assurance premiums generally need to made on a regular basis, the unused relief provisions are of limited application to term assurance arrangements.

Trusts 14.29

Term assurance arrangements written under retirement annuity contract rules can be written into trust, and this will often be appropriate to minimise the impact of inheritance tax.

They can also be assigned, for example, to a mortgage lender.

Retirement benefits 14.30

Retirement benefits under RACs must generally commence between the ages of 60 and 75. This is less flexible than the position under personal pensions, where the age range is 50 to 75.

The only requirement for drawing benefits is age related, and retirement benefits can be drawn before the individual retires if they wish, or can be deferred beyond the date of their retirement, subject only to the maximum age of 75, at which benefits must be commenced.

Benefits are however available earlier than 60 in the event of incapacity (in which case there is no minimum age).

Benefits can also be taken early where the individual is in a special occupation in relation to which the Inland Revenue accepts that an early retirement age is appropriate (see section **13.3**).

Phased retirement   14.31

It is possible to take retirement benefits from RACs on a phased retirement basis, by encashing different contracts at different times, subject to the normal age requirements as discussed in section **14.30** above.

Each retirement annuity contract must however be used to provide benefits starting at a single point in time. Phased retirement is therefore only available if the individual has a number of separate RACs which can be encashed at different times.

As is now the case with personal pensions, many RACs were issued on a clustered or segmented basis, where a single 'plan' was segmented into a large number of separate constituent contracts, each of which could then be surrendered individually.

Tax free cash   14.32

Part of the benefits at retirement under an RAC may be taken in the form of a tax free cash sum. The basis of the lump sum is given in *s 620(3), ICTA 1988*, and this states that the lump sum must not exceed three times the initial annual amount of the remaining annuity.

This means that the amount of tax free cash available is dependent on annuity rates. The proportion of the fund available in this form is greater when annuity rates are at high (ie cheap) and lower when annuity rates are low.

Prior to 1988 (the year personal pensions were introduced) the amount of tax free cash available from an RAC was often around 30% of the total fund, so the introduction of the 25% limit on cash under personal pensions was viewed as a disadvantage. Currently, with annuity rates at relatively low levels, the tax free cash from a personal pension is generally greater than that which would be available under RAC rules. This is one reason why an individual might choose to transfer their fund from a retirement annuity contract to a personal pension at the time of retirement.

Because of the relationship with annuity rates, the proportion of the fund available in cash from the RAC will be greater at older ages, where annuity rates are cheaper.

Calculation of tax free cash

Mathematically, a formula is needed to calculate the tax free lump sum. The description as given in the legislation is circular, in the sense that the cash depends on the annuity, which depends on the residual fund after taking the cash. The necessary formula is:

$$C = \frac{3(F \times R)}{1+3R}$$

where:

C is the tax free cash sum;

F is the available fund; and

R is the annuity rate (expressed as a decimal).

For example, suppose the fund available is £120,000, and the annuity rate is 8% ie 0.08. The tax free cash sum is then:

$$C = \frac{3(£120,000 \times 0.08)}{(1+0.24)} = £23,226$$

The residual fund would be £120,000 - £23,226 = £96,774.

Applying this at the 8% annuity rate would produce an annuity of £96,774 × 0.08 = £7,742.

The cash sum is therefore as it should be: three times the annuity 3 × £7,742 = £23,226.

The break even point between the tax free cash limits on personal pensions and RACs arises where the annuity rate is 0.1111 (ie 11.11%) recurring, so that the cost of each £1 *per annum* of annuity is £9.

Example – Break-even point

If the fund is £120,000 and the annuity rate is .111 recurring, the tax free cash available is:

$$C = \frac{3(£120,000 \times 0.111)}{(1+0.333)} = £40,000$$

The cash sum is therefore 25% of the fund.

If annuity rates are more expensive, the personal pension formula gives the higher cash sum, whilst if annuity rates are cheaper, the reverse is true.

Basis of annuity rate 14.33

The annuity rate used in this calculation can be that for the cheapest type of annuity permitted under the RAC legislation. This would be the rate for a level annuity, payable annually in arrears, with no guarantee or survivors' benefits, and with no proportionate payment in respect of the year during which the individual dies. Once the calculation is made, however, the individual may choose to substitute a different type of annuity, for example one which includes escalation and survivors' benefits, and is payable monthly in advance.

The cash calculation does not have to be redone, and the result in practice will be that the annuity actually paid is often less than one third of the amount paid in cash.

Example – Relationship between cash and annuity

An individual has reached retirement, and has a fund of £100,000 under their RAC. The cheapest annuity rate which can be used to calculate the tax free cash sum available is 8.2%.

The cash sum is therefore:

$$C = \frac{3(£100,000 \times 0.082)}{(1+0.246)} = £19,743$$

The fund remaining to purchase an annuity is £100,000-£19,743 = £80,257.

If the individual chose to purchase the type of annuity on which this rate is based (annual payments in arrears etc), the annuity would be 8.2% x £80,257 = £6,581 per year. The annual annuity amount is then one third of the cash sum.

However, if they choose an annuity payable monthly in advance, with 3% *per annum* escalation, suppose the annuity rate would then be 6.1%. They could still take the same tax free cash sum of £19,743, but their annuity would be 6.1% x £80,257 = £4,896 per year.

Limitation on tax free cash 14.34

For retirement annuity contracts which were first taken out on or after 17 March 1987 (Budget Day in that year) an additional limitation on cash applies. This is that the cash sum under the RAC cannot exceed £150,000.

The intention of this limitation was to produce a parallel provision to the limitation under the 1987–89 occupational pension schemes regime, where the maximum possible tax free cash sum is also £150,000. Under RACs, however, the effect was minimal. This is because the limit is applied separately to each retirement annuity contract an individual has, rather than to the aggregate of benefits under them all.

In the case of a plan issued on a segmented basis, and consisting of 100 RACs (for example), this would mean that the additional limitation on cash from the plan would be to a figure of £15 million. This is unlikely to have any practical impact at all.

Unsurprisingly, most RACs issued on or after 17 March 1987, and before their withdrawal in 1988, were issued in segmented form.

Incapacity 14.35

As already discussed, retirement benefits are available early in cases of incapacity, with no minimum age requirement. The requirements regarding the form of benefit are not altered by incapacity, so the tax free cash formula is unchanged. As with personal pensions, it is not possible to commute all benefits for a lump sum, even if life expectancy is seriously reduced.

Waiver of contribution 14.36

It is possible to include a waiver of contribution provision within a retirement annuity contract, and this operates on the same basis as applies under personal pensions established before 6 April 2001. The basis is covered in detail in section **9.8**.

Transfers to personal pensions 14.37

It is possible for the value of an individual's benefits under an RAC to be transferred, as long as this is done before retirement benefits are taken.

Generally, such a transfer will be made to a personal pension, and personal pension rules will apply. If however an individual has a number of retirement annuity contracts, and, subject to the terms of those contracts, it is possible to transfer from one RAC to another.

There are a number of issues to consider, as detailed below.

Investment issues 14.38

Wider investment choices are available under personal pensions than under RACs. Those who require the flexibility of investing outside of insurance company funds, or who simply find that the range of funds available under their particular RAC is too limited, might wish to transfer to widen the investment potential.

Future investment performance cannot be guaranteed to exceed that available under the RAC however, so the individual would need to have a strong belief in the future potential of the personal pension which receives the transfer.

If an individual wishes to take advantage of the self-invested personal pension route, then a transfer would be necessary as there is no equivalent under RAC legislation.

Contribution limits   14.39

The calculation of contribution limits under personal pensions is distinctly different to that which applies to RACs. Where an individual transfers the value of all their RACs to personal pensions, this would eliminate for ever the opportunity of using RAC limits, including the carry forward of unused relief.

Although this may no longer be an issue after the proposed simplification changes (see **Chapter 15: Simplification of Tax Treatment**), for the moment there could be a considerable advantage in maintaining at least one RAC. This could even be just one segment of a segmented RAC plan, which would be enough to maintain the availability of RAC contribution limits.

Death benefits   14.40

As discussed above, some retirement annuity contracts offer poor benefits on death before retirement, whilst on transfer to a personal pension, the full fund would be available on death. This may be an important issue not only for those in poor health, but also for those some way from retirement who want the reassurance of knowing that the fund they have accumulated would not be lost on death.

Open market options   14.41

Many RACs include an open market option at retirement, allowing the individual to transfer their fund from their existing provider in order to purchase an annuity from a different insurance company with better annuity rates. Before the introduction of personal pensions to replace RACs from 1 July 1988, this was done by establishing a new RAC (called a 'substituted contract').

It is not however now possible to establish a new RAC, even if the intention is merely that it should accept a transfer, rather than be open for any subsequent contributions. If there is another RAC, the transfer can be made to it, but this may not be with the insurer offering the best annuity rates.

If therefore the holder of an RAC wants to use the open market option, this will usually mean transferring to a personal pension.

There are likely to be costs involved in this exercise, and these must be taken into account in determining whether the transfer is advantageous, and may detract significantly from the annuity rates on offer. The different basis of calculating tax free cash under personal pension rules will also be relevant, because the transfer must be of the whole fund, before cash is taken. In current circumstances, the personal pension is likely to produce a higher level of cash than the RAC, so this aspect is likely to make the case for transfer stronger rather than weaker.

Guaranteed annuity rates   14.42

Some retirement annuity contracts offer guaranteed annuity rates and the level at which this guarantee was set will often reflect a higher interest rate environment than is currently in place. Accordingly guaranteed annuity rates may be extremely favourable to the individual, and this may certainly make a transfer undesirable.

However, under many RACs, the availability of guaranteed annuity rates was restricted, for example to retirement at a particular age, or to a particular type of annuity, perhaps a level annuity with no survivor benefits. Where the type of annuity involved does not fit the individual's requirements, it may be that the guaranteed rates are of little or no value. If this seems to be the case, it would nevertheless be wise to investigate whether the individual's other financial affairs could be arranged in such a way that advantage could be taken of the guaranteed annuity rate, for example, by making other provision for a dependant.

Income withdrawals and phased retirement   14.43

Income withdrawals are not available under RAC legislation, and the ability to phase retirement may be restricted by the number of RACs a particular individual has. It may therefore be attractive to transfer to a personal pension in order to utilise one or both of these options.

Again costs are likely to be involved, and these need to be borne in mind. However the increased flexibility under the personal pension regime will appeal to many individuals.

Possible disadvantages 14.44

There are potential disadvantages involved in transferring to personal pensions, particularly if this is done some time before retirement, and therefore before the potential impact on retirement benefits can be quantified with certainty.

In particular, although the tax free cash available from a personal pension is currently greater than would be available from an RAC in most circumstances, this could change in the future, if annuity rates become cheaper. Though this may currently seem unlikely, at the time personal pensions were introduced, it seemed unlikely that annuity rates would fall to a level where the 25% formula for cash was better than the RAC formula.

If this, or one of the other retirement related advantages of personal pensions (for example the availability of income withdrawals) is the main reason for transferring, it may make sense to defer the transfer until the point of retirement. At this time, the effect will be certain, and can be quantified.

Earlier transfer may however be appropriate if the main issues relate to death benefit or investment aspects.

The checklist below summarises the main differences between personal pensions and RACs, and these would be relevant in making the transfer decision.

Checklist – Comparison between personal pensions and RACs		
	Personal pensions	**RACs**
Providers	Life insurance companies; Friendly societies; Banks; Building societies; Unit trust managers ACDs of OEICs	Life insurance companies; Friendly societies
Eligibility	Those with relevant earnings; Non-earners; Some employees in pensionable employment, subject to the concurrency rules	Those with relevant earnings only
Contribution limits	17.5%–40% of NRE or, if greater, the earnings threshold	17.5%–27.5% of NRE
Earnings cap	£99,000 (2003/04)	Not applicable

	Personal pensions	**RACs**
Employer contributions	Permitted	Not permitted
Contracting out	Available	Not available
Basis year rules	Available	Not available
Cessation rules	Available	Not available
Carry forward	Not available	Available
Carry back	Available but limited to 1 year maximum and to contributions paid by 31 January in any tax year.	Available, with two year carry back in limited circumstances. Contributions paid at any time in the tax year can be carried back.
Waiver of contribution	Available	Available
Term Assurance	Available	Available
Retirement benefits available	50 to 75	60 to 75
Tax free cash	25% of fund	3 × residual annuity
Phased retirement	Available	Available, subject to there being a number of RACs in force
Income withdrawals	Available	Not available

15 — Simplification of Tax Treatment

Introduction 15.1

Because of the tax advantages which pension arrangements enjoy, there have always been numerous rules which must be adhered to. In particular, limitations have been placed on aspects such as eligibility and maximum contributions, as well as on the form and timing of benefits. Although this is an unsurprising response from the Government and the Inland Revenue, and is based on a desire to protect tax revenues, it has increasingly been recognised in recent years that the tax treatment of pensions overall has become too complex.

Much of this book has been concerned with these complications, and their practical application. The problem is not just the fact that any particular set of requirements is complex, but that there are many different sets. For example, approved occupational pension schemes are subject to an entirely different set of limits to that which applies to personal pension schemes.

Layering 15.2

In addition, one of the aspects which has caused most concern has been the 'layering' of different sets of requirements. This has arisen because generally, when alterations have been made to pensions legislation, there has been a reluctance to make changes which have retrospective effect. Instead, old rules have often been retained for existing arrangements, with the result that there are many different sets of rules in force at the same time, but applicable in different situations.

This complexity is costly for product providers, difficult and time consuming for advisers, and often probably incomprehensible from the investor's point of view. Many people believe that simplifying the pensions tax regime would go a long way towards encouraging more people to make more substantial pension provision for themselves. Investors will always be reluctant to put money into arrangements which they do not feel they fully understand.

There has even been an inconsistent approach to the layering itself. For example, when major changes were made to the contribution limits for personal pensions with effect from 6 April 2001, these changes were, for the most part, applied to existing as well as new arrangements. However existing arrangements did retain some aspects of the old rules, for example the limitation on premiums for term assurance to 5% of net relevant earnings, rather than the new basis of 10% of contributions paid for retirement benefits.

Furthermore, no changes at all were made at the time to the rules applicable to retirement annuity contracts.

Checklist – Examples of layering

- Different rules for retirement annuity contracts compared to personal pensions, for example the continued availability of carry forward (see section **14.14**).
- The more advantageous calculation basis of tax free cash under pre-Royal Assent personal pension arrangements (see section **5.11**).
- Different basis of operation of waiver under pre-6 April 2001 personal pension arrangements (see section **9.8**).
- Different limits on term assurance premiums under arrangements started before 6 April 2001 (see section **8.19**).
- Different escalation requirements on protected rights accrued before 6 April 1997 (see section **12.17**).

In December 2002, the Inland Revenue published a consultation paper called *Simplifying the taxation of pensions,* which put forward radical proposals for the reform of the tax regime. These are the subject of wide consultation, but it is likely that the main thrust of the proposals will be carried through to implementation.

A possible implementation date of April 2004 was quoted in the consultation paper, though in practice April 2005 may be more likely, given the sweeping nature of the changes.

This chapter summarises the effect of the proposals, particularly on personal pension arrangements, but also discusses some of the wider implications. Because the consultation is ongoing, the position may change over the coming months.

Overview and scope

15.3

The concept behind the proposals for change is to make a clean break with the past, and to abandon the current approach with its different regimes for different products. The new rules will therefore apply to personal pensions (including stakeholder pensions) and retirement annuity contracts. They will also cover occupational pension schemes.

Regimes to be brought under the simplification proposals are:

(*a*)   personal pensions;
(*b*)   stakeholder pensions;
(*c*)   retirement annuity contracts;
(*d*)   occupational schemes – old code (pre-1970);
(*e*)   occupational schemes – pre-1987 approval basis;
(*f*)   occupational schemes – 1987–89 approval basis;
(*g*)   occupational schemes – post-1989 approval basis;
(*h*)   additional voluntary contribution arrangements (AVCs);
(*j*)   freestanding additional voluntary contribution arrangements (FSAVCs);
(*k*)   funded unapproved retirement benefit schemes (FURBS); and
(*l*)   unfunded unapproved retirement benefit schemes (UURBS).

Lifetime limit   15.4

The main feature of the proposed new regime in terms of limits is that it is intended to apply a single lifetime limit to the total value of benefits which can be built up under pensions legislation, with the associated tax advantages. The limit will include both occupational and personal pension arrangements, whether started before or after the date of the introduction of the new regime (generally referred to as 'A day').

In terms of personal pensions, the lifetime limit should be easy to apply, because it will simply relate to the total value of the fund built up at retirement. There are more complex issues involved with occupational schemes which are constituted on a defined benefit basis, because of the need to value the pension rights built up.

It is intended that the lifetime limit should increase, probably each year and probably in line with the Retail Prices Index.

From a purely personal pension perspective, the lifetime limit represents a considerable departure from previous practice where limits have been placed on contributions, but not on ultimate benefits. This could therefore be seen as a significant disadvantage. However, the suggested level for the lifetime limit is £1.4 million, so the number of people who will be affected by it will be modest, at least initially.

The limit may however bite to an increasing extent in the future, if it is increased only in line with price inflation, which historically has lagged behind both earnings inflation and equity related investment returns, at least in the longer term.

Transition   15.5

Because the new regime will encompass existing arrangements as well as new, there will be some cases where the lifetime limit is already exceeded by funds built up prior to A day, or will be exceeded by retirement, even without any further contributions being made.

The Inland Revenue has indicated that transitional arrangements will be put in place to safeguard the position of individuals who might be disadvantaged in this way, though the detailed application of these provisions will need to be worked out during consultation.

Structure of benefits   15.6

The intention is that the way in which benefits are taken under the new regime will conform largely with current personal pension practice. Up to 25% of the fund will be available in the form of a tax free cash sum, with the balance providing an income. The individual will have a choice between annuity purchase and income withdrawals, but whatever form the income takes, it will (as now) be taxed as earned income through the PAYE system.

Excess benefits   15.7

There will inevitably be situations where the individual's fund exceeds the lifetime limit at the point when retirement benefits are taken. The proposal for dealing with this situation is that the excess will then be subject to a special 'recovery tax charge', at the rate of (probably) 33%.

This will be deducted from the excess fund before benefits are paid, but the structure of the benefits provided from the fund remaining after the tax deduction will then be in line with normal rules. This will mean that 25% can be taken as cash with no further tax liability, but the balance would be used to provide taxable income.

The effect of the recovery charge, together with the tax on the emerging income benefit, is likely to be to make overfunding generally unattractive from a tax point of view. Broadly, for a higher rate taxpayer, the effect will be equivalent to tax at approximately 60% on the excess.

The lifetime limit will be policed by the Inland Revenue.

Contribution limits   15.8

As well as the lifetime limit, there will also be a limitation placed on annual contributions. The proposal is that generally, an individual, and/or their employer, should be able to contribute up to 100% of earnings, or £3,600 if greater. It is however suggested that an overriding monetary limit of £200,000 should apply.

Individuals would be responsible for monitoring the application of the annual limit, and this should be straightforward under personal pension arrangements. Essentially any excess contributions would not benefit from tax relief (or there will be a balancing tax charge on the individual where relief is given by payment of premiums net of basic rate relief). It is therefore unlikely to be attractive for an individual to overfund. The effect is to pay a contribution from after tax resources, into an arrangement where a large part of the benefits would emerge in the form of taxable income.

This balance of advantage may be less clear cut where the employer is paying the contribution, though even here, the member will be taxed first on the excess contribution, and then again on the income portion of the eventually emerging benefit. It may therefore be preferable for benefits funded by the employer to be provided up to the annual limit through pension arrangements, but by other means if further contributions are to be made.

Aspects not expected to change   15.9

Although the proposals for change are far-reaching and radical, there are a number of aspects of personal pensions which will remain broadly the same.

These include the essential components of the tax advantages, such as tax relief on contributions, including higher rate where appropriate, and the continuation of the existing tax treatment of the investment returns generated by the pension fund.

Checklist – Areas not expected to change significantly

The following are amongst the main areas where the new regime will not represent any major change from existing practice under personal pensions, though in some cases the new basis will be a significant change from current occupational scheme rules.

- Contributions paid by individuals will qualify for tax relief, including relief at higher rate where applicable.
- Employer contributions will generally be a deductible business expense.
- The employee will not be subject to tax on contributions paid by the employer.
- There will be no National Insurance liability on employer contributions, either for employer or employee.
- The existing tax advantaged treatment of investment returns within the pension fund will continue to apply (though there is no sign of any intention to reinstate the ability to reclaim dividend tax credits).

- Up to 25% of the fund at retirement will be available as a tax free cash sum at retirement.
- Income can be provided by annuity purchase or income withdrawals.
- Income benefits will be taxed as earned income under PAYE.
- Phased retirement will be available.

Major change areas 15.10

Although the new regime is more closely aligned to existing personal pension provisions than those applicable to occupational schemes, there will be significant differences in some of the more complex areas. Many of these areas under existing rules have been designed to solve practical difficulties which would otherwise be encountered by individuals seeking to contribute to personal pensions.

An example of this is the proposal to abolish the carry back facility (see section **4.13**). It could be argued that the maximum contribution levels under the new regime are (for most people) more generous than the existing limits. However, the inclusion of an annual limit on contributions will still mean that in order to contribute with certainty regarding limits, it will be necessary for an individual to be aware of their earnings levels at the time of paying the contribution.

Currently, where there is doubt, the carry back facility allows an individual to have the contribution treated as if it was paid in the preceding tax year rather than the current tax year. The self-employed in particular may find it difficult to be certain of the level of earned income which will be assessed for the current tax year, especially in the opening years of a business. These issues are discussed in detail in section **3.23**.

Because the proposals are only at the consultation stage, it is by no means impossible that some of the facilities which are currently expected to be abolished may remain, or that an alternative way of dealing with such problems will be put forward.

Amongst the other facilities which are likely to be removed are the basis year rules and cessation rules (see sections **3.30** and **3.34** respectively). The removal of these facilities could exacerbate the problems regarding limits which can affect those who suffer incapacity, as discussed in section **9.11**.

Retirement annuity contracts 15.11

Bringing retirement annuity contracts as well as personal pensions into the proposed new regime will also mean the removal of the facility, which is now restricted to retirement annuity contracts, to carry forward unused relief from past years (see section **14.14**). This facility currently allows individuals with these contracts to make up for contributions which have been missed, or have not been paid at maximum levels, during the preceding six tax years.

In practice, the loss of carry forward is unlikely to be disadvantageous to most investors, because the proposed new regime will allow contributions to be made at a level up to 100% of earnings. This is likely to allow contributions at a high enough level to have a similar effect. The existing carry forward facility on retirement annuity contracts is also subject to a limit on contributions equal to the current year's relevant earnings, so the new limit will generally be at least as generous as the old.

The only situation where the new basis will be less favourable would seem to be in the case of a very high earner, with net relevant earnings in excess of £200,000. Currently, given sufficient unused reliefs from earlier years, a contribution equal to relevant earnings could be paid, whilst under the proposed new regime, the monetary limit of £200,000 would be a limiting factor. Clearly such cases would be unusual.

Controlling directors 15.12

An interesting aspect of the simplification proposals is that there will no longer be any special treatment of controlling directors under occupational pension scheme rules. This also has some impact currently for personal pensions, where contributions are funded from earnings derived from an employment which is originally non-pensionable, but in respect of which an occupational pension scheme is later introduced. In these circumstances, the personal pension benefits will reduce the limits on benefits from the occupational scheme. This is discussed in section **11.5**.

It is however specifically stated that the deductibility of pension contributions for directors (not just controlling directors) will be subject to the agreement of the Inspector of Taxes.

Concurrency 15.13

The concurrency rules, under which certain individuals can at present contribute to a personal pension at the same time as accruing benefits under an occupational pension scheme (see section **2.20**) will be redundant under the new regime. This reflects the introduction of a lifetime limit for all pension arrangements, rather than the currently entirely different limitation methods under personal pensions and occupational schemes.

Earnings cap 15.14

Note also that the earnings cap as such would be abolished, since it is unnecessary within a framework which includes a lifetime limit, and an annual limit on contributions with a monetary ceiling. In general this will be a simplification, though under retirement annuity contracts, where there is currently no earnings cap, some individuals may be disadvantaged.

Checklist – Existing personal pension and/or retirement annuity provisions which may be abolished

Amongst the provisions that are expected to be abolished under the simplification proposals are the following.

- Basis year rules.
- Cessation rules.
- Concurrency rules.
- Carry back.
- Differential treatment of RAC compared to personal pensions.
- Carry forward (under RACs).
- Special rules for controlling directors.
- The earnings cap.
- Special rules for concurrent employments.

Areas of uncertainty 15.15

In some ways, the simplification proposals as a whole could be said to be uncertain in that they are subject to consultation. The indications from the Inland Revenue are that the consultation is a genuine and open one, so it is clear that changes may be made in the light of opinions expressed.

However, it is likely that the main points in the consultation paper will form the basis of the new regime, though as already discussed, the transitional arrangements in particular need further development.

Also, there is no indication at this stage of the way in which waiver of contribution will operate under the new regime. The changes made in 2001 (see section **9.10**) have proved less than satisfactory and have resulted in the virtual extinction of this type of protection. Waiver can prove not only extremely attractive, but also very necessary for individuals who become incapacitated. This is particularly true of the self-employed, who are wholly reliant on their own resources.

It may be that the introduction of the new regime will provide a suitable opportunity to reconsider the basis of this benefit.

Taking retirement benefits   15.16

The new regime will allow considerable flexibility in dealing with retirement benefits, though there are also some restrictive aspects in the proposals being put forward.

Retirement ages   15.17

Currently, retirement benefits can normally be taken from personal pension schemes at any time between the ages of 50 and 75, and may be taken on a phased basis (see section **5.5**). Part of the proposed simplified basis is to increase the minimum age at which benefits become available from 50 to 55.

It is certainly true that few people can afford to retire at 50 in practice, and this is a significant part of the rationale put forward for change. The prospect of early retirement is also becoming more elusive. As well as lower levels of investment return and gilt yields (leading to more expensive annuity rates), increased life expectancy has also made early retirement more difficult from a financial point of view. The Inland Revenue argues that it is logical to move retirement ages upwards in this context.

On the other hand, the change would involve a considerable loss of flexibility, particularly for those who might have intended to take benefits on a phased basis to allow them to gradually reduce their working hours over a period of time. This may discourage some investors from putting large contributions into a pension arrangement because it has become less accessible. Indeed, in some cases, it may mean that the individual decides to make no contributions at all.

Indications are that, although this change is unlikely to be introduced as quickly as other parts of the new regime (2010 is the suggested date), it will apply to existing as well as new arrangements. The lengthier timespan for the introduction of this change is intended to allow those currently planning to retire earlier than age 55 to make appropriate alternative arrangements.

Special occupations   15.18

Interestingly, the Inland Revenue has also proposed the abolition of the provision whereby those in certain special occupations can take advantage of an agreed early retirement age. For example, at present, professional footballers can establish a personal pension arrangement with a retirement age of 35. The current provisions are covered in **Chapter 13: Special Occupations**.

Here the thinking is slightly different. Although it is accepted that (for example) a footballer's career is relatively short, and that he will cease to be able to play professional football at 35 or thereabouts, it is pointed out that generally a footballer would not retire from work as a whole at that time. Instead, he would probably take up a different type of work.

This will usually be sustainable to a conventional retirement age, and given that the new career is likely to generate a reasonable income, the need for early pension benefits relating to the special occupation is very limited.

In addition, where an individual does wish to take advantage of an early retirement age, the short available investment period, and the expensive annuity rates applicable at young ages, may make it difficult to build up a substantial income benefit.

The proposed change for special occupations is an issue which is part of the consultation, and it may be that the Inland Revenue changes its mind, though at the time of writing no decision had been made.

Special consideration is however being given to some public sector occupations which currently also enjoy early retirement ages under their occupational schemes (though these are not carried over to personal pension schemes). Examples include the police and fire services. Here it appears likely that the availability of those early retirement ages will be maintained.

Protected rights   15.19

Currently, there are a number of restrictions on taking benefits from any part of a personal pension which is regarded as protected rights. These are covered in section **5.3**.

Amongst the most welcome of the simplification proposals is a suggestion that these restrictions should be removed entirely, and that the normal basis, including access within normal age constraints, and the availability of tax free cash benefits should apply.

Phased retirement   15.20

Phased retirement will be permitted, much as under current personal pension legislation. Currently this facility is not available at all under occupational schemes, but the intention is that it should be introduced. This may reduce the attractions of transferring from an occupational pension scheme to a personal pension in some cases, though whether phased retirement will be available under any particular occupational scheme is likely to be a matter for the trustees of the scheme rather than something which they are legally obliged to offer.

The introduction of phasing would inevitably create some complications from an administrative point of view, so it will be interesting to see how many schemes take up the opportunity in practice.

Phased retirement will affect the operation of the lifetime limit. Essentially the proposal is that the fund (or the value of benefits under a defined benefit occupational scheme) which is accessed at any time is deducted from the lifetime limit to determine the remainder still available. This balance would then be increased each year in line with increases to the overall lifetime limit.

Example – Proposed effect of phased retirement on lifetime limit

An individual has a number of personal pension arrangements, and decides to take retirement benefits from a number of them at age 60. The lifetime limit at the time is £1.4 million and they have not previously taken any benefits from their pension arrangements.

Suppose the total value of the fund under the arrangements which they are currently encashing is £500,000.

After doing so, their remaining lifetime limit is therefore £1.4m – £500,000 = £900,000.

If in the following year, the £1.4m lifetime limit is increased by 5% to £1.47m, the individual's remaining lifetime limit would also be increased by 5%, from £900,000 to £945,000.

Note that although the remaining lifetime limit is reduced, it is not proposed that there will be any reduction in the amount that the individual could contribute. The earnings threshold of £3,600, the limitation to total salary, and the overriding £200,000 limit would all therefore apply in the normal way.

Incapacity and ill-health   15.21

At the moment, benefits under both personal pensions and occupational schemes can be taken early if the individual suffers incapacity. However, different detailed provisions apply, and it is proposed that these should be brought into line.

This would mean that, for the first time, full commutation of benefits would be available under personal pensions (and retirement annuity contracts) in situations where the individual suffers serious ill-health, and his life expectancy is severely reduced as a result.

It is also proposed that in these circumstances the benefits provided would be entirely tax free.

Triviality 15.22

The rules governing the full commutation of pension rights for a lump sum on grounds of triviality would also be brought into line. The proposal is that full commutation should be available on this basis subject to an overall limit on the amount built up through pension arrangements of £10,000 from all sources.

Income withdrawals 15.23

Income withdrawals would be available under the proposed new regime, and the concept will be similar to that which currently applies. There would continue to be a maximum income withdrawal level of 100% of the annuity available, calculated on GAD rates (see section **6.4**). It is however intended to make two changes which will be very significant, if carried through.

Minimum withdrawals 15.24

The first proposal is that the minimum level of withdrawals should be reduced, possibly to a figure as low as £1 *per annum*. This would in effect open up the opportunity to take tax free cash benefits at pension date, but defer virtually the whole of the income benefit until later.

As well as providing a great deal of control in terms of the timing of the taxable income benefit, this will provide welcome flexibility for those who would wish to minimise withdrawals from a purely investment point of view, during times of adverse market conditions. At present, it would be unwise in most circumstances for an individual to invest the whole of their income withdrawal fund in equities or related investments, because of their volatility. Part of the problem is the requirement to take at least a minimum level of withdrawals each year, irrespective of market conditions. As a result, part of the income withdrawal fund will generally be held in a more secure environment, often in cash, but this has the effect of depressing investment returns on the fund as a whole.

The removal of the requirement to take minimum withdrawals (except to the level of £1 *per annum*) would open up wider opportunities for those who are prepared to take a higher level of investment risk. For example, such an individual could invest in equities with a longer term perspective than is currently possible. It needs however to be stressed that in these circumstances the individual will need to be able to provide for their income needs from other resources during periods when they are taking very low income withdrawals from the personal pension.

Age limit 15.25

The second proposed change is that income withdrawals may be permitted to carry on beyond the current maximum age of 75. This is likely to be possible under certain types of arrangement only, including self-invested personal pension schemes (see section **7.39**).

It is not clear at this stage what restrictions would apply to this facility, but this is likely to be welcomed by many individuals, particularly those with substantial pension funds.

It is worth saying that the Inland Revenue is anxious to ensure that the main purpose of pension arrangements continues to be the provision of retirement income, rather than estate planning. It is therefore proposed that if death occurs after the age of 75, whatever the circumstances, it will not be possible for any benefits to be paid in lump sum form.

Where there is a residual fund arising because the deceased was taking income withdrawals, or as a result of payments arising under an unexpired guarantee period, these must be paid in the form of income, which would be taxable. This may significantly weaken the case for continuing withdrawals beyond age 75 in practice.

Annuities 15.26

It is also proposed that there should be some additional options under compulsory purchase annuities.

It will remain possible to build in a minimum guaranteed payment period of up to ten years, and also to provide for survivors' pensions in broadly the same way as at present.

Note however that there are likely to be modifications to the basis under which pensions can be paid to minor children. The new requirement will be that the income must cease by the time the child attains the age of 23, but there would be no link to the continuation of full-time education. (A child who leaves school at 18, takes a gap year and then undertakes a three year course of further education would finish that education somewhere his 22nd and 23rd birthdays, so this seems to be a reasonable change.)

Value protection 15.27

It is also suggested that annuity providers should be able to offer value protection. Currently this is available under purchased life annuities (where it is generally known as capital protection), but not under compulsory purchase annuities.

The concept is that if an individual dies before they have received, through instalments of the annuity, a total amount equal to the purchase price, a lump sum equal to the difference would be payable.

Example – Value protection

An individual takes retirement benefits from their personal pension arrangement at age 65. After taking some benefits in cash, the remaining fund of £80,000 is sufficient to provide an annuity of £6,000 per year, with full value protection.

The individual dies a few years after the annuity starts, and by that time has received total annuity payments of £36,000.

Because value protection applies, a lump sum of £44,000 (ie £80,000 – £36,000) would be payable.

The concept of value protection is likely to be popular in principle, though it is also likely to make annuity rates noticeably more expensive, and this may put off many potential purchasers. This may also result in the development of annuities with different levels of value protection, for example 50% protection, which might represent a reasonable balance between protection and cost.

A further aspect of the proposals for change which will impact in this area is that any lump sum payments made after retirement benefits have been taken would be subject to a tax charge deducted at source of 35%, much in the way that such payments arising under income withdrawal arrangements are currently taxed (see section **6.11**).

Limited period annuities   15.28

It is also intended to allow retirement income to be provided through the purchase of a series of limited period annuities. The concept is that part of the fund will be used to purchase an annuity payable for a specific time period, perhaps of five years. At the end of the five year period, income must be continued, either through the purchase of a further limited period annuity or a lifetime annuity.

The amount of the fund which could be used at each stage would be limited, in order to try to ensure that the fund does not run out. This is likely to mean that the income level available will be similar to that which could be provided by purchase of a lifetime annuity.

The attraction of the limited period basis is that each successive purchase can reflect the individual's circumstances and wishes at the time. For example, if the individual is married when the first annuity purchase takes place, they might choose to include provision for a survivor's annuity. If however their spouse has predeceased them before the second purchase, then the second annuity could be arranged on a single life basis. The result is to limit the extent to which provision for a spouse is made but in practice turns out to be wasted.

Although in principle this is a sensible approach, it will be interesting to see how annuity rates develop to cope with it. The extent of the mortality gain to the annuity fund when annuitants die will be reduced under this basis, and therefore the extent to which there is a cross–subsidy to those who live longest is also reduced. The inevitable result of this will be that annuity rates become more expensive, and the extent of this increase in cost may be more than was foreseen by those who developed these proposals.

Divorce   15.29

The impact of the new proposals on the treatment of pension rights on divorce is also a matter which remains to be resolved during the consultation process.

In particular, under personal pensions, because currently no limits apply to the total benefits available at retirement, the impact of pension credits and pension debits has been limited from a technical point of view (though of course the member's benefits are reduced by the pension debit and the ex-spouse receives the benefits from the pension credit).

Because of the planned imposition of a lifetime limit, the effect on this limit needs to be considered. Within the initial proposals, it was suggested that the pension debit should decrease the lifetime limit (ie be regarded as part of the lifetime limit) of the member from whom benefits are transferred, but that the benefits derived from the pension credit should be additional to the ex-spouse's own lifetime limit. The view has been expressed that in principle this runs counter to the logic of a lifetime limit which is not related to earnings. This may therefore be an area where the initial proposals are amended.

Effect of proposals   15.30

The overall effect of the simplification proposals will certainly be far reaching, though the detailed provisions may change, and the proposals will certainly develop during the period between their publication and their eventual enactment. Those affected and their advisers will need to keep up to date with developments over this period.

In general, a major effect of the new regime will be that advisers will not need to concentrate so much on the minutiae of the operation of rules and limits. It will therefore be possible to place greater emphasis on the retirement planning needs of those seeking to save through personal pensions (and other pension arrangements) and on the relative merits of these arrangements compared with other possible investment vehicles such as ISAs.

The investment aspects of building up and maintaining substantial retirement funds will also take on a higher profile.

The introduction of value protected annuities and limited period annuities will also be useful, and will help to reduce the perceived problems with annuities. These options are likely to appeal particularly to those with modest funds, which are perhaps too small to make income withdrawals a viable option, but who seek greater flexibility and better death benefits than the currently available range of annuities can provide.

As discussed earlier in this chapter, much of the intention behind the changes is to remove some of the complications which may put individuals off making provision for their retirement through pension arrangements. It is therefore to be hoped that the final proposals build on the initial concept of radical simplification.

Index